Global Television Marketplace

Timothy Havens

bfi Publishing

First published in 2006 by the
BRITISH FILM INSTITUTE
21 Stephen Street, London W1T 1LN

The British Film Institute's purpose is to champion moving image culture
in all its richness and diversity across the UK, for the benefit of as wide
an audience as possible, and to create and encourage debate.

Cover design: ketchup

Set by Fakenham Photosetting Ltd, Fakenham, Norfolk
Printed in the UK by St Edmundsbury Press, Bury St Edmunds, Suffolk

British Library Cataloguing-in-Publication Data
A catalogue record for this book is available from the British Library

ISBN 1-84457-104-1 (pbk)
ISBN 1-84457-103-3 (hbk)

Contents

Acknowledgments

While I have often read in other authors' acknowledgments that the writing of a book is not an individual act, it was not until trudging through my own process of writing that I fully realised what these statements meant. This volume has undoubtedly been a collective effort, to which numerous people have contributed their ideas, their time, their research assistance, their support and even their money. Without their aid, this project would have simply been impossible. Chief among these contributors was Dr Rita Zajácz, my wife, who liberally assisted in every aspect of the process, while enduring the stresses and fears that sometimes made me less than a delight to live with. We'll get there yet.

Professors Michael Curtin and Paul McDonald, the editors of this series, both provided remarkably insightful, thorough and speedy reviews of the various drafts of this manuscript, while Michael's friendship and confidence in my project were invaluable for seeing the process through to its conclusion. In addition, two anonymous reviewers for BFI Publishing provided excellent suggestions for improving earlier drafts. Thanks to all of these folks, the book is far clearer, more readable and more intellectually rigorous than anything I could have composed on my own.

The editors at BFI Publishing have likewise kept this project moving along, frequently, yet always gently, enquiring about my progress. I want to thank Andrew Lockett for his initial confidence in the project, Keith Mansfield for taking the reins when Andrew moved on to other pastures and Rebecca Barden for guiding me through the final difficult stages of the process.

Reed-Midem Organisation, NATPE and DISCOP kindly allowed me to attend several of their sales markets, for which I am grateful. I would especially like to acknowledge Bruce Johansen and Pam Smithard of NATPE, Peggy Refford of Reed-Midem and Patrick Jucaud of DISCOP. In addition, dozens of international programming executives gave freely of their time to assist with my research. Without them, this volume would have been impossible.

An earlier draft of Chapter 3 appeared as 'Exhibiting Global Television: On the Business and Cultural Functions of Global Television Fairs', *Journal of Broadcasting & Electronic Media*, no. 47, 2003, pp. 18–36. Used with permission.

I also owe a deep debt of gratitude to the people and organisations who gave their labour and financial support to this book. My research assistants, Alex

Ingersoll, Aya Matsushima, Cate Monahan, Connie Morales, Minkyu Sung and Matt Thatcher made it possible to collect and analyse the large amount of trade journal articles, interviews and data that inform the arguments of the book, even though, on occasion, none of us was really sure what we were doing. The research assistants at the Library of American Broadcasting in College Park, Maryland, took pity on me when I showed up unannounced one summer, dragging out countless boxes of uncategorised materials and obscure old trade journals for me. I would also like to acknowledge the various organisations that provided financial support: the Council for the International Exchange of Scholars for its Senior Fulbright position in Hungary; the University of Iowa's Office of the Vice President of Research for its Art and Humanities Initiative Grant; the University of Iowa's Old Gold Summer Research Fund; the Center for International Business Education and Research at Indiana University for its Non-business Dissertation Research Grant; the Old Dominion University Research Foundation for its Summer Research Grant; and the University of Iowa's Office of International Programs for its Summer Research Grant and several international travel grants.

Finally, I would like to thank my parents, Robert (Pete) Havens and Judy Havens for raising me in an intellectually and emotionally nurturing environment and – perhaps most importantly – for never restricting the amount of television I could watch as a child!

For Rita, who opened up the world for me.

Introduction: Studying Global Television Merchants

When I began studying the global television marketplace eight years ago, I discovered that I was almost completely ignorant about the process of programme exchange among nations. I had already read some of the classics of international communication (Alleyne, 1995; Herman and McChesney, 1997; Mattelart, Delcourt, and Mattelart, 1984; Morley and Robins, 1995; Schiller, 1969; Tomlinson, 1991), but the basic facts of global trade remained a mystery to me. How did decisions about which foreign programmes to air and when to air them get made? How widespread was the phenomenon of television export outside the US? Today, I know that I owed my former ignorance not only to the fact that I grew up in the insular television culture of the US, but also to the paucity of research on television trade. While a handful of scholars have sketched the contours of various dimensions of the global television marketplace (Bielby and Harrington, 2002, 2004; Cantor and Cantor, 1986; Dupagne, 1992; Hoskins, McFadyen and Finn, 1997; Miller *et al.*, 2001, 2005; O'Regan, 1992; Schlessinger, 1986; Tinic, 2005; Wildman and Siwek, 1988), Janet Wasko's (1994) observation that 'the actual process of international distribution and marketing of entertainment [television] needs more careful research' (p. 230) is as true today as it was more than ten years ago.

On one level, then, the purpose of this volume is to describe the process of global television exchange, including the dominant business practices of programme distributors and buyers, and the reasons behind them. On another level, however, these descriptions have a good deal to say about contemporary scholarly debates, in particular the perennial disagreements about the impact of media globalisation on television cultures and industries around the world. In addition, I believe that the framework I develop for examining the television marketplace goes a long way towards reconciling critical political-economic analysis and critical cultural studies of global television (i.e., Meehan, 1999). My main argument is that the business-people who populate the global television marketplace function as gatekeepers, mediating between the economic imperatives of transnational media conglomerates and the fickle viewing pleasures of audiences worldwide. What is more, in order to study how this crucial mediating function works, we need to understand both the political-economic structures of global television and the culture worlds of the businesspeople who operate within its constraints.

My use of the term 'global' throughout this study is meant to signal particular firms and programmes with multinational reach, rather than to suggest that the book covers television exchanges in every corner of the globe. Instead, I focus on those media firms that actively sell their programmes as widely as possible around the world, including companies that range from the largest multinationals to one-person operations. What these firms share is a business model emphasising sales to foreign channels as a significant revenue stream. They are the organisations most intimately involved in constructing today's global television marketplace.

For years, quantitative analyses of aggregate television flows among nations dominated critical research into international programme markets. Beginning with Kaarle Nordenstreng and Tapio Varis' (1974) classic study of the 'one-way flow' of international television programming, this research consistently painted a portrait of a television world dominated by Western-produced programming, especially programming from the US. While later studies (Varis, 1985) discovered increased domestic production in many nations after 1974, the development of regional production centres, and the increasing use of imports in non-primetime hours, they continued to demonstrate a clear trade imbalance between the US and the rest of the world. While these studies did not carry a normative political or theoretical position on the trends they uncovered, they were often used to support claims about creeping Western cultural imperialism (Herman and McChesney, 1997; Schiller, 1969, 1991; Tomlinson, 1991).

By the early 1980s, some audience scholars began to question the premise that the mere presence of such large amounts of American programming worldwide led to cultural standardisation and the impoverishment of local cultures (Ang, 1985; Fejes, 1981; Penacchioni, 1984). Several ethnographically inspired reception studies ensued, documenting the complexity and ambivalence of the uptake of imported television programming among communities in various parts of the world (Gillespie, 1995; Miller, 1992; Valaskakis, 1988). Along with more refined theoretical models of transnational cultural exchange (Ang, 1990; Appadurai, 1990; Caughie, 1990; Robertson, 1994), these studies helped replace cultural imperialism as the dominant theoretical frame in international communications with theories of cultural globalisation and hybridity that emphasise the interactions among domestic and imported cultures, rather than the simple domination of one by the other (Kraidy, 2002; Tomlinson, 1999).

While the complexity of the reception of imported television programming has become a theoretical truism in international communications, the processes of production and circulation of international programming continue to be studied mostly in uni-dimensional, macroeconomic terms. This level of analysis is crucial for understanding the strong-arm tactics of Hollywood and other large media conglomerates in opening up closed markets, threatening the viability of local television and film industries abroad and destroying or homogenising local cultural expression. However, such studies rarely examine how human agents in the global media industries facilitate, mediate, negotiate and resist Hollywood's dominance. For instance, Toby Miller *et al.* (2001, 2005) provide an exhaustive analysis of the history of Hollywood's global dominance of film and television, as well as the ways in which the New International Division of Cultural Labor guarantees that certain territories' creative workers provide casual, semi-skilled labour for Hollywood-controlled productions. Ironically, given their concentration on the forms of dominance that Hollywood exerts, their analysis tends to portray these creative workers as mere cogs in Hollywood's cultural-production machine, rather than as agents whose creative sensibilities and techniques draw from, challenge and potentially transform Hollywood's representational arsenal (Hesmondhalgh, 2002, pp. 160–2).

A lack of attention to how human agents mediate global television trade has led to a good deal of conceptual muddiness when it comes to understanding the dynamics and consequence of global television. One important confusion involves disagreements about the forces that determine global television flows. This debate pits political economists, who argue that structural features of global television determine the kinds of programming that travel internationally and the places where they travel (i.e., Herman and McChesney, 1997), against cultural scholars, who suggest that cultural homologies among exporting and importing nations determine such flows (i.e., Tracey and Redal, 1995).

An examination of the executives who make decisions about television trade allows us to see that these seemingly antithetical theoretical positions are both accurate, if only partially. While a global conglomerate with massive production holdings may, under some conditions, force its programming on the local television outlets it owns around the world, such instances are rare because a local outlet's revenues depends upon its ability to respond to rapidly changing competitive conditions in its immediate surroundings. Likewise, although many television outlets around the world rely on ratings and other forms of audience research, such audiences never have direct decision-making power when it comes to selecting which programmes to import. Rather, local executives act as intermediaries between viewers and exporters, deciding which programmes to purchase and how to schedule them based upon their own understandings of the culture. While structural features of the global television business do not determine programming decisions, they do facilitate interactions among executives within large organisations that can influence such decisions. By the same token, although viewers' tastes and preferences do not decide import choices, importers certainly take into account their knowledge of the local audience and culture, typically formed from a combination of research, past experience and intuition (Bielby and Harrington, 2004).

The model of global television trade that I develop in this volume also helps refine more hybrid models of media regionalisation that attempt to integrate economic and cultural levels of analysis. Joseph Straubhaar's (1991) model of asymmetrical interdependence and cultural proximity suggests that a nation's position in the world system determines how much programming the nation imports, while its 'cultural proximity' to other television-producing nations determines the source of the imports. Thus, if a nation has the financial resources, it will produce its own programming; if not, it will seek imports from the most culturally similar nations it can find.

John Sinclair, Elizabeth Jacka and Stuart Cunningham (1996; p. 8) identify language as a primary marker of cultural proximity, arguing that television programming tends to flow within 'geolinguistic regions', such as Latin America, Greater China and the Arabic-speaking nations. Tom O'Regan (1992, para. 98), meanwhile, suggests that cultural proximities of race help explain US–European programming flows. More recently, Straubhaar (2004) has updated his original thesis to include proximities based in genre, values and themes, in an effort to explain programming flows that seem to eschew the logic of cultural proximity, such as the popularity of Latin American *telenovelas* throughout Central and Eastern Europe. Meanwhile, Scott Olson (1999) turns his attention to the intersection of institutional arrangements and representational strategies, arguing that the 'transparency' of Hollywood programming facilitates its widespread global appeal. While the explanatory power of these hybrid theories offers a marked improvement over the top-down and bottom-up theories of television flow discussed above, they continue to reify the business of television trade itself as a reflection of economic and cultural forces.

The research in this study shows that cultural proximity is not divined from local viewers, but articulated by programming executives worldwide, who develop their ideas about cultural proximity from one another as well as from their local cultures. History, economics, deregulation and international business expansion have created a complex web of relationships among the world's nations and regions, any number of which may be activated during import decisions. As we will see in Chapter 5, for example, the decision by the Hungarian broadcaster TV2 in the late 1990s to import Latin American *telenovelas* and schedule them for older women viewers during daytime slots came from observations of, and discussions with, other television executives in Central Europe, especially Poland and the Czech Republic. When the popularity of *telenovelas* waned, the decision to replace them with US fantasy series came from discussions with television executives in Northern Europe, whose channels are owned by the same transnational conglomerate that owns TV2. In other words, decisions about what kinds of programming to import and how to schedule them often involve a variety of assumptions about programming and audiences that come from both domestic and international sources.

The prevalence of structuralist and culturalist explanations of global television trade has tended to drown out serious analysis of how the business of television trade actually operates. Nevertheless, several researchers working from 'middle-range' theoretical perspectives have explored the links between the business operations of television trade and global programming flows. The term 'middle-range theory' comes from sociologist Robert Merton (1968), whose frustration with both classical sociological theory and positivist social science led him to insist on the need for theory that 'mediates between gross empiricism and grand speculative doctrines' (p. 132). Australian television scholars, such as Sinclair (1999), Sinclair, Jacka and Cunningham (1996), O'Regan (1990, 1992) and Cunningham and Jacka (1996), have been among the most vocal proponents of a middle-range approach to international television that 'is situated between political economy and micro-situational reception studies' (Cunningham and Jacka, 1996, p. 22).

While most of this research has studied international television exchanges in specific nations or regions of the world, some scholars have addressed the process of television trade at the global level from a similar perspective. For example, based on interviews with forty executives and observations at several international television trade shows, Muriel and Joel Cantor (1986) argue against the suggestion that Hollywood forces its programming on markets and viewers around the world. Rather, they write, the process of trade can 'only be described as chaotic, unruly, and unpredictable, with no one really in charge' (p. 512). Although they mainly focus on the role that viewers abroad play in influencing import decisions, they do mention that 'there is a very small group of individuals who specialise in this market. Some of them, buyers and sellers, have known and worked with each other for years' (p. 513). This long-term working relationship, as we will see below, is a central feature of the global television marketplace that leads to a close-knit business community.

In what ways does the business culture of global television shape the transnational exchange of programming? Cunningham and Jacka (1996) identify 'the professional practices of trading in, marketing, and scheduling programs; and the strategic role played by the gatekeepers of the television industries, including managers, commissioning editors, and programme buyers' (p. 22) as crucial factors in their analysis of Australian television exports. Denise Bielby and C. Lee Harrington (2002) take the argument a step further, claiming that the 'culture world' (p. 215) of international business professionals, in particular 'issues of meaning arising from a cross-cultural context, shape business strategies, decisions, and outcomes' (p. 216). Specifically, they look at how programming and promotions must be adapted in various parts of the world in order to appease audiences and buyers.

Picking up on and expanding the insights of middle-range theories of international programme exchange, this volume demonstrates how the business culture of global television exerts a relatively autonomous, overdetermining influence on the processes of trade and flows of programming. Its main argument is that international television executives who promote, sell, purchase and schedule transborder television programming form a unique cultural group, an international jet-set that gets its ideas about television as much from one another as from observations of television cultures in different locales. Everything from the aesthetic possibilities of the medium and understandings of why people watch television to the kinds of meanings viewers derive and the variety of ways of conceptualising viewers' similarities and differences has taken on this hybrid character. Moreover, this is a business culture deeply affected by unequal power relations. In 1997, the most recent year for which such data are available, sales of programming from the seven major Hollywood distributors accounted for 31.6 per cent of all television sales worldwide, at the same time that a small cadre of 77 acquisitions executives consumed 73 per cent of Hollywood's product (Dinerman and Serafini, 1997, p. 1; *Hollywood Reporter*, 1998a). The business culture of global television reflects these imbalances in economic power among different classes of companies, bestowing prestige and wisdom on the most successful firms and executives, whose ideas are followed by producers, distributors and schedulers everywhere.

The constant, worldwide search for programming and ideas is driven by a combination of institutional needs and economic pressures, regardless of whether a television outlet is commercial or non-profit, although the specific pressures differ depending upon where a broadcaster's funding comes from. To begin with, the volume of programming available on the global markets, combined with the uncertain popularity of television programmes when they cross cultural boundaries, leads most buyers to rely on a relatively small number of distributors, from whom they purchase most of their programming. Not surprisingly, many buyers prefer to import shows from producers and distributors with proven track records in international television. For instance, when the producers of the globally popular series *Seinfeld* (1990–98) developed the new series *It's Like, You Know* in 1999, the new series pre-sold in markets around the world, despite the fact that it eventually flopped in the US and was cancelled after a single season. Still, in the absence of other indicators, corporate reputations offer the most reliable guarantee of viewer appeal.

In addition, due to the large amount of preview tapes, programme fliers and emails generated by the promotion of new global programmes each year, the only way that buyers can make their jobs manageable is to rely on a set group of suppliers. Consequently, producers and distributors work hard to establish and maintain positive reputations, and a large part of that effort involves introducing new series on a regular basis. An important dimension of introducing new series consists of identifying or creating worldwide programming trends, which specific series can take advantage of. This worldwide identification and exploitation of the newest programming trends, exemplified most recently by the spread of different genres of 'reality programming', is one of the most obvious and significant ways that the global programming markets influence domestic television cultures (i.e., Waisbord, 2004).

While programming trends offer an obvious example of how the global television market influences television industries around the world, the research in this book offers several examples of this phenomenon. A variety of business decisions, ranging from how to promote programming in international markets and to select specific imports, to how to schedule imported programming and how to discover programming and scheduling innovations, exhibit an intermingling of local and imported television knowledge. In other words, the global trade in television programming includes a good deal of trade in ideas *about* television as well. Moreover, this trade does not take place on a level playing field, but is profoundly distorted by economic inequalities that allow certain companies from certain nations much more control over the discourses of the global television marketplace.

It is at the level of ideas about the possibilities of television, I would argue, that the 'cultural imperialism' of a Western-dominated global media system is the most apparent, rather than in the hidden 'consumerist values' (Herman and McChesney, 1997, p. 189) that supposedly lurk just below the surface of commercial programming. That is, as a generation of television professionals worldwide begins to think about television in similar ways, they likewise define for the rest of us the possibilities (and impossibilities) of the medium, as well as the imaginary connections that bind together different segments of the public both within and beyond the nation-state. These forms of standardisation are far more powerful than the representational strategies of television texts, the meanings that viewers make from television, or global patterns of media ownership. Nevertheless, as the research here attests, the story of global television is not simply one of domination by the powerful; it also includes a good deal of resistance by television professionals who use the global programming markets to produce, purchase and schedule television programmes differently.

In what follows, I have broken down the process of global television trade into three distinct stages – distribution, acquisition and scheduling – which I treat in three different chapters, though this distinction is merely an analytic one, and in practice each moment overlaps and interacts with the others in complex ways. This model for studying global television trade has several advantages. First, it underscores the fact that, at each stage of the process, different firms, personnel, priorities and discourses come together to generate programme trade. Second, it allows us to trace how, in an effort to manage the unpredictable popularity of the televisual commodity, each stage of the process delimits possibilities in each subsequent stage. For instance, when distributors decide to lavish promotional efforts on particular shows instead of others, those decisions will most likely influence purchasing decisions. Finally, the model makes clear how the constant search for corporate profits constructs complex and varied industry discourses that channel, dam and direct programming flows among particular companies, nations and groups.

Before delving into the various stages of programme trade, however, Chapter 1 traces the development of the global television marketplace, looking especially at how regulatory, technological and business practices have increased the global interdependence of television markets, production companies and television broadcasters in many parts of the world. While initially limited to the US and a handful of other nations with commercial television in the 1950s, international distribution 'windows' have, since the 1980s, become central to funding domestic programming at both commercial and public television producers around the world. In addition, the costs of production and increased competition for viewers in markets across the globe have led most broadcasters to seek a balance between domestically produced and imported programming. Furthermore, these international windows have migrated 'upstream' in recent years, often accounting for a good deal of up-front and first-run revenues.

Chapter 2 looks in detail at how different-sized distributors from different parts of the world select, market and sell programming to international buyers, chronicling the kinds of television programming available on the global markets, the variety of companies involved in the global television marketplace and the dominant kinds of promotional activities and personal relationships that distributors establish. The chapter shows how, due to the relative expense and subsequent popularity of US and Western programming around the world, distributors of all sizes, from all corners of the globe, often duplicate Western promotional techniques, making them the standard for the business.

Chapter 3 provides a ritual analysis of global television sales markets, which are industry trade shows held several times per year where merchants come to trade programming and ideas. Although these markets do serve a number of business functions, in particular the establishment and renewal of business relationships, I argue that their primary work is cultural, as they give buyers and sellers a crucial sense of community, at the same time that they provide physical distinctions between participants that help them network effectively and also express the various levels of prestige among them. Because prestige and success are intertwined in global television, distributors and buyers use a variety of tactics at the global markets to demonstrate their prestige. In short, the smooth operation of the business relies on the kinds of cultural work that merchants can only achieve at the markets.

In Chapters 4 and 5, which, respectively, explore how decisions about the acquisition and scheduling of foreign programmes operate, the focus shifts to the national level, because import and scheduling decisions derive primarily from national competitive conditions, and because global distributors typically price and sell rights on a nation-by-nation basis. Indeed, these chapters show that, despite the increasingly global reach of programme distributors and channel operators, the majority of the world's television trade continues to be made up of programming designed for a particular national market, which is subsequently sold into other national markets. Of course, various cultural and linguistic differences among nations account for the continued relevance of the nation-state as the basis of trade. However, industry practices and discourses reinforce and extend the importance of the national as the largest common multiple of social identity. That is, while merchants acknowledge the divisions of race, gender, ethnicity, educational background and the like within the nation, such differences are primarily seen as subdividing an overarching national identity. Not only does this illusion maintain the coherence of *the* national audience, which remains the prime target audience for general entertainment programmers, but it also reinforces acquisitions executives' roles as privileged interpreters of national tastes, thereby securing their clout in an industry that is predicated upon catering to those tastes.

Chapters 4 and 5 both examine decision-making in Hungary, a market with no 'natural' linguistically similar trading partners. Since the collapse of state socialism, Hungary has become a vibrant market for television advertising, as well as a magnet for foreign media investors, particularly Western Europeans. The absence of an inevitable trading partner requires Hungarian buyers and programmers to be particularly conscious of the cultural affinities that underlie their acquisitions decisions, as we shall see in Chapter 4. Based on case studies of the national commercial and public-service broadcasters, as well as two national cable channels, this chapter demonstrates that the main determinants of acquisitions decisions are the competitive environments in which television outlets operate, in particular, the competition for viewers and foreign programme rights. In addition, this chapter shows, through concrete examples, how the business lore of global television circulates and influences local acquisitions decisions.

Chapter 5 looks at how imported programmes are scheduled in Hungary, especially how scheduling innovations occur, and how these innovations influence the placement, the popularity and the fate of programme imports. Scheduling drives acquisitions, because most decisions about the kinds and quantities of programming to import begin when a broadcaster identifies specific holes or weaknesses in its schedule. Moreover, because scheduling innovations occur regularly, though unpredictably, they can have a significant impact on a channel's import profile. The chapter traces three scheduling innovations, including the shift from imported Latin American *telenovelas* to imported US series during daytime, the shift from imported European and US programming to local reality shows in prime time and the development of adult-oriented reality show outtakes in late night. The primary argument of the chapter is that these innovations exhibit features of both locally derived and imported ideas about how to attract viewers most effectively.

Finally, Chapter 6 returns to the international level to investigate how foreign acquisitions and scheduling practices operate at transnational channels, including the global channel Reality TV, the regional channel HBO Central Europe and the ethnic Hungarian channel Duna TV. Here again, we see how the competitiveness of the markets for viewers and programme rights, together with relationships among global television executives and the business lore that circulates among them, determine acquisitions and scheduling choices. Moreover, we see how the global programming markets encourage certain kinds of transnational television channels, while discouraging others.

The research for this volume involved interviews with nearly 100 global television professionals from around the world, including thirty-six distributors, forty-eight buyers and redistributors, and eight people involved in various ancillary industries, many of whom I interviewed more than once. Among distributors, I generally interviewed heads of sales departments or presidents or vice presidents of sales. Among buyers, I interviewed mostly heads of acquisitions or programming departments. Combined, my interviews included people with professional experience in the following markets: Australia, Canada, Chile, China, Columbia, the Czech Republic, Egypt, Finland, France, Germany, Hungary, India, Indonesia, Italy, Japan, Jordan, Kuwait, Latvia, Malaysia, Mexico, the Netherlands, Poland, Romania, Russia, Singapore, Slovenia, South Africa, Spain, Taiwan, Thailand, Turkey, the UK, Ukraine, the US and Venezuela.

Generally speaking, these interviews were conducted in four separate 'waves', and the content of interviews depended roughly on when they took place. During the spring and summer of 1999, I interviewed Hollywood and independent US distributors, as well as buyers from Europe, Latin America, Asia and Africa.

These interviews covered the general processes of television trade, as well as specific buying preferences and sales strategies. In early 2001, I interviewed US and non-US distributors about the ways in which they used the global sales markets, how they constructed their brand identities and their overall sales strategies. The third wave of interviews took place over a two-month period in Hungary during the summer of 2001 and a six-month period in the summer and autumn of 2002. I interviewed acquisitions executives and programming heads of all of the major and minor terrestrial, cable and satellite channels, as well as local redistributors and ratings and advertising executives. Finally, in spring 2004, I conducted a series of interviews with distributors of various sizes and specialities at the Marché International des Programmes de Télévision (International Television Programme Market) (MIP-TV) that addressed their sales and branding strategies, as well as the specifics of how the sales markets work.

In identifying interview subjects, I adopted a snowball sampling method (Lindlof, 1995, p. 128), asking each subject for a list of others whom I might interview. Given the communal and sometimes insular nature of television trade, this method allowed me greater access to subjects and also took advantage of the social networks that already exist in global television. In addition to interviews, I have attended five major international television trade shows and two region-wide trade shows in Central Europe, and have extensively reviewed global television trade journals.

What emerges from this research is the first comprehensive portrait of how the global television marketplace operates. Such a portrait is crucial to any theoretical treatment of television globalisation, since international television executives determine global television flows in the first instance, based on their own readings of the economics of the business and the preferences of their primary audiences.

1

The History of Global Television Sales

The world's television industries have undergone two intense periods of global expansion and contraction. The first lasted from the mid-1950s through the early 1970s, while the second period spans the late 1980s to the present. All of the business practices that are common today in international programme trade were present in the earlier period, including international joint ventures, heavy reliance on international sales to fund production, the amassing of programme libraries to sell worldwide and the formation of buying groups to supply multiple channels of exhibition. What distinguishes these two periods and makes the current one more pervasive and permanent is the multiplication and synchronisation of distribution 'windows' across the globe, which have become central to financing television everywhere. The resulting institutional and economic interdependence of the world's television industries, which requires frequent, close contact among international programming merchants, has led to the formation of a global television business and culture. While domestic television industries continue to follow their own internal political, economic and cultural logics, the global business today exerts an independent influence on domestic industries and the businesspeople who work at the juncture between the global and the local.

HOW TELEVISION TRAVELS
Television programming is sold into what economists call 'windows', which are distinct markets separated by either geography or time, where buyers receive differential access and variable prices. Regarding separation by geography, for instance, the US market contains 210 distinct local markets where a distributor can sell first-run or off-network programmes. Regarding separation by time, a feature film distributor might sell rights first to pay-per-view channels, then to premium movie channels and later to a national network for primetime exhibition. These additional windows are typically referred to as 'after-market', or 'residual' profits, because they do not figure in to the rights holder's immediate profits. However, revenues from these windows do figure in decisions about production budgets for individual projects. Moreover, in recent years, many

distributors have tried to move various distribution windows forward in time, in hopes of recouping their production investments more quickly.

Almost since the inception of television broadcasting, US distributors have treated international buyers as a separate window, and in today's business, distributors in many parts of the world subdivide international windows spatially and temporally. This globalisation of windowing has altered television programming in many parts of the world, enlarging production budgets, standardising the use of recorded rather than live programming, expanding the markets for global television, and requiring almost all television schedulers to seek to balance domestic and imported programmes for economic reasons. Initially treated as residual profits, international windows now frequently account for up-front sales, especially at small and medium-sized companies.

Windows exist because of what is known as the 'public good' or 'joint consumption' feature of audiovisual commodities. As Bruce Owen and Steven Wildman (1992) explain, 'one person's consumption of such a good does not reduce the quantity available to other people. ... The cost of producing a television *program* is independent of the number of people who will eventually see it' (pp. 23–4). By contrast, a private good is a commodity such as food, which, 'if consumed by one person, is no longer available for someone else' (p. 23). Colin Hoskins, Stuart McFadyen and Adam Finn (1997) refer to this as 'the joint consumption characteristic' (p. 31) of television. Many of the unique features of television sales stem from this characteristic. Joint consumption makes windowing possible and appealing because the initial airing does not use up the programme, and 'downstream' windows can take advantage of already-produced programming at minimal additional costs. In fact, this feature underlies much of global television sales, because it is cheaper to buy already-produced programming from the international market than it is to self-produce, even when it comes to programming with high production budgets.

Table 1.1 illustrates comparative costs in 1991 and 1996 of importing programming versus self-producing for European broadcasters. For almost every broadcaster listed, it was cheaper to import than to self-produce, because production requires an investment in studios, crew, hardware, actors, writers, caterers and so forth, while importation involves purchasing only a copy of the original production. In addition, since many distributors make back a majority of their investment from domestic markets, prices in international windows are typically lower.

The public good feature of television means that, theoretically at least, every new programme competes with other new programmes as well as every other programme ever made. A buyer on the international market looking to fill a

Table 1.1: Ratio of Costs for Self-Produced Versus Imported Programming in Selected European Markets
(1991 and 1996)

Country	Channel	1991	1996
Austria	ORF	1.90	1.34
Denmark	DR	5.25	5.26
	TV2	3.12	4.04
France	France 2	2.22	2.01
	France 3	3.14	3.17
Germany	ARD	5.53	5.62
	ZDF	2.98	3.56
Ireland	RTE	6.58	6.86
Italy	RAI	2.90	4.34
Netherlands	NOS	3.26	2.92
Norway	NRK	9.31	7.35
UK	BBC	n/a	2.97
	ITV	1.95	3.56
	Channel 4	3.37	2.52

Source: *Screen Digest* (1997a: 83)

Note:
Numerical values represent how many times cheaper it is to import programming versus self-production. A ratio of
1.0 indicates that costs for imports and self-productions are equivalent.

thirty-minute time slot can purchase an American situation comedy from the
1950s or an animated Japanese series that has yet to be made. In practice, of
course, the competition between old and new shows is not equal, as most television programmes lose a good deal of their value as they grow older or cross
cultural boundaries, moving further away from their spatiotemporal debut window. Hoskins, McFadyen and Finn (1997) note that television programming
faces a 'cultural discount' when it moves beyond the culture it was originally
designed for. Likewise, programmes typically encounter a 'temporal discount'
in windows far removed from their original production date. Thus, while cultural and temporal discounts tend to restrict the circulation of television
programmes to their immediate spatiotemporal locations, their status as public
goods and their subsequent durability tend to encourage wide circulation, both
spatially and temporally. It is this dual tendency within the televisual commodity that explains the expansions and contractions of the global television market
over the past fifty years. In addition, cultural and temporal discounts help
explain the massive price differentials for internationally traded audiovisual
commodities on the world markets (Table 1.2). That is, because buyers only purchase broadcasting rights, which cover a specified number of runs for a
particular geographic area and length of time, rather than a tangible product
with identifiable production costs, distributors can base prices on the buyer's
ability to pay.

The cultural specificity of most television programming means that the
domestic popularity of internationally traded shows is highly erratic, and no

1

GLOBAL TELEVISION MARKETPLACE

Table 1.2: Average Prices Paid by Terrestrial Broadcasters for One-Hour Dramas in Selected Territories (2004)

Country	Average Price (US$)
Albania	250–300
Australia	25,000–35,000
Bangladesh	200–350
Bolivia	250–750
Brazil	4,000–7,000
Canada (English Speaking)	20,000–60,000
France	10,000–50,000
Germany	20,000–55,000
India	1,000–2,000
Iraq	350–500
Israel	800–1500
Japan	45,000–70,000
Mexico	1,500–5000
Saudi Arabia	800–1000
South Africa	2,000–2,250
UK	20,000–100,000
US	1,000,000–2,000,000
Zimbabwe	150–200

Source: *Channel 21* (2004b)

reliable predictors of success exist. Consequently, global television buyers must rely on non-objective measures of potential success, such as reputations, promotional materials, and personal relationships to make purchasing decisions, because one choice is seldom inherently better than another. The unpredictability of any single purchase, complicated by the vast amount of programming to choose from, makes global television 'perhaps the most socially-intimate of all commodity trades' (Mahamdi, 1992, p. 237). Together, then, the public good feature of audiovisual commodities and the unpredictability of their performance have created a vibrant, close-knit business culture of global television sales, which *Broadcasting* as early as 1977 dubbed 'television's own jet-set' (*Broadcasting*, 1977a, p. 88). A buyer from Trinidad and Tobago at the time expressed the sense of community he felt among his fellow television executives at an international trade fair: 'It provides a forum for people to meet,' he said, 'and to realize that, in television, we share the same problems all over the world' (ibid., p. 94).

TELEVISION GLOBALISATION, 1957–72: THE FIRST WAVE
The international exchange of television programmes goes back almost as far as television broadcasting itself. During the 1950s, independent US distributors 'bicycled' kinescopes throughout Latin America (Sinclair, 1999, p. 14). In 1955, Western European nations formed the Eurovision network to facilitate international programme exchanges, an organisation that was balanced in 1957 by a similar arrangement among Eastern bloc nations, known as Intervision (Pollack and Woods, 1959; *The New York Times*, 1957). In other parts of the globe, Central Chinese Television (CCTV) imported programming from the Soviet Union

as early as 1958 (Hong, 1998, pp. 46–7), and the Egyptian series *Hareb Min El Ayam* (1966) (*Fugitive from Life*), played throughout the Arab world in the late 1960s (Darwish, 2004).

Several authors have seen this early period as a formative moment, when many of the current practices of global television developed, including the local adaptation of programme formats from abroad (Moran, 1998); the aesthetic rules of 'satellite televisuality' that aligned the new technology with liveness and progress (Parks, 2003); and the drive to dominate worldwide television by the US networks and the Kennedy administration (Curtin, 1997).

While US distributors may have sold more programming abroad than distributors from other nations, accounting for an estimated 80 per cent of all internationally traded programmes in the early 1960s (*Business Week*, 1962), other nations were hardly idle when it came to international sales. Producers and distributors in the UK, Latin America and Japan also experienced some globalisation, as did Eastern and Western European nations.

For US syndicators in the 1950s and 1960s, numerous international distribution windows opened up as nation after nation introduced television broadcasting. Between 1950 and 1960, television transmission stations worldwide grew from thirty to 1,500 (USIA, 1962). Television broadcasting was introduced in Venezuela and the Dominican Republic in 1952; in Japan and the Philippines in 1953; in Colombia and Denmark in 1954; in Nicaragua, Guatemala, Algeria, Australia, Sweden and Finland in 1956; in Chile, Peru and

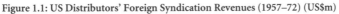

Figure 1.1: US Distributors' Foreign Syndication Revenues (1957–72) (US$m)

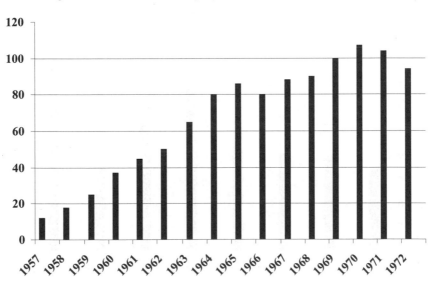

Source: Estimated from trade journal reports

Iran in 1958; in Nigeria in 1959; in Egypt and Norway in 1960; in India and
Saudi Arabia in 1965; and in Jordan in 1968 (Boyd, 1998, p. 184; Jacka and
Johnson, 1998, p. 210; Kato, 1998, p. 171; Okigbo, 1998, p. 234; Syversten and
Skogerbø, 1998, p. 224; Thomas, 1998, p. 201). Most of these upstart broad-
casters relied on US imports to help fill out their schedules. By 1962, foreign
viewers outnumbered US viewers (Seagrave, 1998, p. 36).

Specific revenue data in global television sales is notoriously difficult to come
by, and trying to get reliable figures for these early days is doubly difficult. Nevertheless, a clear portrait of a globalised US television business emerges from
available information. The totals in Figure 1.1, drawn from various trade journal sources, give a sense of the growing importance of international sales for US
producers, as revenues rose from $12 million in 1957 to over $100 million by
the end of the 1960s. These numbers reflect only sales generated by the US networks and independent syndicators, not the major Hollywood studios. US
merchants enjoyed steep sales growth from 1957–64, after which the market
remained steady until 1971, when foreign revenues began to drop off. For
reasons discussed below, the importance of foreign revenues steadily declined
in the early 1970s, even though total foreign sales revenues continued to climb.

A more revealing statistic measuring the level of globalisation is the percentage of overall revenues that US syndicators generated from overseas sales (see
Figure 1.2). This percentage grew substantially from below 20 per cent in 1957
to more than 40 per cent in 1964 (Kroeger, 1966, p. 36). Among syndicators,

Figure 1.2: US Distributors' Percentage of Revenues from Foreign Syndication (1957–64)

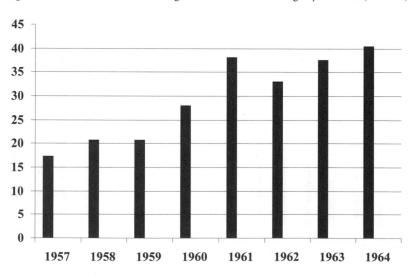

Source: Calculated from figures in Kroeger (1966: 36)

speculation ran high that international sales would soon account for more than half of overall revenues, which had been the case in film distribution for decades (*Business Week*, 1960b, p. 131; Fineshriber, 1960, p. 2). However, international syndication revenues never came close to this mark and, by the mid-1970s, had fallen below thirty per cent of overall sales. That percentage would not regain its earlier levels until the 1990s (Seagrave, 1998: 238–9).

Elsewhere in the world, the excitement over global television was perhaps less hyperbolic than in the US, though many nations did develop a variety of programme exchanges that primarily remained within their immediate geographical regions. In Latin America, for instance, Mexican broadcasting mogul Emilio Azcáraga Vidaurreta began marketing live broadcasts that originated in Mexico City to broadcasters in Latin America and the US in 1954 (Stilling, 1995, p. 234). When Azcáraga Vidaurreta's station in Monterey, Mexico, acquired a videotape recorder in 1958, it allowed his newly formed network conglomerate Telesistema de Mexico (TSM), to expand into foreign programme sales and network investments across Latin America, as well as areas of the US near the Mexican border, becoming the dominant supplier of Spanish-language programming in the Americas (Stilling, 1995, pp. 235–6).

Japanese television industries, meanwhile, were net importers of programming until the late 1970s. The majority of imports came from US distributors, and popular genres ranged from dramas to Westerns to detective shows, depending upon the year (Stronach, 1989, p. 138). Nevertheless, Japanese distributors did export 2,200 hours of programming in 1972, which mostly consisted of sales of animation programming to East Asian buyers (Hara, 2004, para. 23).

Among European distributors at the time, programme trade remained minimal, despite the presence of Eurovision and Intervision networks for programme exchanges in Western and Eastern Europe, respectively. Both Eurovision and Intervision performed similar functions, providing relays among television networks in each nation in their respective organisations. Member nations chose which programmes to place on the Eurovision and Intervision networks and which programmes to broadcast (Pollock and Woods, 1959). Table 1.3 summarises the number of programme hours exchanged via the Eurovision and Intervision systems through 1972. While programme trade increased dramatically during this period, from a combined total of 610 hours in 1960 to 2,262 hours in 1972, the amount of foreign programming remained a small fraction of total broadcast time in all European nations (Eugster, 1983, pp. 224, 227; Pollock and Woods, 1959, p. 110). This paucity of programme exchange resulted from a lack of commercial programme distributors seeking to exploit their products as widely as possible, and the cultural and linguistic difference among nations

Table 1.3: Programme Hours Exchanged Via Eurovision and Intervision (1954–72)

	Eurovision	Intervision
1960	440	170
1961	606	213
1962	586	300
1963	762	392
1964	664	498
1965	743	552
1966	813	496
1967	812	641
1968	898	529
1969	951	877
1970	986	943
1971	1097	873
1972	1138	1124

Source: Eugster (1983: 224 and 227)

in the region. In addition to intra-European exchanges, European public broadcasters also traded programmes to former colonies that shared a language with the exporting state, including British trade with Australia and French trade with Francophone Africa (Fair, 2003, p. 195; Jacka and Johnson, 1998, p. 212), as well as more charitably minded exchanges with Third World nations intended to foster economic and social development (Stephenson, 1967).

A variety of business practices associated with the global television trade today were present by the 1960s, including the formation of industry groups dedicated to globalising distribution, the establishment of international co-production and programme formatting and investment in foreign television broadcasting. As with programme trade, these practices were particularly noticeable among US distributors, although they were also present among distributors in other parts of the world, and some of the practices were pioneered by distributors outside the US.

In 1959, the Motion Picture Export Association of America (MPEAA), a trade organisation representing the nine major Hollywood studios at the time, formed the Television Film Export Committee to focus on improving sales of Hollywood programming abroad (Fineshriber, 1960). That same year, a group of the largest independent television syndicators formed its own organisation known as the Television Program Export Association (TPEA) (Gordon, 1960). Both organisations sought to open new markets for US television distribution, to protect their members from what they saw as unfair quota restrictions on US product in some markets and to drive up prices for US programming. They also got involved in efforts to spread the US model of commercial broadcasting worldwide, especially in the economically mature markets of Western Europe (Seagrave, 1998, p. 75–6).

Programme co-production and local programme adaptations, popularly known as 'formats' in the industry, also became widespread during this period. These business arrangements differed markedly from programme trade in their attempts to overcome the cultural discount that television programming faced outside its culture of origin; they indicated a high degree of globalisation in the production industry because they were sophisticated strategies designed to maximise programme appeal and profits outside the home market.

International co-productions involved partners from more than one nation working together on a programme that was intended for distribution in each partner's home market. Nowadays, many nations have official co-production arrangements with other nations that specify the terms that such agreements must conform to in order to qualify for government funding. In the 1950s, co-productions between American and foreign partners were especially prevalent in the UK, where imported programmes could make up no more than 14 per cent of transmission time, as well as in Latin America, where Spanish-language programming often outperformed imports (Gordon, 1960, p. 1; Myers, 1957).

In 1957, every US network was co-producing with UK partners, as were several of the large syndicators, including Ziv Television Programs and Screen Gems. The most successful of these co-productions, such as *Robin Hood* (1955–60), *William Tell* (1958), and *The Buccaneers* (1956–7), found their way onto the US networks as well (Myers, 1957). On the non-commercial side of programme production, various public broadcasting stations in the US and the BBC began co producing programming in 1971 (Strover, 2004, p. 589). Meanwhile, in Latin America, CBS was involved with co-production in Venezuela, Peru and Argentina through partially owned local production companies in 1966 (Tyler, 1966, p. 33). While European co-productions became a popular way for producers to match the production values of imported US programmes in the 1980s, it was a far less common practice in the 1960s and 1970s (Renaud and Litman, 1985, p. 255; Strover, 2004, p. 589).

Formatting, on the other hand, was a more widespread practice outside the US than was co-production, though formatting lacked its current institutional status and often took place without payments or the knowledge of the original producer. The Latin American *telenovela*, one of the most popular international genres today, began life as a Cuban format of US radio soap operas, which was later adapted to television and spread throughout Latin America (Paxman, 1996). Likewise, several popular Australian shows in the 1960s were unlicensed formats of BBC series (Jacka and Johnson, 1998, p. 212).

When it came to foreign investment in television production and broadcasting services, the US networks led the way, although Mexican broadcasters were also early pioneers in this area, particular in areas of the US where large Spanish-speaking populations lived. In 1966, NBC owned interests in TV stations in Argentina, Australia, Hong Kong, Jamaica, Mexico and Venezuela, and had management contracts to provide advice and expertise to broadcasters in Saudi

Arabia, Nigeria, Vietnam and Venezuela. CBS, in addition to its production holdings in Latin America, had an interest in television broadcasters in Trinidad and Antigua, cable systems throughout Canada and a management arrangement in Israel. ABC held stakes in broadcasters in Canada, Guatemala, El Salvador, Honduras, Costa Rica, Panama, Columbia, Venezuela, Ecuador, Argentina, Lebanon, Japan, the Philippines, Australia, Chile and Bermuda. Through its broadcasting consortium, Worldvision, which consisted of centralised programme-buying and advertising sales operations, ABC also had nearly fifty broadcasting partners in twenty-six nations, as well as interests in production companies in the UK, West Germany and Mexico (Tyler, 1966, p. 33).

In addition to selling programmes themselves, the US network contracted with foreign producers to include their programmes in the networks' international catalogues. For instance, *The CBS International Television Catalog* in 1968 contained programming from the Tokyo Broadcasting Corporation, including *Past Intruding*, an experimental documentary broadcast in the US, Germany, Sweden, Italy and Norway (CBS, 1968). Donald Coyle, the president of ABC's international operations, Worldvision, saw the representation of foreign programming as a potentially lucrative revenue stream in the coming age of global television (*Broadcasting*, 1962b).

Like its North American counterparts, the vertically integrated Mexican network TSM also pursued aggressive foreign investment strategies in the 1960s. By the end of the decade, TSM had partial ownership in stations in Los Angeles, San Antonio, New York and Miami, and targeted other communities along the border with five wholly owned border stations (Stilling, 1995, pp. 235–6). Although Azcáraga Vidaurreta, TSM's owner, was barred from holding more than 20 per cent of these US stations, he successfully orchestrated a variety of illegal manoeuvres that gave him controlling ownership in most of the stations that went undetected until the mid-1980s (ibid., p. 243). Again in a fashion similar to the US networks, Azcáraga Vidaurreta seems to have been less interested in the profitability of these new stations, and more interested in establishing consistent buyers for his programming, whose production costs had already been amortised in the Mexican market (ibid. p. 236). In fact, Erik Stilling credits Azcáraga Vidaurreta with pioneering the now common strategy of internationalisation through the expansion of foreign programming windows.

Ironically, despite their large and potentially lucrative film and television libraries, the major Hollywood studios shunned international television in the 1950s and 1960s in order to protect their international box-office revenues. Foreign ticket sales had accounted for more than half of Hollywood's box office receipts since the early decades of the twentieth century (Guback, 1977, p. 20). Numerous trade journal articles at the time commented on the paucity of feature film sales to foreign television. One *Variety* article from 1963, titled simply, 'Features Abroad Play Minor Role', reported industry estimates that only 10 per cent of revenues from Hollywood feature films came from foreign television outlets (*Variety*, 1963a). An important barrier came from film industries abroad which, like their American counterparts, were uncertain how to deal with the new technology of television. In the 1960s, bans against the sale of feature films to TV existed in the UK, West Germany, Japan and Australia. In addition to concerns about protecting movie theatre attendance, film industries overseas saw television broadcasters as a source of revenue for their own films, and didn't want Hollywood monopolising them (*Variety*, 1960; *Variety*, 1963a; *Variety*, 1963b; *Variety*, 1964).

Limiting sales to international television outlets did little to harm the studios' bottom lines because public broadcasters that paid low prices and bought little product operated in most markets (*Variety*, 1963a). In 1959, a Hollywood feature fetching the highest possible prices in foreign television markets would have brought in less than $30,000 (*Variety*, 1959). By 1978, revenues from sales to foreign television outlets still represented less than 15 per cent of worldwide television and box-office revenues (Renaud and Litman, 1985, p. 249). This was in part because the absence of competition in most markets, combined with the power of local governments to set ceilings on prices, hindered profits, as did quota restrictions on programme imports. In addition, the ninety- to 120-minute length of feature films made scheduling them a challenge, especially at a time when most broadcasters had limited broadcasting hours (*Variety*, 1963).

By the early 1970s, the number of broadcasting hours and television outlets abroad began to stabilise, causing the amount of US imports to level off in most industrialised nations. Latin American and Japanese sales remained consistent throughout the 1970s, but did not grow substantially until the 1980s, when exports from other regional producers such as Egypt and Brazil started to increase as well.

Along with the widespread stabilisation of broadcast schedules, broadcasters around the world also began to increase local production in the 1970s, cutting further into US international syndication revenues. As early as 1966, *Television Magazine* claimed that the US share of foreign television broadcasts had dropped from an average of 30–5 per cent in 1961 to 15–20 per cent in 1966 (Tyler, 1966, p. 32). In addition, the slow pace of commercialisation and the persistence of programme-import quotas kept demand for syndicated US programmes low (*Advertising Age*, 1965; *Broadcasting*, 1960; *Business Week*, 1960a; Myers, 1957; Seagrave, 1998, pp. 95, 101, 103).

One good indicator of the decline in global television sales for US producers in the 1970s is the number of attendants at the annual trade fair, the Marché

International des Programmes de Télévision (International Television Programme Market) (MIP-TV) in Cannes, France, which is the main industry trade
show for international television and was dominated by US programming in the
1960s and 1970s. Attendance at MIP-TV reached its high water mark of 1,680
attendants in 1971, before undergoing steep declines in subsequent years. It was
1978 before attendance surpassed the 1971 numbers (MIP-TV, 2004b). Truly
global programme sales taking place beyond the immediate regional and cultural boundaries would not return in significant numbers until the late 1980s.

CONTRACTION OF GLOBAL TELEVISION MARKETS, 1973–85

In the 1970s, global programme markets shrank for US producers, effectively
bringing the first wave of global programme trade to an end. In addition to
increased production capacity in many nations, regulatory and technological
changes in the domestic US market drew syndicators' attentions to an array of
new domestic buyers, including independent stations and those affiliated with
the national networks. At the same time, new regional distribution opportunities
opened up for Japanese, Brazilian and Egyptian syndicators, while co-productions designed to air in multiple territories became more common among
European, Canadian and Australian producers.

The US Federal Communications Commission (FCC) actively sought to
increase opportunities for independent producers beginning in the 1970s. These
moves inadvertently made international outlets less appealing for both networks
and independent producers. First, the All-Channel Receiver Act of 1962
required television manufacturers to equip new sets with ultra-high frequency
(UHF) receivers, prompting the creation of numerous lower-power, independent stations in need of programming (Sterling and Kittross, 2002, p. 454). By
1966, sales to UHF stations accounted for 10 per cent of all syndication revenues, a 400 per cent increase over 1965 (Williams, 1994, p. 166). Then, in
1970, the FCC passed the Prime Time Access Rule (PTAR) and the Financial
Interest and Syndication (Fin-Syn) Rules, both of which profoundly altered the
US syndication markets. The PTAR prevented local network affiliates in the top
fifty markets from programming off-network reruns in the half-hour prior to
prime time, effectively creating a new window for first-run syndicated programmes. The Fin-Syn Rules, among other things, forbad the broadcast
networks from profiting from the domestic syndication of off-network programming (Sterling and Kittross, 2002: pp. 470–1).

Although nothing in the new FCC regulations prevented the networks from
syndicating their programmes internationally, without domestic syndication revenues, foreign programme sales alone were not sufficient to subsidise network
production costs. By 1972, all of the networks had spun off their international

syndication operations (*Broadcasting*, 1972). Without foreign sales to subsidise the remainder of the networks' international operations, they abandoned those operations as well.

For independent distributors, on the other hand, the PTAR opened an additional sales window for them at more than 600 local affiliates. A wave of mergers hit the independent syndication sector in the 1970s, as production costs rose and networks began cancelling series more rapidly, but those syndicators that remained had much greater profit potential in domestic markets than in the prior decade (*Broadcasting*, 1975a; *Broadcasting*, 1975b). In 1977, *Broadcasting* reported, only 24 per cent of US syndication revenues came from foreign sales (*Broadcasting*, 1977b).

Thus, the two groups that had spearheaded global programme trade in the 1950s and 1960s – the networks and the independents – moved out of foreign syndication for different reasons. The Hollywood studios, meanwhile, benefited more than any other group in the wake of the Fin-Syn, PTAR and UHF decisions, as they now retained the rights to sell their own programming into syndication without sharing any of the profits with the networks. These additional profits further distracted them from television syndication abroad. On the heels of the UHF boom of the 1960s and the regulatory reforms of the 1970s, the 1980s saw the birth of cable networks in the US, which grew from twenty-eight in 1980 to seventy-nine by the end of the decade (NCTA, 2005) and served to further expand domestic distribution windows.

In other parts of the world, due perhaps in part to the retreat of US distributors, a handful of regional distributors enlarged their programme sales in the 1970s and early 1980s. Between 1972 and 1980, Japanese exports doubled from 2,200 hours of programming to 4,585 hours, mostly consisting of animation sales to Asia (Hara, 2004, para. 23). Egyptian programme sales to Arab nations likewise jumped after 1973, prompted partly by the government's rejection of communism and embrace of capitalism following a failed coup attempt. Several independent Egyptian producers began to rent out facilities in nearby countries to escape escalating production costs at home (Amin, 1996, p. 111). For Brazilian conglomerate Globo, the late 1970s represented the beginnings of what would become an active programme export business. Globo sold the *telenovela* *Gabriela* (1975) to the Portuguese state broadcaster RTP in 1975, and the channel bought an additional fifteen Brazilian *telenovelas* over the following ten years. Globo also sold *telenovelas* to buyers in Italy, Latin American, and the former Portuguese colonies of Africa in the late 1970s and early 1980s (Sinclair, 1999, pp. 59–60).

For European broadcasters during these years, international co-productions became more and more popular as a means of maintaining the domestic programming industry in the face of rising costs and cheap US imports with large production budgets. While co-productions did not begin to come into their own in television until the late 1980s and early 1990s (Hoskins, McFadyen and Finn, 1997, p. 24), the practice was nevertheless widespread in the late 1970s and early 1980s. The European Broadcasting Union's *Review* published several articles in the mid-1980s encouraging nations to develop co-production as a strategy to maintain domestic industries and content (Ladouceur, 1984; Wünsche, 1984). Between 1977 and 1979, the number of co-producers seeking partners at MIP-TV grew from seventy to more than 130, most of whom came from Europe (*Broadcasting*, 1977a, p. 89; *Broadcasting*, 1979, p. 44).

Nature documentaries, miniseries and made-for-TV movies dominated the co-productions of the day. Miniseries and made-for-TV movies were the kinds of programming typically bought from the Americans, because few public broadcasters had the funds necessary to mount such expensive projects. Co-production allowed them that option at a time when they felt that US programming was becoming increasingly insular, as US syndicators concentrated on the growing number of domestic buyers. Nature documentaries, on the other hand, were a staple of many European broadcasters, and the common practice of using voice-over narration in the genre made it more easily adaptable to other markets (*Broadcasting*, 1977a, p. 89; *Broadcasting*, 1978, p. 42; *Broadcasting*, 1980, p. 70). In addition to co-production deals, the larger European broadcasters sold their own programming on the international markets at the time. The BBC, for example, brought 140 hours of programming to sell at MIP-TV in 1980 (*Broadcasting*, 1980, p. 68).

Thus, while the main global television distributors scaled back their international operations from the 1970s to the mid-1980s, international programme trade did not disappear. Attendance at MIP-TV rose throughout the late 1970s and early 1980s, posting yearly growth as high as 30 per cent (MIPTV, 2004b). Most attendants were Europeans seeking either to buy American programming or to develop co-production arrangements. However, we can also witness the contours of today's global television marketplace in the steady growth of distributors from around the world looking to peddle their programming. Attendance at MIP-TV grew 400 per cent between 1973 and 1985, from 1,336 to 5,403 participants, attracting merchants from a wider and wider range of territories (*Broadcasting*, 1977a; *Broadcasting*, 1978; *Broadcasting*, 1979; MIPTV 2004b).

TELEVISION GLOBALISATION, 1985-PRESENT: THE SECOND WAVE

Beginning in the mid-1980s, much as in the late 1950s, international windows multiplied due to a flurry of worldwide regulatory reforms that ushered in new commercial broadcasters and new public channels with entertainment-focused profiles (Negrine and Papathanassopoulos, 1990, p. 7). More important, from the standpoint of the global television marketplace, was the spread of cable and satellite channels around the world. Together, these forces again globalised the US production industry. This time, however, Hollywood got far more deeply involved in global television, while the need for programming and added economic pressure on both commercial and publicly funded television producers also led to a globalisation of much of the rest of the world's production industries. By the end of the 1990s, the digitisation of satellite broadcasting, which promised hundreds of premium television channels, reinforced this growing globalisation. However, digitisation brought with it problems of piracy which, along with a shift towards post-Fordist production and financing practices, is leading to a worldwide decline in after-markets and a surge in up-front distribution deals.

Although cable and satellite had provided feeder systems for terrestrial broadcasting for decades in many parts of the world, it was only in the 1980s and 1990s that these media came into their own through a series of deregulatory decisions. Beginning in North America and the UK, cable and satellite deregulation spread swiftly across Europe and the rest of the world. In some cases, deregulation served domestic economic and political purposes, while in other cases national governments were powerless to stop their citizens from receiving foreign satellite channels, leading domestic advertisers to divert money to the foreign satellite operators and prompting demand for domestic channel expansion among businesses and citizens (Negrine and Papathanassopoulos, 1990, pp. 18–20). By 1997, more than 300 million homes worldwide subscribed to either cable or satellite television (*Screen Digest*, 1998). In Europe alone, the number of cable and satellite channels grew from ten in 1984 to more than 250 in 1997 (*Screen Digest*, 1997a, p. 57). Most of these start-up channels depended heavily on imported programming to build audiences and fill out broadcast schedules. In Europe in 1992, 75 per cent of new channels used imported programming for at least half of their schedules (*Screen Digest*, 1992, p. 40).

Unlike the earlier global expansion of markets, this time the major Hollywood distributors were at the forefront of the trend, because their large programming libraries made them uniquely capable of fulfilling the rapidly growing demand for programming worldwide. Gary Marenzi, then president of MGM/UA Telecommunication Group, explained,

> the situation [in international television] is similar to 1985 in the United States when you had various cable networks starting up. You could go to HBO and Showtime with a movie, then broadcast syndication, basic cable and whatever. Then you would start slipping in windows in front of syndication. It's a natural progression that is now happening in the international market. (Walley, 1995)

Figure 1.3: US Distributors' Foreign Syndication Revenues (1984–2005) (US$m)

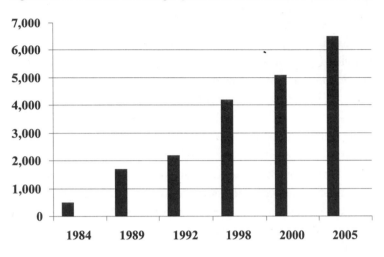

Source: Author's analysis of trade journal reports and Segrave (1998)

In other words, the global television market was becoming more lucrative and complex in the 1990s, just as the domestic market had in the 1980s. Figure 1.3 shows the growth in international television syndication revenues for US distributors since the 1980s, which rose from $500 million in 1984 to $6.5 billion in 2005. Figure 1.4 demonstrates that, much as in the early 1960s, the percentage of US syndicators' revenues earned from overseas sales grew from just above

Figure 1.4: US Distributors' Percentage of Revenues from Foreign Syndication (1985–2000)

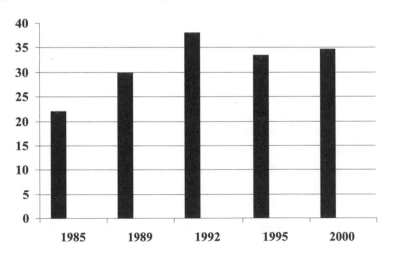

Source: Author's analysis of trade journal reports, especially Egan (1990) and
Hollywood Reporter: Anniversary Issue (1998)

20 per cent in 1985 to nearly 40 per cent in 1992, only to level off to about 35 per cent for the remainder of the decade.

Hollywood probably accounts for about 75 per cent of worldwide television export revenues, although its share of the total number of programming hours traded globally is certainly smaller (Hoskins and McFadyen, 1991, p. 207). Several competitive advantages, owing to the particular circumstances of the audiovisual business and the history of the West more generally, explain Hollywood's dominance. First, English-language programmes can attract a large number of affluent buyers because English speakers are more numerous and have higher per capita incomes than speakers of any other language, owing to the linguistic and economic effects of British and American colonialism. Second, Hollywood distributors enjoy economies of scale *vis-à-vis* other distributors, which allow them to spend significantly more on programming, especially in terms of star power and special effects that help their programming overcome cultural differences, and also keep per-unit costs down. Third, Hollywood distributors take advantage of the growing post-production skills and depressed wages of workers in developing nations to maintain high production values at the lowest possible costs (Miller *et al.*, 2001, 2005).

In addition to the comparative industrial advantages that Hollywood enjoys, the majors' strong-arm business tactics also help account for their growing revenues from global television sales. Hollywood distributors use the draw of their globally popular feature films to force programme packages on would-be buyers, while their vast programming libraries allow them to strike output deals covering vast amounts of programming for several years with large buying groups. Packaging requires buyers to purchase several products in order to obtain the rights to especially popular programming, usually a blockbuster theatrical release. In order to purchase the blockbuster, buyers must also pick up several other films or television programmes that they might not want. In the late 1970s, packages were common in smaller overseas markets, but Hollywood lacked the bargaining power to demand packages elsewhere (*Variety*, 1981). From the late 1980s through to today, however, the presence of several potential buyers in each market, all seeking the most recent Hollywood films, has shifted the balance of power in Hollywood's favour.

Output deals, in which buyers contract for all of the programming produced by a studio over a specified period of time as well as hundreds of hours of older programming, also became prevalent during in the 1990s. Typically, the Hollywood studios are the only distributors that can offer output deals because they are the only ones who produce such vast amounts of programming. In recent years, however, the popularity of these massive output deals has waned, and a number of smaller output deals with smaller distributors have occurred. All of the Hollywood majors struck multiple output deals during the 1990s, mostly with large buyers from the European territories. Table 1.4 summarises several of these deals. While far from exhaustive, this table points out several important features of output deals. First, distributors often separated terrestrial, cable, satellite, pay-TV and pay-per-view rights, distinguishing finely between temporal windows abroad. Second, although most of the deals involved nationally based channels, several with transnational channels were reported, including satellite broadcasters in Africa, Scandinavia and the Middle East. Third, we see that all of the major Hollywood studios entered into or renewed output deals during this period. Fourth, the vast majority of deals included buyers from Western Europe, in particular the large buying groups that owned multiple distribution channels in numerous markets.

One of the largest instigators of output deals in Europe was the German-based conglomerate KirchMedia. According to popular lore, owner Leo Kirch pioneered the first output deal in 1959, when he purchased the rights to 400 films from MCA for 6 million Deutschmarks (Roxborough, 2002). Kirch later resold those rights over a period of time to the national broadcaster ARD (Arbeitsgemeinschaft der öffentlichrechtlichen Rundfunkanstalten der Bundesrepublik Deutschland) and the newly introduced ZDF (Zweites Duetsches Fernsehen).

By the 1970s, Kirch held a virtual monopoly on imported films and television programmes in Germany. In addition to acquiring programming libraries from

Table 1.4: Representative Output Deals of Hollywood Studios (1995–97)

	Buyer	Seller	Types of Rights	Duration (Years)	Price (US$)	Date Reported
Germany	Kirch	Warner Bros.	Pay & digital	10	800	1995
Germany	Kirch	MCA	Pay & digital	10	1,000	1995
Germany	Kirch	Paramount	Pay & digital	10	1,800	1996
Germany	RTL	Warner Bros.	Free	3	240	1995
Germany	RTL	MCA	Free	10	1,000	1995
France	TPS	Paramount	Pay & digital	10	500	1996
France	TPS	Warner Bros	Pay & digital	5	100	1996
France	Canal+	20ᵗʰ C Fox	Pay & digital	5	200	1996
Italy	Telepiu	Dreamworks	All			1996
Italy	Telepiu	Warner Bros.	All			1996
Italy	Telepiu	20ᵗʰ C Fox	All			1996
Italy	Telepiu	MGM	All			1996
Spain	Sogecable	Columbia Tristar	Cable & pay	5		1997
Spain	RTVE	Warner Bros.	Free			1997
Spain	RTVE	Disney	Free			1997
Spain	RTVE	MCA	Free			1997
UK	Channel 5	Warner Bros.	Free	2		1997
UK	ITV	Universal	Free	2		1997
Scandinavia	TV4 (Sweden) TV 2 (Norway) TV2 (Denmark)	20ᵗʰ C Fox	Free	3		1997
Scandinavia	SBS/ TV1000	Columbia Tristar	Pay	4		1997
Netherlands	SBS6	Universal	Free	3		1997
Middle East	Orbit	Warner Bros.	Satellite		50	1997
Middle East	Orbit	Disney	Satellite			1997
South Africa	MNET	Warner Bros.	Pay TV	5	65	1997

Sources: Author's analysis of trade journal reports

RKO and Hal Roach, Kirch imported programming from the US through his rights acquisition company, TaurusFilm, translated the programming into German, and resold the rights to the German public-service broadcasters. Few programmes entered the German market without first going through Kirch's hands (Ewing, 2002, paras 8, 9; *Variety*, 1997a). When governments across Europe moved to deregulate and privatise television in the 1980s, Kirch quickly diversified into broadcasting and pay-television channels. Kirch helped start Sat1, Germany's first commercial broadcaster, with an infusion of programming in 1984 (Ewing, 2002, para. 13).

By 1997, KirchMedia owned the German free-to-air television channel ProSieben, satellite broadcaster Sat1, cable channel Kabel1 and had ownership interests in television channels in Italy, France and Spain. In 1996, the company planned to launch a nineteen-channel direct-to-home satellite service (Herman and McChesney, 1997, p. 98; *Variety*, 1997a). Obviously, such a vast number of channels required the large amounts of programming that only the Hollywood studios could provide, leading Kirch to strike a reported $2.6 billion-worth of output deals with the Hollywood studios in the late 1990s (Brockmeyer, 2002).

Ultimately, Kirch's multibillion-dollar gamble on digital television spelled his demise. In addition to rights to Hollywood films and television programmes, Kirch had spent lavishly on rights for European sports programming, particularly World Cup and Formula One racing rights, giving him the largest portfolio of sports and films rights outside the major Hollywood studios. When adoption rates of digital television in Germany and across Europe continued to fall well short of KirchMedia's projections, operations costs increasingly outstripped subscription and advertising revenues, reportedly causing the company's digital television holdings to lose some $1.3 million per day by 2002 (Brockmeyer, 2002, pp. 23–4). By mid-2002, KirchMedia was embroiled in lawsuits against two Hollywood studios, Paramount and Universal, to try to decrease its debts to the studios, and the company finally filed for bankruptcy in April 2002 (Roxborough, 2002, para. 4). The collapse of KirchMedia marked the end of an era of massive output deals between the Hollywood majors and large European buying groups, helping usher in an age where sellers and buyers tend to measure demand more carefully and earn back investments more quickly.

While buying groups like KirchMedia were not restricted to the European markets, the EU's favourable regulatory conditions certainly encouraged their development. Deregulation across Europe in the 1980s allowed cross-media, transnational investments, which led to the growth of such massive pan-European media conglomerates as Fininvest, Bertelsmann, KirchGruppe and CLT-UFA (Negrine and Papathanassopoulos, 1990, p. 130).

Across East and South Asia, governments were generally less open to broad-cast liberalisation and programme import than in Europe, often leaving terrestrial television under state control, while commercial operations were limited to less lucrative cable and satellite channels with smaller audiences (Cunningham and Jacka, 1996, p. 195; Thomas, 1998, p. 203). Large output deals likewise remained uncommon in Latin American, despite the fact that the region is home to several large buying groups, including Grupo Televisa in Mexico, Organizações Globo in Brazil and Grupo Cisneros in Venezuela. Each of these groups owns multiple television outlets that require large tracts of programming and many had output deals with the Hollywood studios in the 1980s, but both the quantity and the quality of Latin American programming improved during the decade, eliminating the need for output deals in the 1990s at many of the larger broadcasters (Robertson, 1999).

By the late 1990s, the programming strategies of most of the new cable and satellite broadcasters had stabilised, leading to decreased demand for large amounts of imported programming and fewer and fewer output deals. Even many digital platforms, which promise hundreds of channels of premium Hollywood product and are just getting off the ground in Europe, had filled their shelves with output deals by the late 1990s. What is more, the collapse of Kirch-Media has frightened both the Hollywood studios and the large buying groups away from such arrangements.

The emphasis of the Hollywood majors on output deals in the mid-1990s has been replaced in recent years by a turn towards increased local-language pro-duction. Sony Pictures Television International (SPTI) has been at the forefront of this trend, which many see as the future of global programme production (Marenzi, 2005a). SPTI began to develop overseas production arrangements in Europe in the early 1990s, in an effort to guard against down-cycles in global programme markets. In 1991, SPTI negotiated an arrangement with German commercial broadcaster RTL Plus that called for a raft of local productions of SPTI-owned properties, including *Berlin Break* (1993), an action drama series produced in conjunction with RTL Plus. RTL retained German rights, while SPTI sold rights to the series everywhere else (Marich, 1992). At present, the company has local production facilities across Europe, Latin America and Asia (*PR Newswire*, 2002).

Local-language production differs from international co-production and over-seas production because it is designed primarily to sell programming into the local market, rather than into the domestic US or international markets. The strategy recognises the popularity and profit potential of local programming, and identi-fies a long-term strategy to become a major production player in certain large, lucrative markets. As Michael Grindon, president of SPTI in 1999, explained,

When you are looking at a period of five to seven years on the time horizon, an operation of this nature is not likely to be profitable because you have to build production mass and personnel ... But if you are looking at a 10-year time horizon, it becomes a different picture. And we are clearly moving into that stage now. This is not about a quick hit but about building our business in these markets over time (Brennan, 1999b)

The Hollywood studios are in particularly strong positions when it comes to launching local-language operations because they have numerous long-running series with dozens of episodes that can be locally formatted, saving a great deal on script development costs (Marenzi, 2005a). By 1999, SPTI was producing more programming abroad than in the domestic market, including local versions of sitcoms such as *Bewitched* (1964–72), *I Dream of Jeanie* (1965–70) and *Who's The Boss* (1984–92) in Brazil, Germany, Italy, Spain and the UK, as well as several locally developed concepts, especially game shows and talk shows (Brennan, 1999b).

The results of Hollywood's deepening involvement in the global television markets since the 1990s have been manifold. It has created a worldwide programming hierarchy, with Hollywood product at the top. It has expanded international distribution possibilities for others because Hollywood foots a good deal of the bill for global television trade shows. In 1999, for instance, Hollywood distributors spent between $2 and $3 million each attending MIP-TV (Brennan, 1999c). Finally, it has spread many of Hollywood's domestic business strategies to other parts of the world, including deficit-financing of television production, the persistent drive for new product and the organisation and exploitation of distribution windows.

Although US distributors may have benefited disproportionately from changes in the global marketplace since the 1990s, distributors in other parts of the world also began to use international markets to help recoup production costs. In Australia, for instance, a concerted push to revamp the funding of television production made the industry heavily reliant on overseas co-production partners (Cunningham and Jacka, 1996, p. 69). In 2003, British television distributors earned about $371 million from international sales of finished television programmes, and $920 million in total international exports, including co-productions, licensing, formatting and DVD sales, accounting for more than half of total programme sales, including domestic sales (Johnson, 2002; Steemers, 2004, pp. 44, 46). These revenues represent a 400 per cent increase in international sales of finished programmes since 1983 (Johnson, 2002; *Financial Times*, 1984). French syndicators, meanwhile, generated 238.7 million euros ($325.6 million)-worth of television programme sales, co-production sales, and pre-sales in 2003 (*Hollywood Reporter*, 2004a). In Germany in 1998, international revenues were $53.9 million (*Television International*, 1999).

Beyond Europe, distributors in Asia increasingly earn revenue from television programme exports as well. In Japan, the total amount of television programme exports grew tenfold between 1980 and 2001 to nearly 43,000 hours, more than half of which is exported to other East Asian nations (Hara, 2004, paras. 3,4). Television syndicators in Hong Kong, meanwhile, sell their programming widely throughout the Greater Chinese market and beyond. The largest producer-broadcaster, TVB, claims current export arrangements in more than thirty foreign countries (Wilkins, 2004, p. 1130). Even among newcomers to international syndication, export sales are becoming more important: South Korean distributors earned $28.3 million from programme exports in 2003, representing a 77 per cent increase over the previous year (Russell, 2003).

However, some of the greatest growth in global sales outside the US and Europe has taken place among Latin American *telenovela* distributors. As we saw above, international *telenovela* trade dates back to the 1950s, but recently many more distributors in different countries have begun selling their programmes abroad. The number of companies selling *telenovelas* abroad has grown more than fivefold in the past decade, and international sales of the genre grew from $200 million to $341 million between 1996 and 2003, at a time when per-episode prices for the genre were falling (Paxman, 1999; Sutter, 2002).

While Televisa and Globo continue to dominate global *telenovela* trade, Venezuelan and Colombian distributors have become active since the 1990s. Coral Pictures sold the first Venezuelan *telenovela* to Spain in 1991, and its main domestic competitor, Venevision, quickly followed suit (Sinclair, 1999, p. 84). In 1996, Venevision exported *telenovelas* to thirty foreign markets, earning $20 million in sales (Margolis, 1997). In Colombia, the private broadcaster RCN had enormous success abroad with the *telenovela Yo Soy Betty la Fea* (*I Am Ugly Betty*) (1999–2001) in the late 1990s and early 2000s (Burnett, 2002). In addition to these 'major' *telenovela* studios, a number of independents have cropped up in recent years, many of which are based in Miami and predominantly target the US Latino audience (Mato, 2002).

As more *telenovela* distributors have become involved in programme trade, the number of markets that buy *telenovelas* has also increased. Since the late 1990s, East and Southeast Asia have seen a boom in *telenovela* imports, particularly Indonesia, the Philippines and Malaysia, with distributors reporting significant potential in Vietnam, Singapore, Thailand and Korea. Independent producers, including Coral, Telefe, Promark and Comarex, estimate that as much as 35 per cent of their international *telenovela* sales come from Asian markets, and this sector is expected to grow to as much as 50 per cent over the next several years (Burnett, 2002).

Today, television distributors in countries from Singapore to Russia to Venezuela actively export programming to the global television marketplace. In richer nations, where domestic sales can support most of the costs of production, larger distributors typically earn only a fraction of their revenues from international sales. For smaller producers and those in poorer nations, however, international sales often represent a significant portion of revenues.

GLOBAL FINANCING AND PRODUCTION ARRANGEMENTS

As different producers have moved into international television, new types of sales arrangements have become commonplace, including various types of co-production, pre-sales, formatting and repurposing. These new, global forms of production financing derive from a broader economic shift since the 1970s that many have referred to as 'post-Fordism' (Harvey, 1990; Hesmondhalgh, 2002). Post-Fordist business practices include just-in-time production, consumer segmentation and customised products, whereas Fordism tended towards mass production, mass consumption and product standardisation. In the television industry, Fordist principles underlay the US network era that lasted from the 1950s into the 1980s, when a limited number of mass-distribution channels aimed at amassing the largest possible audience with mass-produced entertainment (Curtin, 1996). Deficit financing, which involves a distributor trading up-front production funding for sales rights in the after-markets, became commonplace in the US television industry at the time, because steady interest rates allowed distributors to be patient with syndication revenues. International sales of finished programmes, ultimately designed for the domestic after-market, provided a crucial, but secondary, revenue stream.

In recent years, distributors have been eager to make back their investments as quickly as possible, not least because interest rates have become unpredictable and production costs have skyrocketed. Furthermore, non-Western producers and distributors often lack the financial resources to bankroll production costs for several years, prompting them to seek other kinds of production financing arrangements through the global television marketplace. While all of these financing arrangements have existed for decades, they have begun to eclipse nationally focused deficit financing in even the largest markets.

Co-production involves at least two partners from different nations who each take a creative role in producing a television programme, typically with governmental financing from one or both partner nations. Often reserved for large-budget projects such as made-for-TV movies, miniseries and drama series, co-production offers more up-front funds than either partner could raise independently, and allows them to distribute the finished programme in their domestic markets and various international markets. Traditionally, co-productions in Europe have taken one of three forms: US terrestrial or cable networks co-producing with a European broadcaster, with the US partner retaining international distribution rights outside the broadcaster's home market; British broadcasters co-producing with partners from other English-speaking nations, which provides only minimal additional production funding; and multinational co-productions, typically among French, German and/or Italian producers who share production funding, creative input and international distribution rights (Fry, 2002). The popular miniseries *The Count of Monte Cristo* (1998), for instance, was a French-German-Italian co-production (IMDB, 2005; Kingsley, 2001).

Co-financing and pre-sales are similar to co-production, but they primarily involve only financial interest in the production, rather than creative input. Co-financing is an arrangement whereby producers from various nations pool their money on a single project, but creative control remains with only one producer and the final project is intended primarily for distribution in a single domestic market. Pre-sales, on the other hand, include a single producer and multiple domestic and foreign buyers, who provide money up-front in order to secure programme rights in particular markets. In 1997, for instance, British production house RTF International developed an idea for a travelogue series about the world's various wine regions, which it pre-sold to buyers in Australia, Sweden and Japan, covering about 80 per cent of production costs (Atkinson, 1998).

Formatting involves selling the rights to recreate a popular foreign programme in the domestic market, often with the same set designs, logos, theme music and translated scripts. Global reality formats such as *Big Brother* (1999–) and *Survivor* (1997–) are only the most prominent instances of this practice, which includes dramas, game shows, situation comedies, *telenovelas* and more. The appeal of formatting is threefold. First, it's widely assumed that formatting is less risky than creating a domestic show from scratch, because the format has already proved its popularity in another market. Second, formats are thought to outperform imports of the same programme, because viewers prefer local programming in their own language. Third, format licence fees cost about 20 per cent as much as finished programmes. For format distributors, on the other hand, the business is riskier than sales of finished programmes. Since no standard legal definition of formatting as intellectual property exists, some of the largest format distributors are currently lined up to sue one another over alleged copycat practices. In addition, though licence fees for formats are only a fraction of the fees for finished programmes, they require a great deal more follow-up attention from distributors, including assisting the buyer with a variety of production and promotional tasks (Moran, 1998; Waller, 2005a). Even Endemol, one of the most prominent global format distributors, decided in 2005 to expand its business to include more sales of finished programmes (Jenkinson, 2005a).

Finally, repurposing entails taking segments of already-produced programmes and adapting them to new uses. Repurposing is especially popular in the growing business of mobile television delivery because it provides brief clips that can easily be downloaded on mobile phones. For example, in 2005, Swiss-based Transmedia struck a repurposing deal with a company that owns large amounts of live concert footage to stream video music clips to subscribers' mobile phones (Jenkinson, 2005b). Repurposing has become a vital part of the international market for archived news, sports and music videos. Many documentaries and special reports use archived news footage from international sources, while sports and music programmes often use international sports packages and music videos, with local talent providing introductory and transitional remarks between segments. *Gillette World of Sports*, for instance, which claims to be the most widely distributed television sports programme in the world, uses this technique (Harverson, 1998).

CONCLUSION

The seismic technological and regulatory changes that shook the world television landscape in the late 1980s and 1990s helped open new global markets for producers and distributors everywhere, creating the webs of interconnected media conglomerates, interdependent funding practices and interwoven distribution windows that characterize today's global television business. While the technical capacity for worldwide television broadcasts existed in the 1960s, businesspeople had little concept of the ways in which cultural differences among the world's viewers might channel, block, or redirect the flow of programming worldwide. Instead, when US networks executives spoke of global television, they envisioned a world in which domestically tailored programming would find general entertainment audiences both at home and abroad. Leslie Harris, vice president and general manager of CBS Films, offered a typical assessment in 1958 when he explained, 'In general, tastes are the same everywhere' (*Advertising Age*, 1958). Today, by contrast, the variety of international buyers has grown, as has the number of producers and distributors that primarily target transnational audience segments. Not only do more and more producers in various nations depend upon the global television marketplace to help cover production costs, but producers and channels increasingly strive to overcome differences of national identity by emphasising other markers of identity such as age, gender, ethnicity and lifestyle interests.

The multiplication of global distribution windows over the past half-century exhibit what David Harvey (1990), following Karl Marx, terms the 'annihilation of space through time', by which he means that spatial barriers between markets are no longer central concerns for capital accumulation due to advances in communications technologies and the rapid transport of goods worldwide. In television, international programme distribution was at first limited largely to US and Latin American companies, and foreign windows were predicated on distinct after-markets that were separated by the amount of time it took to conduct trade and transfer programming abroad. The introduction of cable, satellite and digital television in the past decades, however, has multiplied the number of after-markets, first-run markets and up-front markets, while transnational satellite markets have been superimposed over national ones, immensely complicating the organisation of windows. Thus, the newest seasons of *Friends* (1994–2004) in 1999 could be seen in the same week on both NBC and the Middle East satellite channel Orbit. Instantaneous, global communication has not only obliterated time lags in international distribution, it also allows for synchronous, worldwide promotion and exhibition of films and television shows. Alternately, it allows certain audiences privileged access, withholding programming from other audiences in order to build interest (Cohen, 1999).

The ability to transcend spatial limitations on commerce has increased the variety, importance and organisation of various up-front and after-market windows worldwide when calculating potential sales revenues. According to Harvey (1990), 'diminishing spatial barriers give capitalists the power to exploit minute spatial difference to good effect', because multinationals can take advantage of differences in labour costs, tax policies, interest rates and so forth (p. 294). In global television sales, the variety of windows, the prices available in those windows and the relationship among windows in different locations offer multiple possibilities for distributors to maximise profits. To return to the example of *Friends*, Warner Bros. sold new episodes to a national US network, reruns to local US stations and new and rerun episodes in the Middle East to a transnational, pay-satellite service. In the UK, British Sky Broadcasting (BSkyB) held first-run pay-TV rights to *Friends*, while terrestrial broadcaster Channel 4 held second-run free TV rights – an after-market window that does not exist in the US – airing episodes from each new season a few months after its appearance on Sky One (Turner, 1999; Woodcock, 1997). Not only does this example demonstrate the growing variety of after-markets and first-run markets, but also the increasing need to organise such windows carefully in order to maximise returns on investment.

The common practice of deficit financing has been joined by arrangements where production costs are met through pre-sales and co-financing arrangements, in which all parties strive for immediate returns on investment. When possible, most distributors structure their worldwide distribution windows to make the largest profits in the shortest amount of time. Of course, profit maximisation has always been a primary goal of the for-profit culture industries. Again, what is different about the present era is the variety and importance of international as well as domestic windows, particularly up-front and first-run windows. These newer practices have not fully replaced older deficit financing models, but rather have been appended to them. Hollywood, for example, employs both deficit financing and newer practices, depending on each individual project (Marenzi, 2005a).

Economic and technological changes have encouraged this shift to short-term profit maximisation. Uncertain economic times and falling profit margins among Hollywood distributors and others often make it difficult and risky to wait for after-market profits, which are highly susceptible to interest rate changes. In addition, the ease of copying that digitisation and the diffusion of video technology offer can wreak havoc with well-planned windowing, because windows are predicated on the ability to control distribution outlets (Owen and Wildman, 1992, pp. 27, 38). As media corporations have lost their grip on distribution, they have fought back on multiple fronts, including worldwide intellectual property protections, investment in new distribution outlets and restructuring of distribution windows (Curtin, 1996). Obviously, the longer it takes for programming to cycle through various distribution windows, the more vulnerable it becomes to unauthorised copying, so distributors often shorten the time between windows or release programming nearly simultaneously in multiple windows.

The increased drive to maximise short-term profits has sped up the lifecycle for internationally traded television programming, leading to a constant search for the newest programming trends. Much of the buzz and trade press coverage at global television trade shows are efforts to define these new trends. Coupled with the present importance of international windows for producers and distributors around the world, the need for market intelligence gleaned from global trade shows has increased the importance of personal contacts worldwide who can help secure distribution and funding. For these reasons, the business culture of global television sales has taken on a life of its own, independent, yet intimately linked to national television business cultures.

2

Selling Television Internationally

A successful global television sales business requires continuing relationships with an extensive network of buyers and programme suppliers, as well as constant efforts to promote one's programming. One of the most precious commodities for a global television distributor is its reputation, which is intimately linked with its position in the hierarchy of global television sales, its main programming genres and the extent of its distribution network. The major Hollywood distributors, which sit atop of the business, trade in the most lucrative genres and markets, and maintain extensive networks of executives and representatives around the world who keep the lines of communication and promotion open to buyers everywhere. On the opposite end of the spectrum, solo distributors eek out a living by obtaining and selling rights to less popular genres and programming, often to a handful of smaller buyers in a specific region of the world.

As with all businesses, commercial distributors are looking to expand, and because Western buyers from economically powerful nations are both more numerous and richer, we see a distinctly Western slant in many distributors' sales and promotional activities. Even among distributors who don't target Western buyers, Western-style promotional practices are often used to add an air of glamour and universal appeal to their programming. Thus, the business of global television sales is marked by two seemingly contradictory tendencies: first, the focus of large distributors on particular genres and markets leaves other genres and markets to smaller players, keeping entry barriers in global television relatively low; second, however, the inequities in profit and prestige among distributors lead almost all television merchants, distributors and buyers alike, to value Western culture above all others. That is, while many commercial distributors focus on non-mainstream genres and smaller markets, most of them hope for the day when they can sell high-end genres to buyers from large Western markets. Likewise, small buyers strive to become large enough to compete for the rights to the newest movies and series from large Western distributors. While Western production values do not entirely seduce the tastes of global television merchants, the structure of the market does give such values an allure that is difficult to fully resist.

GLOBAL TELEVISION GENRES

In spite of the unpredictable success of internationally traded programmes, certain kinds of programming circulate more readily than others. We can distinguish among internationally traded programming by reference to both format and genre. Formats identify programmes based upon their frequency and length, including episodic series; one-time events, or 'one-offs'; and miniseries, or series with a small number of episodes. In terms of programme length, merchants distinguish among shorts, or programmes less than thirty minutes long; half-hours; hours; and ninety- and 120-minute programmes. Most of the series, one-offs and miniseries sold on the global programme markets have standard lengths: series are half-hours or hours, while most one-offs and miniseries are ninety to 120 minutes in length.

Global television merchants use the term genre primarily to refer to content-based differences among programming, including comedy versus drama, animation versus live action and open- and closed-narrative series. Most genres fall into standard formats, such as the hour-long episodic police drama, the half-hour episodic comedy, or the ninety-minute one-off feature film. While different combinations of format and genre are possible, those that deviate from the standard combinations often have difficulty in global programming markets, because buyers are typically looking to fill scheduling holes of a specified length with programming of a specified type. For instance, ninety-minute episodic French dramas, which are quite popular in their home market, have a notoriously tough time travelling abroad because most buyers only purchase half-hour or hour-long series (Paoli and Williams, 1996).

In terms of total global trade, the most popular genres are drama and film, followed by children's programming, especially animation; light entertainment, a catch-all category that includes talk and variety shows, as well as unscripted 'reality' shows; factual programming, including educational; and television movies (see Figure 2.1). Within each of these broad classifications, the most expensive subgenres tend to be imported from the Hollywood majors or co-produced, while cheaper subgenres are locally produced or acquired from smaller distributors. Thus, Hollywood feature films command the highest prices in most markets, and are frequently the only imported programmes that large broadcasters around the world still air in prime time, while European features, even in Europe, are intermittently traded and generally programmed in non-peak hours (EAO, 2000, p. 3). The US majors likewise dominate the sale of high-end TV movies and miniseries worldwide, although European co-productions that combine funding from a variety of government and commercial sources across the continent, such as the 1998 hit *The Count of Monte Cristo*, have become more prominent in these genres in recent years (Kingsley, 2001). In 2001, for

Figure 2.1: Percentage of Total Global Programme Trade by Selected Genres (1996–97)

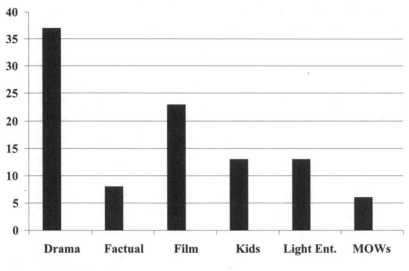

Source: DCMS (1999)

instance, European co-productions, predominantly miniseries and television movies, accounted for 14,000 broadcast hours on Western European channels, an increase of 7 per cent over 1997 (Buonanno, 2000, p. 15; EAO, 2003).

While features and TV movies fetch the highest per-programme prices on the global markets (*Television International*, 2002), episodic series are the most numerous, in large part because their regular daily or weekly scheduling can provide relatively consistent audience ratings for advertisers. Episodic series include animation, action dramas, serials and light entertainment. Again, in all but the richest television markets, most high-end episodic series are imported, while most lower-end product is locally produced. The main exception to this rule, which we will explore below, is animation, which is often cheap to produce and frequently bought from the global markets.

Action dramas, including police/investigative and hospital shows, are the most expensive episodic series to produce, in part because of the frequent use of special effects, single-camera shooting and multiple settings. The Hollywood studios spend between $1.6 and $2 million per episode on hour-long dramas, but receive licence fees of between $1 and $1.6 million from US networks, leaving them to finance the remainder through international sales. *CSI: Crime Scene Investigation* (2000–) was estimated to cost $2.4 million per episode in 2000, while CBS was expected to pay a license fee of $1.1 million per episode (Albiniak, 2003). Due to the high costs of the genre, most markets import action dramas, if they programme them at all. For instance, in 1998 in Spain, the fifth-largest television market in Europe, only 1 per cent of domestic fiction was action dramas, whereas in the larger European markets, the genre accounted for between 20 and 30 per cent of domestic fiction (Buonanno, 2000, p. 18). Although some of this difference may be attributable to the cultural preferences of Spanish viewers, the presence of several US action dramas in prime time suggests instead that Spanish channels were turning to the global markets for action dramas rather than footing the bill for local variants (Berciano, Lacalle and Vilches 2000, p. 68).

At the opposite end of the spectrum are serial dramas, such as soap operas, and 'reality' shows, both of which are cheap and locally produced in most nations. In Iraq in 2005, for instance, the local serial *Love and War*, which cost $150,000 for its first season, was the most popular primetime programme (Worth, 2005). On the other hand, the cheapness of these genres can also make them attractive as imports, especially during non-peak hours or as niche-oriented programming. The global popularity of Latin American serial *telenovelas*, for instance, has a good deal to do with their use by television channels around the world as low-cost imports for niche audiences outside prime time (Burnett, 2002; Escalante, 2004; Sahab, 2004). Reality shows, meanwhile, are usually remade in each market with local talent, making them cheap to acquire and often cheaper to produce than scripted series, because they require minimal sets, no professional actors and no writers. On the other hand, reality shows can hold the promise of impressive ratings, even in prime time, as currently demonstrated by the worldwide popularity of the Swedish reality show *Expedition Robinson* (*Survivor*) and the Dutch reality show *Big Brother*, which have facilitated the genre's popularity in the global television marketplace.

Finally, animation and documentaries are also popular fare on the global television markets, as evidenced by several sales markets dedicated to each genre, including Sunny Side of the Doc and MIPDOC for documentaries and MIPCOM Junior (Marché International des Films et des Programmes pour la Télévision, la Vidéo, le Câble et le Satellite [International Film and Programme Market for TV, Video, Cable and Satellite]) and MIFA (the International Animated Film Market) for animation. Both genres have become more numerous in global programming markets since the rise in speciality cable and satellite channels, and are seen as uniquely suited to global trade because replacing the speech of animated characters or voice-over narrators causes less of a disturbance for viewers than dubbing or subtitling live actors. Although some Hollywood majors such as Warner Bros. and Twentieth Century-Fox carry animation, placing their reputation and promotional muscle behind those series, the genre has glutted the global programming market since the late 1990s due to cheaper computer technologies and the outsourcing of certain tasks to developing countries, which has brought down costs (*Hollywood Reporter*, 1995). Consequently, it is often more cost-effective for channels to purchase rather than self-produce or commission animated programmes. In addition, because more than half the revenues on animated children's series at present come from merchandising, buyers often achieve better ratings from series with global merchandisers behind them that can take advantage of the added publicity from toy advertising, fast food tie-ins, DVD releases and other promotional campaigns (Sofley, 2004a). In 2004, Breakthrough Entertainment, a small Canadian firm, launched its series *Atomic Betty* (2004–) on US cable channel Comedy Central and around the world, with merchandising support from Playmates toy manufacturing, Penguin Books publishing, Wiesner Footwear and Sara Lee Branded Apparel (ibid., para. 14). Obviously, merchandising potential gives Hollywood and US distributors an upper hand in global animation, but the economics of production prevent them from completely dominating the genre.

Prices for imported documentaries, by contrast, are equivalent to drama series in many European markets (*Television International*, 2002), while the genre suffers from generally high production costs and marginal commercial appeal because most are one-offs, rather than series. Nevertheless, in addition to their popularity on niche channels, documentaries can draw good ratings on primetime broadcast schedules, and also serve as prestige programming for some buyers, especially public-service broadcasters. High-end nature and wildlife documentaries are often funded through co-production arrangements, such as the continuing arrangement between the BBC and National Geographic. *Equator*, a multi-part nature documentary co-produced by Natural History New Zealand, German broadcaster ZDF, French broadcaster France5, Japanese broadcaster NHK and Discovery HD, uses state-of-the-art animation and CGI to illustrate what life is like on land and underwater in various spots along the earth's equator (Sofley, 2004b, para. 14). Meanwhile lower-end docudramas are locally produced or imported from smaller companies. In addition, the major Hollywood studios frequently sell documentaries in film packages.

For all genres, a combination of economic and cultural considerations determines their popularity on the global programme markets. Most programmers weigh audience appeal against costs when making decisions about whether to import programming or buy it locally. Thus, genres such as animation and feature film, which seem to maintain their audience appeal well in foreign markets, are more likely to be traded than genres such as situation comedy, which are thought to be intimately tied to their original language and culture. Not surprisingly, large Western distributors dominate the trade in genres that travel best and draw the highest prices. Nevertheless, smaller distributors operating in less lucrative genres are also abundant.

INTERNATIONAL SALES AND PROMOTIONS

Despite vast differences in size and specialisation, many distributors' promotional and sales techniques are quite similar. Almost all focus their promotional energies around a small number of projects each year, relying on high-gloss, printed fliers to promote their programming and inform potential buyers. These fliers look remarkably similar, regardless of whether they come from a major Hollywood studio or a member of the European MEDIA Programme with a single property to sell. Finally, all distributors spend much of their time and effort engaged in personalised selling efforts to maintain and increase the pool of buyers who may potentially be interested in their newest programmes.

Nevertheless, distributors' sales practices differ markedly depending upon their size, scope and corporate identities. The most fundamental distinction occurs among producer-distributors, which mainly carry the programming that they produce, and redistributors, who don't produce original programming, but represent the programming in international markets and take a cut of any rights sales. Producer-distributors encompass not only the Hollywood majors, but also many large public broadcasters, including the BBC, France Télévisions, the Canadian Broadcasting Company (CBC) and NHK, as well as medium-sized and small companies such as US-based Carsey-Werner Distribution and Italian GA & A Productions. Redistributors are frequently small or solo companies that represent a handful of small feature films, documentaries, animated series, specials, or adult programming. Reel Media International, for instance, redistributes master-prints of public-domain movies, documentaries and series. However, some of the largest companies in global television are also predominantly redistributors: KirchMedia, for instance, primarily redistributed Hollywood films and television series prior to 1996 (Parkes, 1996).

The fact that redistributors are able to exist underscores the highly personalised nature of television programming sales: although producers lose some of their revenues by relying on redistributors, it is generally impossible for producers to secure international sales without them (Brown, 2001). Producer-distributors, on the other hand, sell their own products, although they often also operate as re-distributors for smaller producers. Much like smaller redistributors, the large producer-distributors maintain extensive contacts with buyers that allow them to sell rights more widely and more cheaply than an independent producer. Of course, not all producer-distributors are so mammoth: at MIP-TV 2004, the Malaysian producer-distributor Inspedia Animation Studios was selling its only animated series to date, *Johan, The Young Scientist* (Ooi, 2004).

We can also identify differences within the categories of producer-distributors and redistributors. Perhaps the most salient distinction among producer-distributors is that of non-profit and commercial producer-distributors. Typically, non-profits rely on a tradition of expertise in factual programming, educational children's programming and 'serious drama' when promoting and selling their wares. YLE, the Finnish public broadcaster, brings dozens of documentaries, animated series and youth series to MIP-TV each year. A company's focus on either a single programming genre or a diverse programming library offers another level of distinction that holds good for both producer-distributors and redistributors, and also allows us to explore different promotional practices. Finally, it is worth noting that, while nation of origin does influence some of the subtleties of promotion, most companies have practices quite similar to others in the same category, regardless of whether they are commercially or publicly funded, general or niche distributors. In what follows, we will explore the promotional and sales practices of a large Hollywood producer-distributor, a niche producer-distributor, a publicly funded producer-distributor and a solo redistributor, giving a sense of the range of ways in which global television distributors sell their programming and the cultural underpinnings of those practices.

GLOBAL SALES PRACTICES AT HOLLYWOOD DISTRIBUTORS

Despite their continued dominance of the global television marketplace, Hollywood producer-distributors have had to work harder and harder in recent years to maintain their foreign revenue streams. While the Hollywood majors continue to derive the vast majority of their revenues from sales of finished programming originally designed for the domestic US market, they have had to explore other kinds of programming and funding options, in particular co-production, local production and formatting (Marenzi, 1999). Along with these developments, the majors have had to focus more on promoting their programmes to overseas buyers and audiences in order to secure the best prices and the most lucrative time-slots in the largest markets.

Much as in the US, Hollywood producer-distributors in foreign markets primarily develop programmes with wide appeal aimed at general audiences, leaving a number of holes for niche programme distributors even in those markets where they are most active. In addition, it is important to note that the Hollywood majors do not dominate production activities in foreign markets in the way that they do in the US. Rather, the parts of the world where they invest most heavily in local programming are precisely those markets with powerful economies and strong local production industries. Nevertheless, the Hollywood studios continue to have the deepest pockets of all producer-distributors in the world, which allows them to produce programmes in the most popular genres in different international markets and to promote those programmes effectively.

Paramount International Television, a division of Paramount Pictures, is a typical international television distribution wing of a major Hollywood studio. Its business strategies reflect the truism that global television distribution consists of two kinds of firms: those with diverse business operations spanning a range of genres in the most lucrative markets in the world, and those that focus on a handful of less profitable genres and markets. Paramount Pictures Worldwide Television divides its programming operations into three divisions: Domestic Television, International Television and Worldwide Pay Television, each headed by a division president. Domestic Television is responsible for the production and distribution of all television programming in the US. The Worldwide Pay Television division is primarily responsible for Paramount's cable and satellite channel holdings in the US and abroad, as well as selling programming that its pay-channels produce or acquire rights to. The International Television Division, meanwhile, handles the majority of Paramount's programming-related activities outside the US (Marenzi, 2005a; MIPTV, 2004a).

Three departments comprise the International Television Division – Sales, Marketing, and Business Development and Co-production – suggesting that these are the three most important sectors of the division's business. The Sales Department handles the sale of all finished television programming, including any rights acquired through co-production. The Marketing Department designs advertising campaigns to attract both international buyers and their audiences, including a variety of press releases, advertisements and press junkets to help promote programming in the buyer's market. Finally, the Business Development and Co-production Department directs the myriad joint ventures that Paramount engages in around the world, including local productions, co-productions, co-financing, formatting and co-distributing. The name of this division was changed in 2002 to include co-productions, reflecting the growing importance of such projects to Paramount's international operations (Feiwell, 2002).

Within each department of the International Television Division, several executives are assigned to different regions of the world. These include vice presidents of sales to Australia and the Far East, Europe, Canada and Latin America, and sales directors responsible for the UK, France and Northeast Asia. Paramount also employs a vice president of European operations, based in Italy, who oversees sales to Italy as well as the company's extensive European production and co-production activities, which are centred in Rome. Altogether,

Paramount maintains permanent sales offices for Latin America, Europe, the UK, France, Italy, Australia and the Far East, Canada, Japan, and South Korea.

Paramount's various offices in Europe, including separate executives assigned to specific nations, reflect the relative importance of these markets for the distributor. Meanwhile, Far East operations, including sales to Southeast Asia and China, are grouped together with Australia and based in Sydney, and sales to Brazil, Africa and the Middle East are handled by agents or redistributors (MIPTV, 2004a). Not surprisingly, the assignment of high-level executives and the reliance on dedicated sales offices abroad roughly reflects Paramount's main sales markets, which are Germany, the UK, Italy, Spain, Canada, France, Australia and Scandinavia-Benelux, in order of importance (Marenzi, 1999). Neither is the organisational structure of Paramount's global television operations markedly different from that of its fellow Hollywood majors, who typically distinguish between the pay-TV and video-on-demand business, the sales business, and the co-production and joint-venture business while maintaining several sales executives throughout Europe, Australia and Canada, with fewer in Latin America and Asia, and agents in the Middle East and Africa.

Because Viacom, Paramount's parent company, does not report Paramount's international television sales broken out from total foreign operations in its various financial reports, it is impossible to estimate Paramount's yearly revenues from international television. Furthermore, all of the Hollywood majors are tight-lipped about foreign sales revenues. Nevertheless, Gary Marenzi (1999), the President of International Television from 1997–2004 confirms that more than half of total revenues from a single Paramount television series produced for the domestic market can come from international sales. 'I think, on a super successful show right now, if you project forward ten years in both the US and international markets of what percentage international would represent, I think it would be thirty-five percent or so,' he explains. 'On a show that's less successful, that's where international really bales you out. On a show that's less successful, international would be probably over fifty percent of the revenue.' This happens because less successful shows may not achieve a three-year domestic network run, and thus be unsaleable in domestic syndication.

As with all of the Hollywood distributors, Paramount's most important genres in terms of international sales revenues are feature films, drama series and made-for-TV movies (Marenzi, 1999). These are the genres that have the highest production costs and tend to attract a wide general audience, which makes them valuable as primetime or access-primetime programming at general entertainment terrestrial and cable channels, which tend to pay higher licence fees than smaller niche-oriented channels. The size of the production budgets, including the presence of Hollywood stars in features and television movies, makes it difficult for non-Hollywood producers to turn out such programming. Thus, Hollywood producer-distributors are clearly dominant when it comes to these prestigious, high-priced genres.

As we saw in Chapter 1, major Hollywood distributors like Paramount experienced a surge in sales to foreign television outlets in the 1990s, which has slowed in recent years due to increased domestic production in many parts of the world and greater competition from other distributors. Consequently, especially in the richest markets, the majors today face a much harder sell than in the past, and rely heavily on marketing and promotions to maintain their sales margins. Promotions begin with the process of selecting which programming the distributor will carry. All of the majors pick up distribution rights to particularly attractive programming from other companies. Often, these deals involve network series for which the Hollywood studio provides distribution support and advance funding in return for a variety of fees that get covered before the original producer turns a profit (Marenzi, 2005b). An alternative arrangement involves programming initially distributed by another company that becomes a major US hit, after which a Hollywood distributor will swoop in and take over international distribution. Because the surest predictor of a programme's success in international markets is strong domestic performance, US network hits enjoy widespread appeal among buyers and command high prices, and can also move other programming in the distributor's library (Kaner, 1999; Marenzi, 1999; Puopolo, 1999). The high prices that buyers pay, however, increasingly come with the expectation that distributors will provide personalised promotional assistance, as described below. Not only do smaller distributors lack the network of potential buyers that the major distributors have, they also lack the marketing support that buyers have come to expect with high-end product.

Given the limited promotional resources even of the major Hollywood distributors, not all programming receives an equal amount of promotional effort. As mentioned, the most popular programmes in the domestic market are the most heavily promoted internationally. At MIP-TV 2004, for instance, Paramount focused its promotional efforts on *Navy NCIS* (2003–), a freshman series broadcast on CBS that has performed quite well in the ratings, especially among hard-to-reach young men. While successful network series continue to receive marketing support after their debut season, most of the attention is lavished on the newest series. In years when a studio does not have a network hit, it is likely to hedge its bets across a small number of moderately performing series, as was the case with Paramount at MIPCOM 2002, when it featured four new drama series that either aired on US cable networks or turned in less-than-impressive network ratings: *Haunted* (2002) on UPN, *The Dead Zone* (2002) on USA, *Hack* on CBS (2002) and *Keen Eddie* (2002–4) on Fox. In addition, break-out stars or cross-promotional opportunities can lead a distributor to promote certain programmes over others. Warner Bros. International Television in 1999, for instance, heavily promoted *The Jamie Foxx Show*, a moderately performing Fox series, because of the eponymous star's film contracts with Warner Bros. 'We actually internally have a big push with *The Jamie Foxx Show*,' explained Michael Puopolo, manager of international research for Warner Bros. International Television, 'because we really feel that if he gets established from a movie-career perspective, then the series will move. If Jamie Foxx's films take off, look for the popularity of the series ... to do the same' (1999).

In addition to promoting a limited number of new series to buyers, Hollywood distributors increasingly provide extensive, personalised support to help their more prized buyers market programming to advertisers, journalists and viewers in the buyer's market. In the 1990s, the major distributors typically provided the same promotional material that they produced for the domestic market, including kits with star interviews, advertising promos and press releases. None of these promotional kits was tailored to international markets, leaving buyers to design their own marketing campaigns. Beginning in the 1990s, Hollywood distributors began to develop offices that assisted with such promotional campaigns. Puopolo of Warner Bros., for instance, reports that much of his time is spent conducting research for international buyers' promotions, including discovering the length of Superman's cape to assist an Asian buyer with a promotional contest (1999). Today, marketing executives assist with all facets of buyers' promotional efforts, helping design local campaigns, providing research and talent appearances, and wining and dining local advertisers and journalists. Twentieth Century-Fox Television Distribution, for instance, designed a press junket for European journalists – one from each country – to meet stars and producers of their top-rated programmes in Los Angeles in 2002. In addition, the distributor produced a series of star interviews with greenscreen backgrounds that came with their series, allowing buyers to drop in local sites or station logos behind the stars (Sofley, 2002, p. 15). Such efforts have not only increased the price of high-end television product, but also complicated the sales contracts and negotiations.

Despite efforts at localised marketing and promotions by the Hollywood distributors, their programming typically remains aimed at an undifferentiated US primetime audience, thus diminishing its overseas appeal and sales. While blockbuster television programmes such as *Friends* and *ER* do appeal to foreign buyers and viewers because of the global cachet of US popular culture, most of the programming sold by the majors is seen as 'idiosyncratically American' (Schapiro, 1991, p. 29) and does not find its way into primetime schedules abroad, which keeps prices down. Paramount's Marenzi (1999) explains:

Unfortunately, at the studios, there is still a bit of myopia that this is a domestic business. And the big pay-off is if you get a hit show in the US and it goes to sixty-six episodes and it's strippable. Selling ... a show like that, you can make over a million bucks an episode or more if it's really successful. And that kind of upside doesn't exist internationally. ... So that's why they're still focused on developing stuff for the US, because the biggest upside is when you get a hit show in the US.

Of course, the expansion of the studios into co-production, local production and co-financing arrangements has changed this dynamic, as these arrangements allow them to continue producing their high-end programming for the domestic market while developing programmes abroad that are aimed at international markets.

As the Hollywood distributors have moved into localised programme production activities, they have tended to focus on the most lucrative foreign genres with widespread audience appeal, including miniseries, made-for-TV movies and action dramas, in some instances squeezing local producers out of the business or requiring them to work together with Hollywood. However, local producers frequently welcome Hollywood's involvement because it leads to increased production funding and increased revenues, which can be used to cross-subsidise local producers' other projects. Local programme activities include co-producing, which involves producing programmes designed for distribution in multiple markets. Paramount's *Largo* (2000), the extreme sports Canadian co-production *Cliffhangers* (2000) and various animated series co-produced with French, German and Belgian producers are examples of this strategy (Brennan, 1999e; Marenzi, 1999). Industry-wide, this arrangement is most common between Hollywood and producers or broadcasters in the UK, Australia, and Canada, although Paramount has also co-produced with Spanish cable giant Sogecable, and headquarters its European co-production facilities in Rome (Brennan, 1997; Marenzi, 1999, 2005a).

For Paramount, however, local production remains a more common form of non-US production activity than co-production. Local production involves setting up a production company in a foreign country, often with local investors, and producing programming for that market through the partially owned subsidiary. In 1998, for instance, Paramount struck a deal with German production company Ufa for both English-language co-productions intended for the European market and a number of projects aimed solely at the German market (Kirschbaum, 1996). Again, Paramount's Marenzi explains, 'We're going to become a lot more local. We believe it's just inevitable that if you want to maintain your share of the market, you can't just be an American programme supplier. You have to be a global producer and distributor' (Bortin, 1998). In addition to these arrangements, Paramount has also become active in selling programme formats and formatting its programmes in overseas markets (Marenzi, 1999, 2005a).

GLOBAL SALES AT COMMERCIAL NICHE DISTRIBUTORS

While the Hollywood majors focus on general entertainment programming in expensive genres, a flood of smaller, niche-oriented producer-distributors survive on lower-budget productions that sell to speciality cable channels and broadcasters that programme non-primetime slots for specific audience segments. Most of these niche distributors specialise in one of the handful of programming genres that global television merchants consider capable of transcending national boundaries: documentaries, children's animation, action-adventure series, erotica, soap operas, sports and music television. Small distributors dedicated to these genres often rely heavily on international sales revenue and are particularly vulnerable to changes in the global marketplace that rush different genres into and out of popularity. On the other hand, large niche producer-distributors with strong domestic revenues typically use international sales to help defray production costs and are less vulnerable to the tides of the global markets. Nevertheless, even for these large operations, changes in the global marketplace can have serious profit implications, particularly when domestic and foreign generic tastes change at different paces.

A common genre for distributors to build their businesses around is the Latin American *telenovela*, which international buyers usually use as daytime fare to attract older women viewers. Even non-Latin American distributors, such as the US independent producer-distributor Promark, specialise in the genre (Jenkinson, 2005a). The world's largest *telenovela* exporter, Televisa Estudios, is the international distribution wing of Grupo Televisa, the main media conglomerate in Mexico, which includes broadcasting, satellite and cable operations throughout Latin American, North America and Europe, as well as magazine publishing. Televisa has long been a provider of Spanish-language television programming to other Latin American nations and the Latino community in the US, but began to rise to prominence in international television distribution beginning in 1980, when it sold the *telenovela Los Ricos También Lloran* (1979) to the Soviet Union (Tegal, 2001).

Since 1980, the international distribution division of Grupo Televisa has undergone various organisational changes. Until 1998, a division known as Protele handled international television sales through a Miami-based office that sold programming to Latin America and a New York-based office that sold to North America and the rest of the world. A separate subsidiary, Televisa International, handled Televisa's other international operations, in particular its investments in television channels in Spain and the US. Until 1994, Televisa maintained ownership interests in Latin American broadcasters, but abandoned those investments due to instability in the advertising markets across the region for what it calls 'affiliate' agreements. Basically, its fifteen affiliates in Latin America get broadcasting rights to all of Televisa's television productions in return for 15 per cent of advertising revenues earned with Televisa productions (Paxman, 1998; *Variety*, 1997b). In 2003, Grupo Televisa combined Protele and Televisa International under the name Televisa Estudios, in part to identify itself less with the importation of Mexican programming and more with the production of US Latino programming (Hecht, 2003b). It is interesting, though by no mean surprising, to note that the simple act of naming in global television sales is a cultural act with economic consequences. Today, Televisa Estudios maintains sales staffs in Madrid, Miami and New York that are responsible, respectively, for sales to Europe, Latin and North America, and Asia and Africa (Televisa Estudios, 2004).

The international trade in *telenovelas* dates back to 1958, when Telesistema Mexicano (TSM) acquired a videotape machine and began exporting *telenovelas* to the US and Latin America. By 1976, the national Mexican broadcasting monopoly Televisa, which had incorporated TSM years earlier, exported 12,000 hours of programming, mostly *telenovelas*, to the US and Latin America (Fox, 1997). Televisa remains the most prolific exporter of *telenovelas*, boasting a catalogue of nearly 60,000 programming hours and international sales revenues of $153 million in 2002 (Sutter, 2002). About one-third of international sales revenues come from the US, another third from Latin America and the final third is split among European and Asian territories (Burnett, 2002; *Variety*, 1997b). Not unlike the Hollywood majors, Televisa experienced a surge in international *telenovela* sales in the 1990s, which has since dissipated, especially in Europe, requiring changes both in its marketing strategies and its international programming catalogue (Fraser, 2002).

Televisa's promotional efforts are strikingly similar to those of the Hollywood majors, although the growing disconnect between the target markets for *telenovelas* at home and abroad poses distinct problems for Televisa. As with Paramount, Televisa promotes its newest *telenovelas* most heavily, particularly those with strong domestic ratings in Mexico. At MIP-TV 2004, *Amar Otra Vez* (*Loving Again*) (2003–4) was Televisa's spotlighted *telenovela*, a relatively expensive project starring Mexican pop star Iran Castillo and a top-performing series in Mexico. In addition to its spotlighted projects, Televisa adopts what it calls an 'assembly-line approach' to producing cheap *telenovelas*, which are largely sold as filler programming for newer channels in small markets, although

the European pay-television channel Romantica also buys large tracts of Televisa *telenovelas* to help fill its twenty-four-hour *telenovela* schedule (Fraser,
2002). According to Guillermo Canedo White, head of international sales at
Televisa Estudios, 'The ability to mass-produce gives us a competitive product
in terms of pricing and audience' (Hecht, 2003a). Despite Canedo White's mention of the competitiveness of its programming among viewers, price seems to
be the primary consideration for most buyers when purchasing *telenovelas*. That
is, because *telenovelas* are usually placed in daytime schedules and attract small
audiences that bring in minimal advertising revenues, buyers tend to make purchasing decisions based mainly on price, rather than audience appeal of
particular series (Balogh, 2001; Biltereyst and Meers, 2000: 402, p. Escalante,
2004; Sahab, 2004).

With the exception of the Spanish market, where Televisa's *telenovelas* have
frequently aired to large audiences in prime time, the company focuses its promotional efforts on different markets and different time-slots than do the
Hollywood majors, in order to carve out a niche in the global television marketplace. One of Televisa's main marketing challenges comes from the fact that
telenovelas tend to target broad, undifferentiated audiences during prime time
at home, while international buyers use them to target niche audiences in other
dayparts, most commonly older women during daytime (Fraser, 2002). In Hungary, for instance, broadcasters programmed *telenovelas* in late morning and
early afternoon slots throughout the late 1990s for women viewers between
thirty-five and forty-nine. Consequently, a gulf has developed between the preferences of Central and Eastern European viewers, who prefer 'classic'
telenovelas that tell the story of lovers estranged by class differences, and domestic Mexican audiences, where younger-skewing *telenovelas* featuring
contemporary social issues draw better ratings (AGB Hungary, 2002; Balogh,
2001; Escalante, 2004; Fraser, 2002; Sahab, 2004).

In addition to targeting different demographics than the Hollywood majors,
Televisa has also targeted different markets. *Telenovelas* have achieved their
most consistent sales in less affluent markets that cannot fill their entire broadcast schedules with locally produced programming. Although popular in Western
Europe in the 1980s due primarily to their cheapness, *telenovelas* have travelled
most successfully in other Latin American markets, Eastern Europe and
Southern and Southeast Asia. The exception has been Spain, where Televisa's
telenovelas have often been used as primetime fare, but in the past couple of
years, consolidation in the Spanish production sector and increased competition
has led most broadcasters there to rely more on locally developed *telenovelas*
(Biltereyst and Meers, 2000, p. 398; De Pablos, 2002).

The strongest market for imported *telenovelas* has always been the US Latino market, which has traditionally been ignored by the national networks and the Hollywood majors who supply them (Avis, 2001). The interest in *telenovelas* in South and Southeast Asia, on the other hand, has been more recent, and includes such markets as Indonesia, the Philippines and Malaysia (Burnett, 2002). While Televisa is more active in the US market than the independents and thus unlikely to see such a significant percentage of revenues from Asian buyers, the company nevertheless sees great growth potential there. Currently, Televisa is eyeing the Indian market as its next area of expansion (Hecht, 2003a). The structure of Televisa's sales staff reflects these geographic emphases, with different sales managers assigned to cover Latin America, North America, Europe and Asia and Africa (MIPTV, 2004a).

The changing international market for *telenovelas* has resulted in a levelling off in Televisa's foreign revenue growth rates over the past five years, even as such revenues have come to represent a larger and larger share of overall revenues. In 2002, international sales of Televisa's *telenovelas* generated $153 million, or about 7 per cent of overall income, up from $62 million in 1995 and representing an increase of about 3 per cent of gross profits over seven years (Standard & Poors, 1997; Sutter, 2002; *Variety*, 1996; Worldscope, 2005). While this percentage may seem small, especially compared to what the Hollywood studios earn from overseas television markets, we must remember that Televisa is an integrated media conglomerate with extensive holdings in broadcasting, cable and magazine publishing around the world. Thus, comparing Televisa's international *telenovela* sales to its overall revenues is equivalent to comparing Paramount International Television's sales to the overall revenues of Viacom. If we compare sales of all Latin American *telenovelas* outside of Latin America to the total advertising revenue generated within the region, we find that international rights sales account for about 21 per cent of all revenue generated by Latin American versions of the genre (Sutter, 2002).

While international sales have since 1996 come to represent a growing proportion of Televisa's revenues, competition among distributors and production costs have increased, while prices are lower in most markets. The number of distributors selling *telenovelas* abroad has grown fivefold since the mid-1990s, and now includes the Hollywood studios. The competition among distributors at home and abroad has driven up production costs, as producers use more stars, better writers, more exotic locations and flashier post-production techniques to differentiate their programming. Meanwhile, prices for *telenovelas* on the global markets began to fall in the late 1990s. 'Russia was paying $1,200 per hour, now they're paying $ 800; Indonesia was paying up to $1,200, now it's $700,' according to Germán Pérez Nahím, then head of Venezuelan distributor, Venevision (Paxman, 1999, p. 74). These lower prices mean that distributors must increase the number of markets where they sell their programming in order to maintain overall foreign sales revenues (Guider and Tasca, 2000; Herman, 2002; Paxman, 1999).

Televisa has taken three approaches to dealing with the increased competition among *telenovelas* in recent years: it has developed co-production arrangements and *telenovela* formats, segmented the audience for *telenovelas* at home and abroad, and tried to expand its library beyond the *telenovela* genre. The classic *telenovela* remains the dominant form in Mexico today, but Televisa has developed new subgenres to target children, teens and young adults separately, incorporating animation, music videos and reality shows. Increased action sequences and topical themes, such as drug addiction and AIDS, have come to dominate teen-oriented *telenovelas*, which frequently feature pop stars and music-video scenes. Children's *telenovelas* mix the melodramatic format with animation. And, Televisa recently sponsored a reality-show vote-off contest to pick the actors for an upcoming *telenovela*, combining the *telenovela* with the reality genre (Fraser, 2002). In addition to helping Televisa compete for audience niches in the Mexican market, these new subgenres can be sold or formatted abroad for similar audiences. Thus, rather than addressing an undifferentiated, domestic audience, the newer forms address multiple niche audiences at home and abroad. However, the 'edgy' programming that niche audiences find most appealing can cause problems with buyers. 'We have one example, *Clase 406*, and it was for teenagers and it talked about all these issues, drugs, rape, and we could never put it on air in [Central and Eastern Europe],' explains Claudia Sahab, the director of European sales at Televisa. 'We really tried and we couldn't. They were not interested' (Sahab, 2004).

Televisa has also taken to expanding its co-production business in order to maintain its profit margins in particularly important markets, much like the Hollywood majors. Although Televisa has long co-produced with Spanish partners, it only recently began co-producing for the US Latino market, and has even started reselling these co-productions in Latin American markets. Since it deals primarily with smaller, independent companies when co-producing in the US, Televisa typically retains international rights to the projects. In addition, Televisa is looking to establish a major co-production venture in India. Local formatting of *telenovelas*, too, is likely to become an important revenue stream for Televisa in the near future. Finally, Televisa's expansion into a wider variety of programming genres domestically has expanded the variety of genres for which the company holds global rights. In addition, the uncertainties of the *telenovela* market have spurred a desire to diversify Televisa's programming library to guard against down-cycles in the genre. Today, Televisa's library includes reality shows, comedies, dramas and variety shows, in addition to *telenovelas* (Fraser, 2002).

The final challenge that Televisa faces comes from the encroachment of the Hollywood majors into the *telenovela* genre, demonstrating how Hollywood tries to corner the most lucrative markets, as well as the ways in which other kinds of distributors must adjust to Hollywood's presence. José Escalante, vice president and general manager of Coral International, explains the general concern among *telenovela* producers regarding Hollywood's involvement in *telenovela* production. 'The stronger [the majors] get, producing good-quality *telenovelas*, the more difficult it's going to be for us,' he explains. 'It is going to be competition. We have to be prepared for it. They're majors, we have to remember that' (Escalante, 2004). Obviously, the concern here is that the majors will take over *telenovela* production, muscling current producer-distributors out of the business with their large production and promotional budgets, as well as their reputations.

Televisa, then, has adopted many of the same strategies as the Hollywood majors, in an effort to maintain international revenues in an era of increased global competition. These strategies include co-productions, promotional campaigns and formatting. However, Televisa faces special challenges due to its concentration on a single internationally traded genre, such as the genre's erratic popularity with buyers, the encroachment of larger distributors into *telenovela* production and differences in how channels at home and abroad use the genre to target viewers. Consequently, Televisa has moved to develop more niche-oriented *telenovelas* that can target the same audience segments at home and abroad. It is important to note in this respect that Televisa has integrated other genres into the *telenovela* in an effort to leverage both the company's and the genre's global reputation, rather than abandoning *telenovelas* altogether.

The challenges faced by Televisa are not dissimilar to those faced by niche distributors of all sizes, in particular the need to guard against down-cycles in a genre's global popularity. As a genre's fortunes rise and fall in different markets around the world, due to changes in niche-audience preferences and the programming practices of one's primary buyers, the revenues of a niche distributor can change unpredictably. Larger niche-distributors try to diversify their programming libraries in order to deal with this uncertainty. Endemol International, for instance, the Dutch distributor best known for its reality-show format *Big Brother*, has recently expanded its programming library to include scripted series such as *telenovelas*, in order to insulate itself from the fluctuations of the market in reality shows. Smaller niche distributors, on the other hand, may have more difficulty branching out into other genres, and may remain vulnerable.

PUBLIC BROADCASTERS AND THE GLOBAL TELEVISION MARKETPLACE

Like commercial niche-distributors, many non-profit broadcaster-producers have come to rely upon the global television marketplace to aid in programme production. For smaller public broadcasters, the global market has become not so much an economic necessity as an integral part of their remit to serve the local production sector and improve its reputation by attracting buyers for independent, domestic productions. These distributors face problems similar to the commercial niche-distributors explored above, as well as the added challenge of squaring their non-commercial identities with their commercial functions in the global marketplace. In addition, when it comes to branding themselves and promoting their programming to buyers around the world, non-profit distributors adopt strategies quite similar to commercial companies.

Japan's public-service broadcaster, Nippon Hoso Kyokai (NHK), produces some of the most actively traded public-service programming on the world markets. Founded by US occupation forces after World War II on the model of the BBC (Hilmes, 2003, p. 55), NHK is a non-commercial entity whose primary function is to serve the Japanese citizenry. Not surprisingly, then, NHK does not extensively produce, programme, or distribute large quantities of violent Japanese anime, a globally popular genre, though non-violent animation is NHK's second most popular export. Rather, NHK's most popular genre with foreign buyers is the documentary.

Much like its European public broadcasting counterparts, NHK has a long tradition of factual programming. Its location in East Asia and the strength of the Japanese economy has made wildlife documentaries, especially those featuring uniquely Asian animals such as Pandas, NHK's signature product, because it was for a long time the only broadcaster in the area capable of producing such expensive programming. In recent years, NHK has taken advantage of the growing high-definition television (HDTV) boom in Asia, Europe and North America to extend its brand into high-end, high-definition documentaries. Drawing on its established expertise in documentaries and the long association of Japan with superior electronic technologies such as HDTV, NHK has moved to become one of the foremost producers and co-producers of documentaries whose soundtrack and cinematography are specifically designed for HDTV (*Television Business International*, 2003). Along with sports and feature films, wildlife and nature documentaries are generally seen as genres uniquely suited to the technology of HDTV.

NHK produces its own documentaries and also co-produces with other public broadcasters, particularly those in Europe, North America and the Australian continent, as well as Asian, European and North American commercial documentary producers such as Discovery and National Geographic. As with most co-productions, NHK's partners retain distribution rights in their home markets and perhaps the wider geolinguistic region, while NHK retains rights in Asia and the Pacific Rim. For instance, in 2000, NHK partnered with German public broadcaster ZDF and independent commercial French TV group, Télé Images, to produce a science documentary series named *Space Millennium*, in which ZDF got German-speaking rights, Télé Images got non-German European rights and NHK retained Asian and South American rights (*Screen Digest*, 2001).

NHK's non-profit status in Japan complicates its global sales activities because the broadcaster is legally barred from profiting from international rights sales. Consequently, an intermediary, the Media International Company (MICO), handles international distribution of NHK's programmes and pays what it calls a 'copyright fee' to NHK. Prior to MICO taking over NHK's global sales in 1991, the company was represented by a quasi-for-profit distribution wing, NHK Enterprises, founded in the 1960s, which today focuses primarily on programme production. In 2004, MICO's programming library included more than 1,000 NHK titles, representing about 7,000 hours of programming (Sakamoto, 2004).

MICO utilises sales agents and redistributors to sell its programming for both practical and historical reasons. Originally, NHK Enterprises, MICO's predecessor, sold mostly to public broadcasters in large European markets, which made intermediaries familiar with European customs, executives and languages indispensable. More recently, such arrangements have become less necessary, because the acquisitions process has been rationalised and more and more of NHK's sales, especially its HD programming, go to non-terrestrial, commercial channels. Nevertheless, since many of the redistributors are large companies with good-sized programme libraries, NHK's programming benefits from inclusion in the redistributors' catalogues. In addition, some of these redistributors, such as Télé Images, have become partners on HD programming, and keeping the relationship with them increases such partnership opportunities. MICO relies on redistributors in France, Germany, Taiwan, Thailand, Spain and the Middle East, and uses its own sales representatives for other territories. Although the company splits its rights into DVD, video, terrestrial and pay windows, they typically assign all of the rights to their redistributors, though they retain transnational pay-TV rights for themselves. In addition, the company holds merchandising rights to NHK's animated characters (Sakamoto, 2004).

One of the most striking features of NHK's promotional and marketing materials is that it is produced in English, a practice repeated across the sales floor at MIP-TV. The 'screeners' that play on the HDTV at the NHK/MICO booth are subtitled in English, and all of the flyers and catalogues are in English.

Illustration 2.1: At the NHK/MICO sales stand, HDTV programming is featured, subtitled in English. MIP-TV 2004.

In short, English is the *lingua franca* of global television sales, as most contracts are written in English and scripts for translation are provided in English, regardless of the original language of either the distributor or the buyer.

NHK's promotional materials make clear that they are specifically targeting European buyers or, at least, buyers with European sensibilities. The broadcaster's promotional DVD at MIP-TV 2004 concentrated on HD programming, featuring nature, wildlife, history, arts, science and human interest documentaries. With the exception of the nature and wildlife documentaries, all of these programmes had distinctly Western themes, including a documentary about the global marketing prowess of Yao Ming, the Chinese basketball star who plays for the Houston Rockets, and soccer superstar David Beckham; another about Rembrandt's portrait *Night Watch*; and a third about the Paris Opera's performance of *William Tell*. The DVD's opening sequence begins with a quote from Genesis, in English of course, which provides the titles for the ensuing sections of the introduction, which are made up of clips from various documentaries grouped together under headings like 'Light', 'Creatures' and 'Mankind'. The soundtrack for the introduction includes audio from the documentary clips and a score composed of European classical and new age music. Obviously, several of the features of this promotional DVD suggest that it is aimed at European and US buyers. Moreover, because this is NHK's primary promotional DVD for all buyers in the world, it demonstrates how the economic power of Western buyers leads to promotional practices that privilege Western culture as the standard of quality in promotions.

NHK's concentration on documentaries and its use of international contacts groomed at the global sales markets to facilitate co-production activities is repeated at public broadcasters across Europe. International sales at smaller public broadcasters, such as YLE in Finland, TV Channel Russia and Netherlands Public Broadcasting also focus on documentaries, and use their international sales to develop and renew relationships with potential co-producers (Charvadze, 2004; Kriek, 2004; Moore, 2004). One unique feature of these smaller broadcasters is that they often represent independent programming from their home markets. International sales, then, are less about helping defray production costs of already-produced programming or securing partners for the broadcaster's future projects, and more about helping independent producers in the broadcaster's country find outside funding, which feeds the development of the production sector, thereby helping to fulfil part of the public broadcaster's remit. Notice, however, that this support is only open to independent producers who work in genres that are seen as adding to the education or cultural distinctiveness of the citizenry, particularly documentaries, children's animation and feature films. Smaller public broadcasters and the independent companies they represent rely heavily on international film and television competitions, such as the Banff Television Festival, to promote their projects. According to Alexander Charvadze (2004), an international sales representative for TV Channel Russia, nomination for an award at Banff virtually guarantees sales to Western European markets, and a winning entry guarantees North American sales.

The reliance of smaller broadcasters on global sales fairs leads to a variety of potential business relationships that may benefit the broadcaster or the domestic television industry. Thus, global sales revenue may not be the only reason for attending the markets for these smaller organisations; in fact, it may not be an important reason. This fact holds true for other small organisations as well, especially non-commercial ones. The British Film Institute, for example, does make sales at MIP-TV, but one of the primary functions of the market is to search out new producers and renew relationships. John Flahive (2004), the sales manager for the BFI, explains, 'International sales is very much about having a relationship with the producer who made the film, because they basically give you the film.' The BFI's catalogue, which consists of about 100 art and experimental films, mainly appeals to buyers from public broadcasters, especially 'second channels', or the smaller cousins of the large public broadcasting channel, which often schedule the films in late-night slots (Flahive, 2004).

Thus, despite the fact that larger distributors can corner the market in the most lucrative genres in the largest markets, a number of other genres circulate to other markets, buyers and time-slots. These include such apparently 'non-commercial' genres as documentaries and experimental films. Unlike commercial broadcasters such as Televisa, these boutique and non-commercial distributors are less driven to expand into more and more programming genres, because they build their brands specifically around non-commercial programming. In addition, these distributors are perhaps even more reliant on the global sales markets and the relationships they groom there to facilitate a variety of non-selling business functions. Nevertheless, the inequities in the market have their impact here as well, because buyers from the comparatively richer nations of the West are the most appealing international buyers, and the promotional efforts of even non-commercial distributors are aimed at such buyers.

THE SOLO DISTRIBUTOR AND THE GLOBAL TELEVISION MARKETPLACE

Thus far, the distributors profiled in this chapter have been based in a single nation that provides the majority of their distribution revenues, while global sales generally provide a crucial, yet secondary, revenue stream. However, a number of companies rely almost exclusively on global sales for their very existence, including both minor distributors, often run by one or two people, and independent producers who sell their own programming worldwide. These are the companies that are most affected by the preferences of buyers and global trends, and as such they keep their ears closely to the ground to guard their very survival, as a single deal can vault them into prominence or spell their demise. These companies can exist due to their close and long relationships with a relatively small group of buyers and distributors in a single region of the world, which gives them market intelligence that large distributors lack. The observations that I make in this section are based on interviews with half a dozen minor redistributors and producer-distributors, but the majority of the section draws on a solo Hungarian distributor, János Kovács (not his real name), with whom I spent four days at MIPCOM 2002 and whom I interviewed again at MIP-TV 2004. In addition, we have had several conversations before and after these sales markets.

János Kovács defected to France and eventually the US in the early 1980s, at the age of sixteen. He worked his way up through the ranks of a medium-size television production company throughout the 1980s, after which he moved into sales at Warner Bros. He spent a few years in international sales at Warner Bros., but left to pursue a career of producing and directing films. After a stint of producing erotic films for Playboy and Penthouse, he wrote, directed and produced a feature film that received some theatrical distribution in the US and Europe, and also played on HBO. Kovács does not have rights to the film he directed, but did retain rights to several of the erotic films he produced and has acquired rights to other programmes over the years. In the late 1990s, Kovács returned to his native Hungary, in part with the declared intent of improving the state of the Hungarian entertainment industry.

Kovács attends both MIP-TV and MIPCOM sales markets, as well as some regional markets. At MIP-TV and MIPCOM, he registers as a sales agent for a friend's company that supports a booth at the market, giving him a home base where he can meet clients and potential partners, without having to endure the costs of his own booth. The majority of Kovács' sales revenues continue to come from his adult films. While he does not promote them in any way, he explains that buyers tend to know who at the markets has a cache of erotic films 'under the table'. Apparently, a network of buyers of adult programming walks the markets looking for titles to acquire, and it is easy to make a good living distributing the genre. It should also be noted that a number of companies, including Mainline Releasing and Playboy International, openly sell adult programming. However, several minor distributors like Kovács, who are trying to break into other kinds of programming, don't want to get identified as distributors of adult programming, because it seems that many people in 'legitimate' global sales look askance at those who deal in erotica.

At MIPCOM 2002, Kovács brought a new series and a new film to the market to distribute. Both the film and the series were Hungarian, and he had a slick, professional flyer for each project made that explained the basic plot and other programme features in English. Kovács also had a 'screener' tape with the most exciting scenes of both the series and the film edited together with a compelling soundtrack and English subtitles. Unfortunately, because Kovács was merely a guest in the sales booth, he could not convince his partner, who had paid for the booth, to play the screener on the booth's single television set. Instead, Kovács' partner played his own screener. Consequently, Kovács' products had little exposure and little opportunity to attract passers-by. He left the market without any sales or any firm interest in his Hungarian product, though he did net several sales of rights to his erotic titles.

MIPCOM 2002 was Kovács' first attempt to sell Hungarian programming at a market. The most important lesson he learned, he said, was that he should have dubbed the screener into English, rather than subtitling it. According to Kovács, as soon as a buyer hears characters speaking in Hungarian, they tune out and complain that none of their viewers would be interested in programming from such an obscure culture as Hungary. However, if he dubbed the programming into English, buyers would be less conscious of the origins of the programming and therefore more positively disposed to it. Kovács has not, to my knowledge, tried to sell other Hungarian programmes at a sales market, so his speculation must remain speculation. Still, I take his reporting of buyers' reactions at face value, and his idea to create what he called a more 'universally appealing' screener by dubbing in English demonstrates the degree to which distributors' perceptions of buyers' preferences for Western-looking and Western-sounding programming shape their promotional choices.

Kovács had previously operated primarily as a redistributor, picking up programming rights at market and trying to sell them to Hungarian channels, at one time obtaining Hungarian broadcast rights to all of the recent winners of the Cannes Film Festival. These solo redistributors trade off of the relationships they have with buyers, hoping to corner rights to particularly attractive programming in the markets where they operate before other broadcasters or redistributors can. Cecilia Hazai, the founder of Twin Media, for instance, nabbed Central European rights to *Pokémon* from US distributor 4Kids Entertainment before the series became a smash global hit, and has built a reputation for herself as a distributor of children's animation (Hazai, 2001). In addition to programme sales, Kovács uses the sales markets as a place to groom relationships for other projects. When I ran into him at MIP-TV 2004, he was working on finalising a co-financing deal between two acquaintances, a financier and a producer, for which he would collect a finder's fee.

Kovács' story demonstrates the variety of money-making opportunities that global television offers for solo redistributors who are able to respond to market conditions and trade in less sought-after or discredited programme genres than the larger distributors. Even – or perhaps especially – at this level, the preferences of Western buyers influence promotional efforts. Although Western buyers may not be the main targets of their promotions, solo redistributors design Western-style promotional materials to add a touch of class and appeal to their programming.

Small producers, too, find a variety of ways to increase profits through the global markets, particularly those who operate in genres with widespread global appeal, such as children's animation. Kok Hong (Andrew) Ooi of Malaysian Inspedia Productions brought a single, unfinished animated children's series, *Johan, The Young Scientist*, to MIPCOM 2003 and MIP-TV 2004. His main purpose was neither to make sales nor to secure funding to finish the product, though he had completed a pre-sale to a Middle Eastern children's channel to help defray production costs. Rather, his attendance was the opening salvo in what he termed a 'kamikaze' promotional strategy: through the appeal of the series and the relationships they groomed at the markets, he hoped to get an idea of the kinds of programming Inspedia should develop in the future. In addition, he hoped to coax some of the larger animation producer-distributors to use Inspedia's production facilities and expertise for future projects (Ooi, 2004).

In many ways, then, these small producers and distributors are the most truly globalised of all the participants in global television sales, in the sense that they depend most on non-domestic markets for their production and promotion ideas, as well as their revenues. Consequently, they are also the most influenced by price and capacity differentials in the global markets that make Western buyers the most coveted, leading to Western-oriented promotional strategies and, most likely, production decisions.

CONCLUSION

Sales executives at the Hollywood majors insist that they do not dominate global television sales, that their programming faces increasing competition in growing television markets everywhere, that they have had to adapt their strategies to take account of the uniqueness of foreign markets and that the complexities of keeping pace with changing economic and competitive environments around the world mean that only in genres with high entry barriers, such as action films, can they continue to enjoy their once-dominant position.

No doubt, all of these observations about the global television markets are accurate. However, Hollywood in particular, and Western distributors in general, benefit from the dominant economic position of Western markets in other ways. First, they continue to control much of the market for the highest-priced genres, leaving others to cobble together funding from international sources to fund or defray production costs for more niche-oriented programming. Second, Western markets boast the largest numbers of affluent buyers, prompting both large and small distributors to focus their promotional efforts on Western buyers through the use of Western cultural values in their promotional materials, including language, music and themes. Third, the ritual divisions of the markets, examined in the following chapter, guarantee that Western executives' opinions and practices remain the most highly respected among all participants, thereby lending to their practices an aura of quality that other distributors emulate, and buyers expect.

3

Global Television Trade Shows

If the worldwide multiplication and co-ordination of distribution windows has spurred the development of a global television business culture, global television fairs serve as that culture's high holidays, where the main categories, divisions and rhetorics of cohesion become available for analysis. Officially known as 'sales markets' or 'trade shows', they include MIP-TV (Marché International des Programmes de Télévision, or International Television Programme Market), NATPE (National Association of Television Programme Executives) and MIPCOM . Each of these global television markets has a slightly different participant base and business function, but all of them offer condensed microcosms of the business culture. This chapter takes a ritual approach to analysing global sales markets, demonstrating how the cultural distinctions that the sales markets provide not only streamline the global exchange of programming, but also confer prestige on participants, which is one of the most valuable commodities in the global television marketplace. In addition, the sales markets provide the illusion of scarcity, which is necessary to maintain high prices and demand for new product.

MAJOR GLOBAL TRADE SHOWS: MIP-TV, NATPE AND MIPCOM

Television programming fairs can be divided into three types: global fairs dedicated to programming trade of all genres from all nations; regional fairs, where distributors from the region exhibit their wares for international buyers; and genre-specific fairs that focus on particularly popular international genres, such as reality programming or documentaries. In addition, television rights for films are sold at international film festivals. Here, I concentrate on global television fairs, which serve as the primary sites where members of the global television sales community come together.

MIP-TV, held every spring in Cannes, France, is the premiere global market for television programming. Begun in 1963 as a place for European buyers and American distributors to trade programming, MIP-TV has grown into a truly international event. As Table 3.1 shows, companies representing more than 100 nations generally attend MIP-TV. This number has remained quite constant over the past decade, attesting to the fair's international flavour. In addition, the number of companies has increased by approximately 20 per cent over the past ten years, reflecting both the growth in international television trade and the importance of MIP-TV in conducting trade. For many distributors and buyers, MIP-TV is the only international trade show that they can afford to attend (Al-Mugaiseeb, 1998). In the late 1990s, Hollywood producers began to scale back their presence at MIP-TV, but increases in mid-season replacements, which take the place of cancelled series on the American broadcast networks beginning in January, have rejuvenated Hollywood's interest in MIP-TV because it gives them a venue for selling such series internationally (Brennan, 2000).

NATPE, held alternately in Las Vegas and New Orleans each January, was founded in 1963 as a US programming trade show. However, the international contingent has grown significantly in recent years (see Table 3.1). In fact, the decision in 1993 to hire Bruce Johansen, a well-known international distributor, as CEO reflects NATPE's efforts to be 'known throughout the global television industry as the leading association for content professionals' (NATPE, 2004). NATPE's relevance for domestic television syndication has suffered in recent years due to consolidation in the syndication business and station ownership. While representatives from hundreds of stations around the country used to buy programming from dozens of syndication companies, since the relaxation of ownership regulations in the US Telecommunications Act of 1996, group owners have swallowed up local stations and centralised programme buying in to a single corporate office. At the same time, a handful of companies have come to dominate domestic syndication. However, while domestic syndication 'implodes' (Johansen, 2001), the international contingent continues to rise, growing more than 50 per cent between 1996 and 2001 (see Table 3.1).

Table 3.1: Attendance at MIP-TV, MIPCOM and NATPE (1992-2002)

	MIP-TV		MIPCOM		NATPE	
	Participants	Countries	Participants	Countries	Participants	Int'l participants
1992	9008	101	7803	76	8674	1185
1993	9164	103	8242	84	11,277	
1994	9565	99	8499	85	11,652	
1995	10,225	107	9240	91	15,750	
1996	10,578	104	9776	92	17,694	2975
1997	10,901	103	10,145	96	16,751	
1998	10,518	102	10,428	90	17,250	
1999	10,791	101	10,571	88	17,440	
2000			11,786	89	17,520	4380
2001	11,049	90	9943	85	20,348[1]	4585
2002	10,217	92	10,209	90	10,125[2]	

Source: MIPTV (2004b); MIPCOM (2005); NATPE (2002)

Notes:
1. The attendance figure for NATPE 2001 in part reflects relocation of the conference from New Orleans to Las Vegas, which is more readily accessible to Hollywood-based executives.
2. According to NATPE officials, this number reflects a significant drop for 2002 due to the economic downturn in general and the uncertainty following September 11.

Finally, MIPCOM, founded in 1985 and sometimes referred to as MIP-TV's younger brother, takes place in Cannes each autumn. Initially designed to include a wider range of buyers than MIP-TV, including video distributors and cable and satellite channels, MIPCOM today draws essentially the same participants as MIP-TV. MIPCOM is geared more towards selling US programming than MIP-TV, because American sellers have autumn ratings data with which to demonstrate the popularity of new programming. MIPCOM attendance grew more than 50 per cent between 1992 and 2000, before plummeting briefly in October 2001 in the wake of the 11 September terrorist attacks (Table 3.1). The remarkable growth of MIPCOM has paralleled the growth in international television trade over the past ten years, suggesting a connection between programming fairs and the smooth operation of international sales. Furthermore, the creation of MIPCOM demonstrates the degree to which Western programming and companies dominate international television trade. While the Hollywood majors make most of their deals with larger buyers at a regional trade fair called the Los Angeles Screenings in May, MIPCOM offers a venue for programming that was not sold at Los Angeles and for buyers who did not attend the Screenings (Roxborough and Masters, 2001).

THE BUSINESS STRUCTURE OF GLOBAL TELEVISION SALES

Before addressing the cultural dimensions of global television programming fairs in depth, I want to examine the structure of the global television industry whose representatives meet there to trade programming. Such an analysis explains the institutional forces that bring together global television merchants year after year when the direct economic benefits of the sales markets are intangible.

Paul Hirsch (1972) has examined the organisational structure of the book publishing, record and film industries, concluding that these industries exhibit a proliferation of contact personnel on the 'input' (product selection) and 'output' (promotion and marketing) sectors of the individual organisation. While his analysis does not address the television industry, it can productively be adapted to demonstrate the organisation of international television trade (see also Turow, 1997). Hirsch argues that uncertainty is the dominant feature of the culture industries. Cultural commodities such as television require substantial capital investment, but their popularity and subsequent revenues are unpredictable. Therefore, numerous sales and marketing executives are needed at the organisation's output boundary to ensure that the products receive favourable critical evaluations and that they are sufficiently differentiated from and promoted against competitors' products. In addition, the industries require a steady stream of new products at the input sector, which in turn leads to a large number of industry representatives who seek out new material (Hirsch, 1972).

Global television markets form at the intersection between sellers' output boundaries and buyers' input boundaries. That is, distributors market their finished programmes to international buyers through advertisements placed in the trade press, promotions at sales markets, direct-mailing of videotapes, e-mail, and in-person sales calls. Meanwhile, buyers constantly scan a range of possible imports for those most likely to succeed on their channels, sifting through stacks of advertisements, trade press reviews and pilot videotapes, attending numerous regional and global sales events, and receiving sales representatives, international co-producers and independent distribution agents in their offices.

According to Hirsch (1972), contact people at the output boundary of the culture industries engage in a variety of efforts to ensure commercial success, including 'linking the organisation to (1) retail outlets and (2) surrogate consumers in mass-media organizations' (p. 651). In the book industry, for instance, retail outlets include bookstores, while surrogate consumers are book reviewers whose opinions can make or break a new release. Because of the importance of surrogate consumers, promotional representatives expend a great deal of time and effort trying to sway their opinions. Global television trade shows incorporate both of Hirsch's linking strategies because they operate as the retail outlet where the organisation's contact people and the surrogate consumers meet. That is, although buyers are the primary consumer in international television sales, they ultimately serve a surrogate function because the success of an imported programme lies with viewers. Though independent, buyers' choices are never wholly their own. Instead, they receive their authority because they lay claim to being privileged interpreters of viewers' tastes, much like book reviewers. Consequently, distributors work hard to court buyers, and programming trade shows provide the primary setting for these efforts.

Despite the structural importance of global television markets, executives frequently question their economic importance, especially when it comes to the most immediately obvious characteristic of the markets: their sheer promotional extravagance. Everywhere on the sales floor loom mammoth billboards advertising new series, while lavish sales 'stands' reach to the ceiling. Warner Bros. International plastered a whole wing of the Palais de Festival in Cannes with giant Looney Tunes characters at MIP-TV 1999. MGM had lion cubs on display in a glass cage at NATPE 2001. Commenting on the complexity of preparing the sales floor, one trade show organiser explained, 'It's like building a city' (Smithard, 2002).

As one ventures further onto the sales floor, one glimpses a vast array of perquisites, or 'perks'. Several stands feature free, non-stop food or drink, while other giveaways and celebrity photo sessions lure participants to vendors' stands. At NATPE 2001, executives lined up at the Paramount stand to have their pic-

Illustration 3.1: This advertisement for MTV Networks International gives a sense of the scale of promotional activities at MIP-TV 2004.

tures taken with cheerleaders from the now-defunct XFL (Extreme Football League), a short-lived American football league co-owned by World Wrestling Entertainment and NBC, and played catch in the long hallway outside with palm-sized promotional footballs. When a particularly attractive giveaway or photo opportunity begins, word spreads across the sales floor like wildfire. In addition to the extravagance on the sales floor, several companies sponsor exclusive soirées after the floor closes. When King World International launched its remake of *Hollywood Squares* at NATPE 1998, for example, it hosted a private Elton John concert at the New Orleans Superdome, where it introduced the secret celebrity 'center square', Whoopi Goldberg (Lawrence, 2002).

Such tales of extravagance and their ensuing price tags have led many in the business to question the significance of programming fairs, especially because large distributors who shell out millions of dollars attending them claim to make few important sales there (Brennan, 1999c). Industry executives and trade show organisers have clashed publicly on several occasions over these issues. In 1999, Buena Vista Television International skipped MIP-TV, leading to speculation that other Hollywood distributors might follow suit (Brennan, 1999d). At NATPE 2002, the domestic wings of every major studio forwent sales stands for more subdued business meetings at a nearby Las Vegas hotel, and that practice has now become common (Johansen, 2002). While most executives agree that trade shows provide an important time and place to network with current and potential clients, they cast a wary eye on the extravagances of the programming fairs.

Commentators have generally treated the extravagances associated with sales markets as unnecessary indulgences, similar to corporate jets or bottomless expense accounts that need to be eliminated in the current era of corporate belt-tightening worldwide. However, business management and marketing researchers generally conclude that, although their impact cannot easily be quantified due to the complexity of purchasing decisions and the variety of other sales efforts that buyers encounter, trade shows remain effective sales tools, offering a variety of 'pre-sale' or 'non-selling' opportunities that are crucial to future sales, especially with regard to products that entail complex purchasing decisions (Gopalakrishna *et al.*, 1995; O'Hara, 1993).

Researchers agree on the presence of four main kinds of non-selling activities at trade shows that will interest us here: establishing and renewing relationships with buyers, gathering information about the industry and competitors, creating awareness of new products and crafting corporate images (Gopalakrishna, *et al.*, 1995; Herbig, Palumbo and O'Hara, 1996; O'Hara, 1993; Rice, 1992). In addition, Lisa Penaloza (2001) suggests that trade shows serve important cultural functions such as establishing the identities of participants, instructing them in the business culture and fostering commonsense assumptions about how the industry functions. I will argue that, at least when it comes to global television trade shows, these business and cultural functions are interwoven through the process of ritualisation that occurs at the sales markets.

GLOBAL TELEVISION MARKETS AS RITUALS

The importance of surrogate consumers and the personalised nature of selling in international television require that distributors and buyers have frequent contact. Global programming fairs offer efficient settings for this task because they bring everyone together at a common place and time. Fred Cohen, President of King World International, explains that his company attends MIP-TV because 'all my buyers are here, all my customers' (Brennan, 1999a, p. 6). Kevin Sullivan, President of Canadian Sullivan Entertainment, sounds a similar note about NATPE: 'It's an important place to meet European buyers' (Kelly, 1995, p. 50). In fact, networking among executives is perhaps the most commonly accepted business function of global trade shows. But, the importance of global television markets extends far beyond such rational business functions. Sales markets provide a ritual space that allows participants to think of themselves as members of a coherent global television business community, even as they articulate differences of prestige, scarcity and corporate identity that animate the business processes of global television sales.

In his review of the literature on ritual in critical anthropology, Nick Couldry (2003) insists upon seeing rituals not as practices that smooth social differences, but as processes whereby social inequalities are naturalised through specific ritual acts. In this section, I adopt Couldry's insights in order to examine global television markets as rituals, where the shared definitions, boundaries and values of the global television business culture get expressed through a variety of concrete practices. These concrete practices allow for the smooth functioning of global television sales, even as they elaborate and naturalise divisions among participants. Expressed through the ritual space of the marketplace by a variety of physical boundaries, these divisions distinguish among buyers and sellers, naive newcomers and wise veterans, important and insignificant companies. The physical space of the sales stand provides a key terrain for articulating the corporate identities of distributors, which in turn facilitates the process of product differentiation among competitors and helps buyers and sellers find one another in the crowded marketplace.

Rituals occur within a 'ritual space' that patterns the actions of participants, especially through the establishment and crossing of boundaries. These physical boundaries both exhibit the main categorical distinctions within the culture and naturalise those categories by embedding them in our physical actions and cognitive processes. In addition, the categories associated with the boundaries of the ritual space suggest the underlying values of the culture which, in the case of global television sales, revolve around prestige. Prestige means power in global television sales, including the power to maintain high programme prices and wide distribution, to shape programming trends, and to rise above one's competitors.

Participants at global television markets encounter a variety of boundaries that begin before they even reach the market. International participants must leave their nations of origin and pass through national border checks before arriving at the site of the market, thereby differentiating them from their fellow national citizens. It is important in this respect to recognise that many participants are among the elite in their nations, for whom international travel may not be uncommon, but each specific instance still reinforces the distinction. Even though some participants come from within the borders of the nation, they generally participate in other sales markets that occur abroad.

For almost everyone, passing into the city where the sales market takes place involves entering a site steeped in media ritual, where the division between those 'inside' and 'outside' the media are particularly keenly felt because of the close and frequent contact among media personalities and 'ordinary' people. Los Angeles, where the Screenings are held, is the heart of Hollywood, especially for international visitors, while Cannes, the site of MIP-TV and MIPCOM, has similar connotations due to the yearly film festival, though it also exudes an atmosphere of upper-crust culture because of its miles of designer shops and its location on the French Riviera. Las Vegas, meanwhile, where NATPE takes place every other year, may be a less elite location than Cannes, but it remains a popular site for Hollywood star-gazing. The businesspeople in the entertainment industry are limners who are neither fully inside nor outside the media world. According to Couldry (ibid., p. 12), this distinction between being 'inside' and 'outside' the media is the primary ritual distinction that modern media make. However, crossing into Cannes, Los Angeles, or Las Vegas clearly identifies these people not only as members of an internal jet-set, but also as members of the entertainment industry, a fact reinforced by the presence of television personalities at the markets.

At the doorway to the marketplace, participants cross the most important ritual boundary that the sales markets construct, symbolising their entrance into the culture of global television sales. Only those with proper credentials can cross this threshold, marking the distinction between those who are part of the global television business and those who are not. In Cannes, crowds of curious bystanders milling near the entrances help reinforce this distinction. Some of the clearest examples of promotional excess appear immediately inside the doorway, from billboards promoting new series to costumed characters handing out fliers. The emotional impact of these excesses, especially at the first market I attended, was quite powerful. What I described in my field notes as 'pop culture overload' adds an emotional dimension to the cognitive distinction between those inside and outside the world of global television sales.

Why is it necessary for businesspeople in global television to feel as though they are a part of a larger culture? The answer lies in the importance and unpredictability of international markets for programme buyers and sellers. Buyers need imports to programme their schedules effectively and economically, while sellers need international sales to cover their production investments. However, the uncertain success of television programming, especially when it crosses cultural boundaries, combined with the vast amount of potential programming and potential buyers to sort through, make personal relationships crucial for international sales to operate efficiently. Buyers lack any reliable predictors of the success or failure of their purchases, but no one wants to miss the newest global trends. Consequently, buyers typically rely on a handful of distributors who have reputations for successful international programmes and with whom they have long-term relationships. Thinking of themselves as members of the same culture helps buyers trust that they are getting programming of predictable quality that will likely perform as expected with audiences.

For sellers, on the other hand, a shared culture provides them with a consistent set of buyers for their new programming. More importantly, a shared culture allows all participants to trust that negotiated business arrangements will be honoured, including prompt payment of rights fees and delivery of programming, as buyers and sellers come from different nations with different laws. In addition to the underlying institutional reasons, global television merchants have good career reasons to think of themselves as members of the same community. Executives with experience in international sales move frequently between companies, and a personal reputation in global television is a requirement for such positions.

ARTICULATING DIFFERENCES AT THE GLOBAL TELEVISION MARKETS

The ability to enter the marketplace designates one as a member of the global television business but, once inside, the creation of distinct spaces with varying degrees of accessibility within the marketplace establish significant differences among participants. The most important distinctions, which anthropologists call 'category differences' (ibid., p. 28), distinguish among buyers, sellers and observers. These different categories of participants are formalised through name badges that let the numerous security guards determine who has access rights. For instance, colour-coded badges at NATPE 2001 (see Table 3.2) differentiated between buyers and representatives from various television channels, who made up the highest class of participants; exhibitors and celebrities, who made up a second tier; and representatives of various support businesses, who comprised a third. As a rule, buyers have the greatest freedom of access to restricted spaces. Within these categories, a variety of secondary differences work to establish and naturalise divisions among prestigious and upstart companies, large and small organisations and various kinds of buyers and sellers that help facilitate networking and promotional activities at the sales markets.

Secondary differences among participants get mapped onto the sales floors of the markets. At MIP-TV 2004, the Palais des Festivals was divided into seven primary sales halls, with numerous ways of distinguishing exhibitors within each hall. The largest hall was the main sales floor, which housed nearly 350 sales stands, or about 60 per cent of exhibitors. A wide hallway bisected the main sales floor, leading from the stairway at the entrance of the Palais at one end to a large, sunny café and bar area at the other end. On either side of the hall stretched thirteen rows of stands, some of which lay near the near the main hallway and included internationally successful companies such as the Canadian Broadcasting Company and Carsey-Werner International, and some of which were hidden in barely accessible nooks. Exhibitors of all stripes rented space on the main floor, though the vast majority were small companies with a handful of series, films, or concepts to sell, while many of the buyers were independent

Table 3.2: Badge Colours of Selected Participants at NATPE 2001

Blue	Red	Green
Broadcast Network	Exhibitor	Advertising
Buyer	Exhibitor/Buyer	Distributor/Syndicator
Cable Network	Celebrity	Public Relations

Source: NATPE (2001)

Illustration 3.2: The common practice of selling advertising space on stairways in the Palais des Festivasl is an example of promotional excess.

redistributors. These tend to be the people who are most dependent upon markets like MIP-TV to conduct sales, as it offers one of the only opportunities for buyers to find new distributors, and vice-versa. During the first few days of each market, the main sales floor is thronged with people, and a frenzied din of voices and video clips fills the air. Crowds press for espressos and other drinks at the main bar, while a long wait for the handful of available tables leads participants to camp out on the stairway leading to an emergency exit. At times, the number of bodies and the full sunshine streaming in through the glass ceiling above the bar can make the entire main sales floor uncomfortably warm.

The second-largest sales space was the Espace Riviera, which lay up a flight of stairs from the main bar. Nearly 100 exhibitors set up shop here, including several, such as MTV Networks International, Granada International, Paramount and Radio Television Española, that had large reception areas and a number of meeting rooms. The difference in atmosphere between the Espace Riviera and the main sales room was palpable. Sales stands here ran three or four times larger than the average stand on the main floor, and higher ceilings

Illustration 3.3: The bar area is a popular meeting place for global sales executives. This picture was taken on the final day of MIP-TV 2004, traditionally a quiet day.

Illustration 3.4: This overhead view gives a sense of the size of the sales stands and the atmosphere in the Espace Riviera. Courtesy of Reed-Midem.

allowed for much larger exhibitions. More striking, however, was the distinctly different mood of the space which, while active and crowded, lacked the intensity of the main floor below. In large part, this difference was owed to the fact that stands were spaced further apart, which made for more isolated conversations and a more subdued climate.

Nothing prevented participants who were based on the main floor from entering the Espace Riviera, but exhibitors who set up shop there were making a statement that they were successful enough to afford the higher prices of these larger stands: they either had large financial backing or had been successful enough in international sales to 'move up', and these exhibitors generally expected buyers with larger wallets than those who trolled the main sales floor below. Alexander Charvadze, an international sales representative for TV Channel Russia, which had moved from the main floor to the Espace Riviera beginning with MIP-TV 2004, explained the change as follows: 'Last year, we located on the first floor, and it was not so good, ... because there's not so big companies [sic]. For example, here's Beta Films, who is one of the biggest distributors in Europe, here's Granada. Good neighbours, and so it's good for us' (2004).

While many exhibitors on the main floor employed receptionists who triaged visitors and controlled access to meeting rooms in the back of the stand, in the Espace Riviera, this practice was widespread, and the size and extravagance of the restricted spaces grew. Several companies here, including CBS International, Paramount and MTV Networks International had large patios overlooking the Mediterranean where participants could escape the rush of the market and relax with free drinks and food. Access to these spaces was determined by personal contact with sales executives, usually through appointments set up months in advance, and getting a meeting simply by showing up at the stand was nearly impossible.

In terms of the mood created and the prestige of the exhibitors, Exhibition Halls A, B and C fall somewhere between the main sales floor and the Espace Riviera.

Illustration 3.5: The secluded Paramount International Television patio overlooks the Mediterranean.

Each of these halls is smaller, housing between four and eleven companies, some of whom have good-sized stands with meeting areas that look out over the sea, while others are as humble as the humblest stands on the main floor. Canadian-based Chum City International, a successful distributor of formats, series and feature films has for years had a modest stand in Hall A across from RTV Slovenia, whose stand was little more than a table and chairs. These smaller exhibition halls attracted two classes of exhibitors: good-size distributors who felt that they didn't need a large number of co-exhibitors to attract buyers, and smaller companies who did little international business. The moods in each of these halls was decidedly more subdued than in either the main floor or the Espace Riviera because the small number of stands tended to attract few wanderers.

On the third level, Exhibition Hall G contained some twenty exhibitors, many of whom were among the most prominent names in international television, including Discovery Channels International, Alliance Atlantis and the BBC. Most of the large stands in this area were located in their own antechambers or hallways off the main third-level hallway. Along the main hallway lay a number

Illustration 3.6: The BBC Worldwide sales stand sits apart from other stands in Exhibition Hall G at MIP-TV 2004.

Illustration 3.7: Discovery Communications' sales stand lies in a sunken antechamber in Hall G. MIP-TV 2004.

of smaller distributors in modest stands similar to those on the main floor, such as the Bulgarian National Television stand. Despite the prestige of the larger distributors in this hall, they remained generally accessible, and the volume of traffic through the hall was high, allowing smaller distributors access to a good number of passers-by, although it seems unlikely that most of them would have been in the market for the programming sold by the smaller distributors.

Exhibition Hall H, on the fourth level, housed four sales stands in a large space that provided the most refined and peaceful atmosphere of any of the exhibition halls. The sales stands here were massive, and included Universal Television International, Endemol Entertainment, Fremantle, Southern Star, RTL and Telefe International. Several of these stands were shared by two or more companies, such as Fremantle and RTL or Endemol and Telefe. Except for occasional wanderers who stopped in to gawk at the stands and take pictures, almost everyone who came into this hall had an appointment.

Immediately outside Hall H, on the fourth and fifth levels, are the cheapest sales stands in the Palais, which are associated with the European Union's

Illustration 3.8: The Endemol/Telefe sales stand in Exhibition Hall H offers a large degree of privacy and a relaxed atmosphere. MIP-TV 2004.

Illustration 3.9: The reception area for the collection of independent television producers associated with the MEDIA Programme sits at the top level of the main stairway in the Palais des Festivals. MIP-TV 2004.

MEDIA Programme. The MEDIA Programme is designed to facilitate the production and region-wide circulation of European-produced audiovisual materials. At the top of the escalator to level four sat a clearing-house for members of the MEDIA Programme, consisting of a reception area and two long racks of fliers for the programming handled through MEDIA. Typically, each company has a representative who attends the sales market and meets with interested buyers, though a single representative may work for several independent producers at once. These companies have sales stands along the hallways on the fourth and fifth levels that consist of metal chairs and a TV/VCR hook-up, surrounded by a metal cage. Here, companies such as the British Film Institute and the Norwegian Film Institute set up shop. Again, only buyers interested in specific distributors or those looking for non-commercial and independent programming walk among these stands. In fact, the MIP-TV 2004 'List & Maps of Stands' does not even designate which companies are located in the more than thirty stands used by MEDIA Programme participants (MIP-TV, 2004b). For most of the days of the market, the mood surrounding these stands

Illustration 3.10: The typical sales stand for MEDIA Programme participants includes metal chairs and a TV/VCR hook-up, surrounded by a metal cage. MIP-TV 2004.

can best be described as desolate, although at numerous times each day things do get lively, especially at the bar on the fifth level.

Finally, a handful of sales stands sit apart from others in their own halls or isolated spaces. Generally, these are the largest of the large stands and belong to the powerhouses of the global television business, such as Twentieth Century-Fox Television Distribution and Warner Bros. International Television. For the past several years, Warner Bros. International Television has maintained one of the largest, most visible and least accessible sales stands at MIP-TV and MIPCOM. Located directly above the main entrance, access to the Warner Bros. stand is gained from the second level of the Palais. A mural depicting great moments in the history of film-making at Warner Bros. stretches fifty feet across the length of the stand, below which lie two entrances to the sunshine-filled meeting rooms. A large front desk staffed with several receptionists greets visitors as they come up the escalator to the second level, and two gangplanks guarded by velvet ropes and security guards lead over the main Palais entrance below into the sales hall. The Twentieth Century-Fox Television stand encompasses all of Exhibition Hall E, which lies at the top of an unmarked staircase on the third level. Meeting rooms line the hallway that leads from the reception desk to a secluded outdoor patio, and receptionists and security personnel guard the entrance to the hall.

Restricting access to sales stands adds an allure of desirability to distributors' products, which is critical in an industry where purchasing decisions rest largely on hunches. The challenges of national, regional, racial, ethnic and historical differences associated with international television trade make it tough for buyers to figure out which imported series will work in their markets. For one thing, the success of a series in one market by no means guarantees success in other markets. In addition, methodologically consistent ratings data from around the world has only recently started to become available (Mahoney, 1991), but even ratings data cannot explain the reasons behind a series' performance, and there-

Illustration 3.11: The well-guarded Warner Bros. International Television sales stand restricts entry to authorised visitors only. This picture was taken on the final day of the market, when few people are around. MIP-TV 2004.

fore cannot effectively guide future buying decisions. While some buyers screen imports for focus groups, the relative cheapness of imported programming discourages the practice in most markets. Furthermore, buyers rarely conduct follow-up research to discover whether viewers responded to the same elements in imports as focus group participants did, so again buyers have few objective criteria on which to base their decisions (Duran, 1999; Mulder, 1999).

Lacking objective criteria, buyers usually rely instead on a distributor's track record in international sales, with the expectation that distributors' new series will perform as well as their previous ones. Restricting access to sales stands and sales agents gives visible evidence to the claim that one's programming is widely sought-after. One commentator writes that 'part of what a station is buying is the promise and grandeur and power of a major syndicator or studio' (Bednarski, 2001, p. 21). It should be noted, however, that distributors' reputations probably have little impact on the popularity of programming with viewers abroad, except that large, successful distributors can guarantee larger promotional budgets for imports. For instance, few viewers in the US, much less worldwide, are aware that Warner Bros. distributed *Friends* or that Viacom marketed *The Cosby Show* (1984–92).

The lack of access to sales stands and exhibition halls also creates artificial scarcity in an industry where product is abundant. Again, because of the public good nature of television, programming is quite easily and cheaply traded, which tends to drive down prices. In order to maintain high prices and demand, distributors use temporal scarcity to try to enforce product scarcity. That is, because executives at the large distributors cannot possibly meet with everyone during the few days that the markets are open, the scarcity of time becomes a way to artificially restrict buyers from product.

In addition to the boundaries that distinguish certain sales halls and distributors from one another, sales markets like MIP-TV offer a variety of even more restricted spaces. At MIP-TV 1999, a VIP tent sat on the lawn outside the Palais, where only MIP-TV officials, guests and other VIPs were allowed. The tent had a large, indoor seating area and an outside café with covered and uncovered tables set up on the grass, where one felt that the business of the market was much further away than just a few yards. A number of distributors host swanky, private parties after the sales floor closes on yachts docked behind the Palais. Typically, these high-profile parties mark anniversaries, especially successful programme sales, or other important milestones for the sponsors. About twenty different distributors sponsor yacht parties during each market. In addition, as mentioned above, several mega-distributors host exclusive, invitation-only soirées at local hotspots or remote chateaux in the French Riviera. An invitation to one of these exclusive parties illustrates that one has 'arrived' in international

Illustration 3.12: The Fremantle Media yacht, anchored outside the Palais des Festivals, hosted swanky, after-hours parties at MIP-TV 2004.

syndication, and attendance at the global programming fairs is crucial for gaining access to these select in-groups (Lawrence, 2002).

While the physical space of the Palais des Festivals allows participants to think of themselves as members of a cohesive global television business community, all of whom come together at the same place and time each year, the marketplace also articulates a number of differences among participants through various boundaries, including different exhibition halls, privileged access to sales stands and other areas and inclusion or exclusion from after-hours parties. These boundaries establish which companies and executives have prestige, and which do not. Distributors spend lavishly to demonstrate their success, as they strive to achieve or maintain positions among the elite in global television.

The differences established among participants in the global television sales markets are not merely the secondary effects of a global television economy, but are integral to the business of global television trade. Prestige, which can only be conferred by one's colleagues in the business, is one of the main commodities on display during the markets. Explaining his organisation's reasons for attending MIP-TV, TV Channel Russia's Charvadze (2004) says,

> I think first is respect, and second is money, because [we] have without sales already enough money. But this feeling that people know your channel in Europe … because if they know you, they buy your product, if they know you, they want to co-produce with you, if they know you, they just understand that you are stable and that you are a good partner.

It is important to note that the prestige felt by Charvadze comes from the recognition of his organisation among European executives. In this way, power differences in the world system help determine the level of prestige bestowed by the 'respect' of other organisations. According to Charvadze, TV Channel

Russia is the 'Warner Bros.' of the former USSR nations, or the most important and prestigious programme supplier, but he considers the respect of executives in the more lucrative European markets more important. In this way, worldwide power relations based on economic differences determine cultural power relations that come from the ritual practices of the global television markets. Economic relations, however, offer only the crudest distinctions among participants; within these broad divisions, a number of finer cultural distinctions help construct different corporate identities and manage the flow of 'buzz' about market trends.

CONSTRUCTING CORPORATE IDENTITY THROUGH SALES STANDS

Within the different sales halls of the marketplaces, the boundaries between exhibitors are marked off by sales stands, which serve as the most visible expressions of corporate differentiation and identity, or brands. While the stands follow the same general layout, they tend to take three different paths in constructing brands: genre-based brands, nationally or ethnically based brands and universal brands. In addition, many distributors link their branding efforts to a particular programme they are spotlighting at the market, in an effort to generate buzz among their fellow participants.

Exhibitors follow one of two broad strategies when constructing their sales stand: while almost every stand has a reception desk and meeting areas, one set of exhibitors follow a maximalist strategy that highlights the volume of programming that they sell; the other follows a minimalist strategy that highlights a single series or, simply, the corporate logo. Most exhibitors staff their reception desk and even their sales team with young women, most of whom are white and many of whom are blonde. Here, the gender distinctions within the industry become clear. To some degree, this practice harks back to an earlier time when buyers were mostly men, which is no longer the case. A random sample of acqui-

Illustration 3.13: Distributor em.tv used a 'maximalist' strategy in designing its sales stand for MIP-TV 2004, which emphasised the variety of programmes for sale.

Illustration 3.14: Distributor France Televisions followed a minimalist strategy in its sales stand design for MIP-TV 2004, which emphasised the corporate brand rather than the amount of programming on offer.

sitions executives at MIPCOM 2002, for instance, reveals roughly equal numbers of men and women, a fact that may reflect a glass ceiling that keeps women from rising above the level of programme buyer in their organisations. One distributor I interviewed suggested that the reason so many women are receptionists and sales agents is that the owners of the sales organisations, who are typically men, think women are unlikely to start their own businesses and steal clients. Apparently, some women take advantage of this sexist stereotype to gain experience and contacts before starting their own companies.

For distributors, branding is a cultural tool of significant economic importance that allows them to differentiate themselves from the competition. Branding adds value, or brand equity, to a distributor's products by imbuing them with desirable qualities (Keller, 2000, p. 115). In crowded markets where it is difficult to distinguish between competing products, such as global television sales, 'corporate identity carries a bigger share of the responsibility for sustaining [profit] margins' (Hatch and Schultz, 2000, p. 13). As channel competition and competition among various video distribution systems have become more intense, branding has evolved into a vital component of sellers' and buyers' strategies, especially in a digital world, where brands promise predictable textual experiences across multiple audiovisual platforms, including television, the internet and mobile devices. Digital television channels often provide predictability by concentrating on a small number of genres, and many global television distributors also specialise in these same genres.

Product brands, based on actual or perceived attributes of products, are the most common type of brand (Olins, 2000, p. 58). Programming genres and subgenres form the primary product market in international television, around which many distributors build their corporate identities. Gardening for Real People, Inc. and The Sportsman's Showcase with Ken Tucker, for example, use the subgenres of 'how-to' gardening and outdoor programming, respectively, to distinguish themselves on the sales floor. 4Kids Entertainment, which made its mark distributing the globally popular *Pokemon* series, built its brand and its sales stand around numerous animated characters at MIP-TV 2004. As increased channel capacity worldwide has fragmented television audiences into smaller and smaller niches, served by increasingly focused speciality channels, such niche-distributors have flourished. However, some of the largest corporations in international television also build their brands around programming genre. Carsey-Werner International, King World International and Playboy TV International all have established themselves as global experts in ensemble situation comedies, game-show formats and erotic programming, respectively.

While channel growth has increased the value of niche programming, the most profitable genres sold at the fairs are still those that reach the widest and most lucrative audiences. Large corporations concentrate on programming designed for such audiences, and their efforts to attract buyers from channels that target broad audiences create holes for niche-providers. International television trade, then, does not homogenise cultural differences: instead, it searches out differences and structures them into a coherent hierarchy based upon perceived economic value. These hierarchies are never inflexible, however, because industry changes can alter the popularity of certain programming genres. Carsey-Werner International capitalised on revised attitudes about the international marketability of comedies in the early 1990s (Dupagne, 1992; Tobin, 1990), while Playboy TV International has benefited from worldwide growth in pay-per-view channels, which are often willing to carry adult programming (Davies, 1998).

Perhaps the most effective brand identities in international television come from a combination of proven ability in a programming genre and a clear national image. Slick American action dramas, Latin American *telenovelas*, Australian documentaries, German police dramas and Japanese animation all offer

Illustration 3.15: Distributor 4Kids Entertainment designed its MIP-TV 2004 sales stand around its signature genre, children's anime.

good examples of this strategy. In the minds of many buyers, these nations are synonymous with these genres. However, given the small number of programming genres seen as capable of international export and the vague images that some nations conjure up in buyers' minds, this form of branding is unavailable to many distributors.

Although the business management literature has long recognised that nation of origin can positively influence sales of certain products, O'Shaughnessy and O'Shaughnessy (2000) argue that national identities are generally too multifaceted to provide the clarity that successful brands require. Instead, a nation's reputation in certain product categories is more likely to influence purchasing decisions, as happens when a consumer purchases a Swiss watch over a comparable Mexican one. In these instances, individual producers, such as Bulova, can benefit from the overall prestige of the nation. While the distinction between reputation and national image is important, we also need to recognise that national reputation in specific products must be built and maintained. In international television, part of the strategy that distributors employ to build a reputation involves exhibiting a recognisable national image at market, which draws on associations with the nation that buyers presumably already carry.

Under certain buying conditions, nation of origin becomes more salient. Studies of purchasing behaviour have identified several ways that people make buying decisions, including impulse-buying, habit-buying and deliberate buying. Deliberate buying occurs 'when no single option is superior to others' (ibid, p. 62), and is often accompanied by risk. In such instances, nation of origin has the greatest influence on purchasing decisions because it can help identify one option as superior. As we have seen, because of the high risk of failure of imported programming, programme buyers are quite deliberate in making buying decisions. Thus, nation of origin is likely to be an important consideration in international television syndication.

Many exhibitors try to leverage national identity to increase brand equity. NATPE 2001 featured sales pavilions dedicated to programming from Belgium, the UK, Canada, Germany, the Netherlands, Quebec, Ireland, Korea, the Nordic countries, Spain, Italy, France and Switzerland. The French pavilion, for example, drew on two recognisable French images: a French-style café, large enough to give it the ambience of an open-air café in the otherwise cramped exhibition hall, surrounded by brightly coloured facades of quaint, seventeenth-century French buildings, which housed the sales rooms of the pavilion's forty-two corporate sponsors.

Individual sales stands also make frequent use of nationally distinctive colours, architecture and decoration. At MIP-TV 2004, Indian commercial

Illustration 3.16: The sales stand of the Egyptian Radio and Television Union (ERTU), Egypt's public broadcaster, featured nationally distinctive accoutrements at MIP-TV 2004.

broadcaster Zee TV adorned its sales stand with puppets, swag lamps, brightly coloured fabrics and a traditional Indian puppeteer to advertise its new branded line of 'alternative lifestyle' programmes dubbed 'Asian Mantra'.

If properly managed, a strong national image acts as a family brand for a variety of genres and distributors, increasing the levels of the brand hierarchy and creating flexibility. Recognisable family brands 'allow access to global associations that consumers may have toward the company [or nation]', while sub-brands associated with particular genres 'can help customers better understand how products vary' (Keller, 2000, p. 126–7). Hence, the French pavilion draws on the image of France as a cultured nation at the level of the family brand, while French animation companies distinguish themselves from Japanese companies by selling slower-paced series that highlight historical, educational and fantastic themes. Meanwhile, Zee TV's 'Asian Mantra' programmes featured documentaries, lifestyle and talk shows focused on spirituality, sexuality, tribal wisdom and other topics typically associated with India. Just as a national brand cannot succeed without a distinct product

Illustration 3.17: A traditional Indian puppeteer adds a touch of Indian culture to the Zee Networks sales stand at MIP-TV 2004.

category, individual genres receive added differentiation and desirability through the creation of a strong national brand.

The attempt to create a slice of France or India at sales markets runs counter to the conventional wisdom that international sales require producers around the world to copy Hollywood's aesthetics. If these distributors hoped to emphasise the similarity between their programming and American-style programming, they would have made quite different exhibition decisions. Instead, they are trying to build brand equity through cultural distinctiveness. Of course, the degree to which a few tables and some cardboard cut-outs express the full complexity of French culture is debatable. Still, as McCrone, Morris and Kiely (1995) argue regarding efforts to construct a brand identity for the Scottish heritage industry, the commodification of national culture may be limiting, distorting and stereotyping, but it is never politically vacant or univocal. Commodified cultural expressions can serve radical as well as conservative political ends.

Producers from nations that have been trading programming internationally for a long time and those with strong national or ethnic associations are well positioned to use branding in this manner. Distributors without readily identifiable national or ethnic images or those that do not have expertise in a particular programming genre find branding more difficult. South Korea's MBC Productions, for example, brought 96 programmes to NATPE 2001, but little in the programming, promotional materials or exhibition design identified the series or the producer with Korea. In short, it had a weak brand identity, in part because MBC did not create a clear Korean image. Because nations with long histories in television production dominate the most lucrative programming genres, it is difficult for new entrants to discover a profitable niche. Nevertheless, new opportunities regularly emerge. Recently, for example, we witnessed the remarkable success of reality formats like *Survivor* and *Big Brother* from Western Europe, which has now become synonymous with the genre. Zee TV's efforts to corner the market on the 'alternative lifestyle' subgenre with Orientalist images of Indian culture reflects a similar strategy.

As distributors become more and more successful, many of them chafe against the confines of their national identities and seek independent corporate identities. In spite of the usefulness of national identity for branding, most of the buyers I spoke with felt that cultural differences between their audiences and imported programmes cause difficulty (Hoskins and Mirus, 1988). While national identity may help a distributor build a brand presence, those who can avoid nationalist associations may benefit from appearing more universal. Warner Bros. International, for instance, crafted its presence at MIPCOM 2002 and MIP-TV 2004 self-referentially around a series of animated scenes from

Illustration 3.18: Warner Bros. International Television built its brand identity at its MIP-TV 2004 sales stand self-referentially, around animated recreations of film-making history at the studio.

Warner Bros. movie history, imbuing the company with attributes of classic cinema and longevity of international appeal.

THE CULTURAL ECONOMY OF 'BUZZ'

Along with branding, the management of 'buzz' is one of the most important business functions performed by the rituals of the global sales markets. The multiple distinctions among participants that emerge from the establishment and crossing of boundaries facilitate the four business functions of international trade shows, as outlined above: establishing and renewing relationships, gathering information about the industry and competitors, creating awareness of new products and crafting corporate images. A key component to each of these functions is the management of buzz at the marketplace, which helps explain their signature promotional excesses. To be effective, buzz must circulate among those participants who are most likely to respond, and the creation of various networks of participants through the markets' ritual processes facilitates this circulation.

We have already seen how ritual boundaries sort participants into various categories. This process governs the establishment and renewal of networks among participants with similar interests and reputations. In other words, the rituals of the marketplace encourage participants to think of themselves both as *different* from some and *similar* to others. Effective networking is complicated by the volume and diversity of attendants with varying budgets and business priorities. From the distributor's perspective, price differentials among the world's buyers are extreme, ranging in 2004 from as much as $2 million per hour of programming in the US networks to as low as $30 per hour in Cuba (see Table 1.2). From the perspective of those who purchase programming, certain genres and national brands 'travel' better across cultural boundaries. Michael Puopolo, Manager of International Research for Warner Bros. International Television, expresses a common refrain when he says that 'better than any other culture, American culture transfers well to the rest of the world' (1999). In addition, different buyers are seeking different kinds of programming, while some distributors specialise in certain genres and not others.

The arrangement of sales spaces and differential access at the global sales markets create numerous in- and out-groups that facilitate networking by allowing some interactions while discouraging others. Girts Licis (1999), head of acquisitions and sales for Latvian Television, who was attending one of his first global markets at MIP-TV 1999, reported that sales agents from large US and European distributors would not meet with him. The difficulties that newcomers have doing business at the marketplaces are not limited to small buyers dealing with Hollywood distributors. Neophyte producers looking to sell their product who lack a network of business contacts also have difficulty getting meetings with potential buyers, who are busy meeting with sellers with whom they already have long-term relationships (Brown, 2001).

One of the most effective ways to break through such barriers is to create buzz around one's products or companies. Quite simply, buzz refers to business-related word of mouth that circulates year-round, but becomes more intense and concentrated in the 'incestuous environment' of global television markets (Smithard, 2002). Although buzz is a vital aspect of global television sales, it has received almost no attention from media scholars. Industrial economists, however, have written about the role of buzz in global industries generally. Bathelt, Malmberg and Maskell's (2004) definition is worth quoting at length here:

> Buzz refers to the information and communication ecology created by face-to-face contacts, co-location, and co-presence of people and firms within the same industry and place or region. This buzz consists of specific information and continuous updates of this information, intended and unanticipated learning processes in organized and accidental meetings, the application of the same interpretive schemas and mutual understanding of new knowledge and technologies, as well as shared cultural traditions and habits within a particular technology field, which stimulate the establishment of conventions and other institutional arrangements. Actors continually contribute to and benefit from the diffusion of information, gossip, and news by just 'being there.' (p. 38)

In other words, buzz is a cultural phenomenon, in the sense of a symbolic activity engaged in by a specific society, which has unique business consequences. In this way, buzz is a 'cultural economic' activity that demonstrates the interdependence of cultural and economic practices within the global television sales business (see Du Gay and Pryke, 2002).

Trade journals provide much of the grist for sales-floor buzz at the global markets. Fair organisers publish their own daily recaps of news, and dozens of trade journals run special daily issues available only on the sales floor, including *Variety*, *Hollywood Reporter*, *Television International* and *Television Business International*. Participants tear through stacks of these free journals for the latest information, making the trade journal stands one of the liveliest areas of the market, typically containing dozens of special publications. Debbie Lawrence, Managing Director of Lippin Group's London Office, which handles public relations at the television fairs for several large American and European distributors, explains the importance of trade journal coverage at the fairs plainly: 'To be one of the main distributors of drama and not to be in the daily drama feature [of the organiser's publication] is seen as a disaster' (2002). Thus, part of the purpose of trade journals from the distributors' perspective is to ensure that they and their firm become part of the sales-floor buzz.

The buzz that emanates from the trade journals is an effort to discover the 'next big thing' in global television trends, a phrase commonly found in trade journal articles about the sales markets. A great deal of effort goes into this endeavour, bearing witness to the fact that programming from abroad influences domestic television cultures in nations around the world. Jörg Langer, managing director of T&G Films in Berlin, explains,

> I see MIP as a unique instrument for getting an overview of the market situation. What are the trends? What is being internationally produced? More series, singles, docudrama, docusoap? In Germany we have all the trends in the following year, so I get an idea of what we can do. On the other hand, I get an impression of what our competitors are doing.' (Brown, 2001, p. 44)

In addition, participants share more quotidian business information. Kaisa Kriek, the programme sales manager for Netherlands Public Broadcasting, for example, told me that she shares pricing information with fellow public broadcasting representatives and European distributors whom she knows well (2004). Also, several distributors confirmed that they maintain a collective 'blacklist' of untrustworthy buyers. Both of these activities require significant trust among participants, which the close-knit networks created by the sales markets' differentiation strategies help make possible.

The search for the newest trends extends to individual programmes, which distributors try to promote through buzz. In fact, most of the promotional excesses discussed above flow from the effort to create buzz about new programming. Buzz surrounds celebrity appearances and giveaways on the sales floor, large release parties at the sales stands, and star-studded, invitation-only

Illustration 3.19: Levymann
Entertainment constructed its
sales stand around its newest
programme offering, *Itty Bitty
Heart Beats*.

galas. All of these promotional efforts share a similar goal of generating excitement and interest around new series, a goal perhaps best served by global
television trade shows. Again, Lippin's Lawrence explains, 'Television markets
are certainly a time to be focused on new shows and therefore [to] create buzz
for all new programming' (2002). Similarly, Bruce Johansen, former President
and CEO of NATPE says, 'Obviously, I am biased, but I think it would be very
difficult to orchestrate buzz without the focus of a trade meeting. … Trade
shows themselves create buzz that radiates onto the product' (2002). Promotional efforts at the sales fairs also reflect Hirsch's (1972) insight that the
culture industries must differentially promote new product, lavishing some with
extensive attention while letting others flounder. Because of their unpredictable
performance, organisations overproduce new products in the hopes that a small
percentage will catch on, and then heavily promote only those that they consider
the most likely to succeed.

The role that buzz plays in creating favourable impressions of programming
and distributors, and the presumed influences that such impressions have on
eventual buying decisions, goes a long way towards explaining the obvious
extravagances of the global programming fairs. Because buyers function as surrogate consumers in international television, distributors can focus their
promotional efforts on courting their favour, rather than trying to create programmes that appeal to viewers around the world with unknown and
unpredictable tastes. This practice rationalises the process of global television
sales and makes manageable the otherwise insurmountable task of trying to
understand the cultural affinities and differences between specific national and
subnational groups and specific television series or films.

A textbook example of a distributor's effort to create buzz through promotional excess occurred at NATPE 2001 with Universal Studios' feature film,
How the Grinch Stole Christmas (2000), a remake of the animated Dr Seuss

classic, starring Jim Carrey. Universal Television built a twenty-foot tall replica of Mount Crumpit, the mythic home of the Grinch, to house its sales staff. On the first evening of the market, Universal hosted a cocktail party featuring bright green cocktails in glasses bearing Grinch stickers and music from the film's soundtrack played over loudspeakers. The main attraction was the Grinch's pet dog, Max, supposedly the same dog that had appeared in the film. Max entertained guests with a variety of tricks and sat for pictures with a long line of guests, all the while wearing a pair of antlers that the Grinch had tied to his head in the film in order to make him look like a reindeer. As with all such photo opportunities at the markets, buyers formed a separate line that received priority over other guests, again reinforcing the main category distinction between buyers and others at the markets.

The cocktail party for *How the Grinch Stole Christmas* was announced in the trade press and the *NATPE Daily News*, and accompanied by full-page advertisements in several trade journals. Anyone who missed these announcements, however, could not help but notice the loud music blaring across the sales floor. Attracted by the music, I made my way through the other sales booth to the Universal stand, where I saw about 100 guests wandering through the sales stand, crowding the stairs to get free drinks at the bar on the second level and milling about in the aisles in front of the stand. Unlike many such parties, this was an open event, and everyone on the sales floor could attend, get free cocktails and food, and have their pictures taken with Max the dog.

Ironically, Universal's Grinch-inspired cocktail party was not primarily designed to promote the film. By the time of NATPE 2001, Disney/ABC had sewn up all domestic cable and broadcast rights to the film until 2014, with the first airing not scheduled until 2004. Thus, domestic executives, who made up more than three-quarters of attendees at NATPE 2001, could not have bought rights to the film even if they had wanted to. Instead, the decision to spotlight *How the Grinch Stole Christmas*, instead of a television series that was available to all buyers, seems to have been designed primarily to call attention to Universal's overall programming catalogue, and secondarily to promote the film to international buyers. Universal's strongest new syndicated series in 2001 was the dating game show *The Fifth Wheel* (2001–4), but at the time of NATPE, the series had sold only marginally well, and was nothing to build a promotional campaign around. Likewise, the studio's best performing new network series, *The District* (2000–4), had garnered only mild interest among international buyers. *How the Grinch Stole Christmas*, on the other hand, was one of the top-grossing films of 2000, and had been released worldwide only one month earlier. Thus, in the absence of a break-out television series to support its promotional buzz, Universal chose instead to capitalise on the buzz that already surrounded *How the Grinch Stole Christmas*, in the hopes that it might net some international sales and also spill over to the rest of its programming.

CONCLUSION

Understanding the global television markets as rituals, where the divisions of the global television business are constructed and naturalised, helps us appreciate the role that the business culture plays in facilitating international trade. The complexity of buying decisions, the importance of global sales revenues and the magnified uncertainties surrounding the local appeal of globally traded television programming all frustrate effective global television sales. In order to function effectively and efficiently, the global television marketplace requires close relationships among buyers and sellers, clearly defined corporate identities and up-to-date information about new programming trends, all of which get communicated through the ritual practices of the global television markets.

Differentiation is a cultural practice enacted through ritual that serves specific business functions in global television trade. Global sales markets are the primary sites where these differentiations occur, because all distributors and buyers compete with one another in global commercial television trade. In addition, the most precious commodity – prestige – can only be conferred through cultural practices such as those we witness at sales markets. These practices also create artificial scarcity, which keeps both demand and prices high for large distributors. In other words, to function effectively, the process of global television sales requires the cultural practices outlined in this chapter. Hence, the shared assumptions, blind spots and power relations inherent in the business culture of global television shape the business practices of television industries everywhere, profoundly influencing which programmes and genres travel worldwide.

Few television merchants, however, operate exclusively in the global marketplace. Most distributors continue to be heavily dependent upon domestic markets for much, if not most, of their revenues. Likewise, buyers compete primarily in their domestic markets, as they wrangle with others for the most promising imports, formats and co-production opportunities. In the remainder of this volume, we will explore the programme purchasing and scheduling practices of national, subnational and transnational television channels.

4

Buying International Programming

The business of global television remains mostly a multinational endeavour, where distributors whose primary income originates in domestic markets sell programming to television channels abroad that target national or subnational audiences. As Owen and Wildman (1992) note, the price differentiation that characterises the global trade in television programmes is predicated on the ability of sellers to separate buyers and distinguish between those who are able to pay higher and lower prices. Otherwise, they note, 'all customers will represent themselves as buyers with a low willingness-to-pay' (p. 29). In global television, the nation-state serves both of these functions. First, because most terrestrial and cable channels continue to be organised along national lines due to historical circumstances and regulatory differences, the nation-state provides an effective mechanism for separating buyers from one another. Second, varying GDPs among nations allow sellers to determine differences among buyers' abilities to pay.

Practically speaking, the division of programme rights by nation means that the main competitors that buyers face when trying to purchase programme rights come from other buyers in their domestic market. Whether a buyer works for a speciality cable channel or a general entertainment terrestrial broadcaster, in most markets around the world, someone else will be interested in the same programme rights. In this chapter, we examine programme import decisions in depth, in particular the balance between national competitive and cultural conditions and the pressures and power differences of the global programme markets. The main purpose of the chapter is to explore the degree to which television buyers exercise independent decision-making when it comes to foreign acquisitions. Ultimately, I will argue that several forces, including channel identity, the market for viewers, the global programme markets and an outlet's ownership profile and funding sources determine the degree of independence in such decisions. In order to facilitate the analysis, much of the chapter provides extended case studies of acquisitions decisions among several kinds of buyers from a single national market.

STUDYING PROGRAMME IMPORT DECISIONS

The processes whereby buyers select programming from the global marketplace have received almost no scholarly attention. This lack is probably due to the fact that most scholars tend to view such choices as the manifestations of larger economic and business processes, rather than imaginative acts that require human agents to reconcile their perceptions of audience preferences with their understanding of the pleasures available in imported texts, all within the limits that acquisitions budgets allow. Buyers are far more than rational economic actors; they are cultural interpreters of popular domestic and global trends.

Despite the general scholarly neglect of foreign programme acquisition, three important insights about the process have been documented. The first and most obvious insight is that buyers everywhere seem to look first to linguistically and culturally similar programmes. Buyers across Latin America, North America, Europe, the Middle East, Asia and Africa exhibit this tendency, selecting programming originally shot in the same language or programming from cultures with similar religious or historical backgrounds (Sinclair, Jacka and Cunningham 1996; Steemers, 2004). This observation, however, can depend upon current political relations between the importing and exporting nations. Nations in the Caribbean, the Middle East, Greater India and Greater China, for instance, have at times restricted imports from culturally proximate nations because of concerns about their potential political impact in the importing nations (Amin, 1996, p. 102; Miller, 1992, p. 176; Ray and Jacka, 1996, p. 95; Chan, 1996, p. 146). The second insight about acquisitions decision-making is that a buyer's budget determines the degree of effort put into finding culturally proximate material. Thus, small buyers and those purchasing programming for less lucrative time-slots frequently make decisions almost exclusively on price (Steemers, 2004, p. 29).

Finally, local institutional, cultural and political forces shape buyers' choices. For instance, the decision to import the Australian soap opera *Neighbours* (1985–) at the BBC in the late 1980s stemmed from increased competition from commercial broadcasters and an effort to develop a more populist identity for the BBC, as well as a political and cultural shift to the right (Cunningham and Jacka, 1996, pp. 122–6). Meanwhile, the decision by the Dutch public broadcaster VARA to import *Flying Doctors* (1986–91) from Australia in the late 1980s resulted from the taste preferences of its acquisitions executives, who preferred BBC-style programming, as well as the communal aspects of the series, which fitted well with the broadcaster's remit as a socialist channel (ibid., 160–4).

While few in number, these examples demonstrate that decision-making about acquisitions is an active, embedded process, in the sense that such decisions derive from what Cunningham and Jacka term the 'television ecology' of a nation – a complex combination of historical, cultural, social, economic and technological conditions (ibid., 16–17). Any thorough understanding of acquisitions must account for the interaction of these various forces in specific instances. Several recent studies have demonstrated how domestic ecologies shape the process of programme distribution in specific countries (ibid.; Steemers, 2004; Tinic, 2005), but such research has tended to pay less thorough attention to the domestic complexities surrounding acquisitions decisions.

What is more, most of the research addressing acquisitions has looked at large terrestrial broadcasters in nations with little or no foreign investment in their broadcasting industries (Sinclair, Jacka and Cunningham, 1996; Steemers, 2004). As global media conglomerates have sought to acquire television channels worldwide, serious questions about the independence of domestic acquisitions decisions and their cultural relevance have arisen (see Herman and McChesney, 1997). Despite such concerns, incidents of conglomerates using outlets abroad simply to dump programming or spread their costs over a wider range are rare and usually limited to niche channels in small markets with few competitors. More commonly, each television outlet in a large conglomerate is primarily concerned with maximising audience ratings and advertising revenues in its specific market, and decisions about how best to achieve that goal are largely left to local programming and acquisitions executives.

At television channels around the world, acquisitions decisions begin with an examination of the current schedule, with an eye towards underperforming series that need replacement. Even at non-profit broadcasters, where considerations of culture and politics may trump sheer viewing numbers, procedures exist to decide which shows to cancel, renew, create and purchase from domestic or international sources. Typically, these decisions coincide with the main global and regional markets that acquisitions executives attend, especially MIPCOM in the autumn and MIP-TV in the spring, representing another example of how global television markets, specifically the television seasons of large European and North American nations, influence programming practices in other parts of the world. Most large channels employ separate programming and acquisitions departments, with the programming department responsible for identifying amounts and types of imports – and occasionally particular programmes – while acquisitions executives make specific import decisions and negotiate prices within the parameters set by the programming department. At smaller channels, programming and acquisitions are often handled in the same department. Finally, some companies that own channels in multiple territories retain centralised programming and acquisitions departments for all of their channels.

Despite the fact that most acquisitions executives make their own decisions about which programmes to purchase, they are nevertheless influenced by the global programming markets in a variety of ways. They share acquisition ideas with fellow buyers abroad, particularly those in the same region or global conglomerate. They rely on a handful of international distributors, with whom they have long-term relationships, for most of their new imports. They constantly scan the markets for the hottest new distributors and shows whose reputations, as we saw in the previous chapter, get built at the global sales markets. And, like all members of the global television business, they tend to be seduced by the grandeur of the largest distributors and programmes with the highest production values. In this sense, much like the scheduling decisions explored in the following chapter, acquisitions decisions are often hybrids of domestic and foreign cultural perceptions about what kinds of programming might interest domestic viewers.

For all of the reasons discussed thus far, it makes sense to analyse closely acquisitions decision-making in a single national market. While such a decision inevitably diminishes the general application of my findings, I believe that the benefits of such a method outweigh the drawbacks. Acquisitions and scheduling decisions have generally been treated as transparent, if not mechanical, when, in fact, they are deeply embedded cultural-economic practices, and specific domestic conditions are most often the key to understanding them. Indeed, I believe that studies of global television trade in general are in a position not unlike audience reception studies in the early 1990s, when a number of scholars began to privilege the particular over the general in order to infuse what had been an administrative, positivist enterprise with a cultural studies sensibility that emphasises human agency, contingency and complexity (Ang, 1991; Morley, 1992). My research here is designed to contribute to such a project.

Although I supplement my analyses here with examples from other territories, I have chosen primarily to examine the Hungarian market, for a variety of reasons. Hungary offers a unique opportunity to explore buying and scheduling practices due to its linguistic isolation and rapidly commercialising television landscape. Often described by Hungarians as 'an island in a seas of Slavs', Hungary shares a language with no other nation, and therefore does not have a natural trading partner when it comes to television programming, which often circulates within 'geolinguistic' regions (Sinclair, Jacka and Cunningham, 1996, p. 8). Instead, Hungarian buyers must rely on other cultural markers when making acquisitions decisions, causing their decision-making processes to be more complex, deliberate and available for analysis.

Since the collapse of state socialism in 1989, and particularly since the introduction of commercial terrestrial television in 1997, the Hungarian market has rapidly commercialised, and now boasts three national terrestrial broadcasters, a dozen or more cable and satellite channels and a number of local and regional channels in a nation of 10 million inhabitants. In 1998, Hungarians watched more television than any other nation in Europe (EurodataTV, 1999). Hence, Hungary has numerous buyers and channels, providing a rich variety of purchasing and scheduling practices to examine.

Hungary also sits on the border between the West and the East, having been part of the Ottoman Empire, the Habsburg Empire and the Soviet Empire, so there are good historical reasons to expect that its cultural imports might be similarly mixed. The fact that they are instead dominated by programming of Western origins suggests the degree to which the kinds of economic and prestige differences we have studied thus far shape acquisitions practices.

Finally, the scant research on acquisitions and scheduling to date has been conducted in affluent markets such as the US, Western Europe and Australia. The practices of smaller markets such as Hungary that depend heavily on imported programming and foreign investment depart markedly from those of the larger markets. In fact, the Hungarian experience is perhaps more common worldwide than the relatively independent acquisitions and scheduling practices of larger and richer nations.

PROGRAMME IMPORTS AT HUNGARIAN COMMERCIAL BROADCASTERS

Commercial, nationwide, terrestrial broadcasters have the greatest need for imported programming because they repeat programming less frequently than cable channels and, unlike their non-profit counterparts, often have lower local-content requirements and can run more minutes of advertising per hour, thereby increasing their advertising revenues and acquisitions budgets. Hungary supports two commercial terrestrials, RTL Klub and TV2, both of which attract about 40 per cent of the national audience on any given day. The public broadcaster, Magyar Televízió (MTV), by comparison, averages about 15 per cent of viewers (AGB Hungary, 2002).

Both TV2 and RTL Klub are majority-owned by Western European media conglomerates, with Hungarian partners maintaining roughly 25 per cent of voting rights. Luxembourgeois media powerhouse CLT-UFA, itself a subsidiary of Bertelsmann, AG, is the majority owner of RTL Klub, while Scandinavian SBS Broadcasting controls 49 per cent of the voting stock of TV2. Both CLT-UFA and SBS Broadcasting own a number of television channels throughout Western and Eastern Europe. In addition, Disney has part ownership in TV2 through German television producer Tele-München Fernseh, while UK production firm Pearson owns more than 20 per cent of RTL Klub. Local owners include the production house MTM Communications, which controls 28 per cent of TV2's voting stock, and the state monopoly telephone company MATÁV (Gálik, 2004).

The presence of two commercial broadcasters with roughly equivalent ratings profiles in a single national market has a marked impact on acquisitions and programming strategies. In fact, this competitive structure is perhaps the single most important factor determining acquisitions strategies. Even the largest distributors must deal on the buyer's terms in markets where a single terrestrial channel dominates, while competition among two rivals makes the market more of a seller's market since it encourages competitive bidding. Of course, in some especially poor or especially small markets, large distributors such as the Hollywood majors refuse to sell their programming in hopes of encouraging region-wide buying cartels (Licis, 1999), but in most cases even terrestrial channels from poorer nations can drive a hard bargain if they are the only viable buyer. For instance, at a regional trade fair, I overheard a conversation between a buyer from the dominant Macedonian channel, A1, and the European sales manager for MGM in which the latter promised to work with the former to provide as much or as little programming as he needed, including the newest titles. Meanwhile, in markets where the audience is split among three or more rivals, sellers can play one buyer off against another in order to get the highest prices for their programming, and bidding wars for especially sought-after programming often break out.

Having two strong terrestrial channels, as in Hungary, keeps prices generally high, though not unreasonably so most of the time, while encouraging very similar channel profiles and acquisitions strategies at both channels, so long as one channel doesn't outperform the other significantly for a long period of time. Huw Wheldon, the managing director of BBC television when commercial rival ITV was introduced in 1955, may have been one of the first programmers to recognise this trend towards programming standardisation in a two-market channel. 'The brute fact is that pure competition ... forces the companies into a deeply like-against-like situation,' he explained (Wheldon, 1971, p. 8). Although Wheldon only partly realised it at the time, while his observation was correct, it primarily addressed the situation in a two-channel market.

In the Hungarian market, RTL Klub and TV2 compete with one another not only for audiences, but also for particularly sought-after programming, most often new Hollywood releases and top-performing US series. These are the kinds of imports that consistently find their way onto primetime schedules at general entertainment broadcasters across Europe, Latin America and some territories in the Asia-Pacific region, because they are the only ones that seem to attract a broad, undifferentiated audience regardless of the country where they air. A survey of films broadcast on television worldwide, for instance, found that television channels strive to 'broadcast popular and family-oriented films that have been international box office hits and have had a good run in local movie theaters' (*Screen International*, 2000a). Such films tend to be from Hollywood, and even domestically produced films have difficulty getting on the air at broadcasters across Europe (*Screen International*, 2000b).

Both RTL Klub and TV2 field two-person acquisitions teams who split up purchasing duties geographically, with one focusing on European (or European and Australian) distributors and another focusing on the US and 'the rest of the world', although few, if any, acquisitions come from the rest of the world. This breakdown differs from some broadcasters in other territories, which divide acquisitions by genre. However, since certain regions and nations often specialise in specific genres, as we saw in the previous chapter, both ways of dividing acquisitions are roughly similar. The acquisitions team is responsible for viewing pilot tapes that distributors send, maintaining contact with distributors throughout the year and keeping tabs on new global programming developments through trade journals. At TV2, the acquisitions team is supported by an extensive research department that not only assesses imported programming in the Hungarian market, but also looks at the performance of acquired programmes in Poland, the Czech Republic and Germany. In addition, relationships with other buyers in the region as well as other channels in the larger channel group all serve as potential sources of information about programme offerings and performances for acquisitions executives.

Unlike the typical characterisation of acquisitions in most scholarly literature, then, these buyers are not forced to buy programming from the major studios, even when the studios have partial ownership in the channel. Neither do the conglomerate owners bulk-buy programming from the major studios to take advantage of volume discounts and distribute it to their affiliated channels, though this practice does occur at some small cable channels, as explored below. As one of the acquisitions executives at TV2 explained, commenting on the different channels in SBS's channel portfolio, 'what is a need for a Polish cable channel ... or for a Romanian cable channel or for a Danish smaller television [sic], is not what a larger channel in Hungary needs' (Szőllőssy, 2002). In other words, for commercial broadcasters, advertising revenues in the domestic market, based upon ratings with the domestic audience, are the main drivers of acquisitions decisions. Nevertheless, because of their involvement with the business culture of global television sales, buyers' perceptions of what kinds of imports will work in their markets are not wholly dissimilar from those of buyers in other territories, especially when it comes to high-ticket primetime imports. For instance, the hit US series *Desperate Housewives* (2004–) has been sold into more than 100 territories, including primetime sales in the UK, Germany, Italy, France, Australia and Hong Kong (Brennan, 2005). These similar perceptions explain why it is possible for conglomerates to operate independent channels in multiple nations and still take advantage of bulk pricing deals with large distributors.

Acquisitions decisions at both RTL Klub and TV2 are made in close consultation with scheduling executives. The process begins with an evaluation of current programming rights that are already 'on the shelf'. Based on these evaluations, holes in the schedule are identified and plans for acquisitions to fill those holes are drawn up, usually with a rough idea of which programming genres will fill which holes. Furthermore, both channels programme new Hollywood releases several times per week during prime time, so acquisitions executives are always on the lookout for the newest hit films, as well as especially popular US drama series and the occasional, exceptional sitcom. Once these general decisions have been made, acquisitions executives go about viewing screeners, reading promotional fliers, reviewing plot summaries on the internet and contacting distributors about their new programming.

Executives at both channels reported that they maintain close relationships with about twenty European producer-distributors as well as the major Hollywood studios on a regular basis, from whom they most typically acquire series. These distributors, including UK-based Carlton International, German-based ZDF Enterprises, Dutch-based Endemol Productions and French-based Télé Images, enjoy a privileged place among buyers at RTL Klub and TV2, who pay close attention to new programming from these distributors and reserve most of their time at the markets for meetings with them. Additionally, RTL Klub and TV2 buy programming from new distributors whom they more often meet at film festivals such as MIFED, mostly one-time films or specials. Not surprisingly, the acquisitions executives at both RTL Klub and TV2 work with the same general group of distributors, both in the US and Europe, and competition for the best, new programming from these distributors is the impetus behind acquisitions executives' efforts to maintain continuing contact with these programme providers (Balázs, 2002; Szőllőssy, 2002; Zaras, 2001). The practice of relying primarily on a set group of distributors year in and year out is common among all buyers, who typically fill up their meeting schedules for the markets months in advance with well-known sellers and the occasional new distributor. One buyer, identified only as a 'veteran MIP-goer' explains, 'it's essential to have a fully filled-out dance card before you even land in Cannes' (Guider, 2004, p. 6).

Maintaining a close relationship with distributors gives a channel privileged access to the most promising new series and films, although the impetus among Hungarian buyers for building relationships is different with the major Hollywood studios than with European distributors. With European distributors, the goal is to be the first to put in a bid for new series or features, because distributors make decisions quickly. With Hollywood distributors, on the other hand, Hungarian buyers strive to maintain contacts because the comparatively low prices in Hungary mean that sales executives don't want to spend a lot of time negotiating among buyers. Unless the buyer maintains consistent contact, sellers are apt to 'forget' about certain buyers because they are not large clients. Thus, size and purchasing power of the domestic market have a determining influence on the relationships between buyers and distributors, as does the size of the distributor.

In terms of genre preferences, buyers from both of the main commercial channels primarily look for series from Europe and feature films from the US, although the buyers at TV2 professed a greater affinity for US series than their counterparts at RTL Klub. Feature films are primarily acquired from the Hollywood majors, and include the newest theatrical releases once those films have been shown in theatres. In their efforts to acquire new releases, Hungarian broadcasters wind up with packages that include a number of series and specials that they otherwise would not acquire. In previous years, especially when the Hungarian channels had output deals with the studios, they picked up many unwanted series, but acquisitions officials at both broadcasters claimed that, after years of developing relationships with the sales teams at the studios, they were now able to exclude most unwanted series from film packages. Nevertheless, buyers have two options when bidding against their competitors for Hollywood blockbusters: increasing the prices they are willing to pay, or increasing the amount of programming in the package. Since the Hungarian channels are often unable to increase their prices substantially, they rely more often on larger packages as a strategy.

In addition to Hollywood films, both channels acquire a large number of European films, particularly from the UK, Germany and France. In part, the use of European films results from Hungarian and EU regulations, which stipulate that 51 per cent of the programming on a terrestrial broadcaster must consist of European productions, including Hungarian productions (ORTT, 1996). However, no one I spoke with considered that target a burden; rather, the use of European films was seen as inevitable, given that Hungary is a European nation. Series, particularly primetime series, come mostly from German and Hollywood sources. French, Australian and Canadian series, particularly those that target a teenage and young adult audience, are also purchased on occasion. Finally, in the late 1990s and early 2000s, both channels purchased a number of *telenovelas* from Latin American distributors, particularly those located in Mexico, Brazil and Venezuela. More recently, however, those purchases have dried up due to perceived changes in audience preferences and the abundance of *telenovela* rights already on the shelves.

The acquisitions practices of the commercial Hungarian broadcasters reveal a reliance on imported programming to fill genres that are too expensive to self-produce, or that appeal to non-prime time niche audiences. In this manner, their practices are similar to broadcasters across Europe and throughout the world, which, since the mid-1990s, have tended to decrease their use of imported US series during prime time while increasing domestic productions (Akyuz, 1996). However, Hungarian broadcasters tend to use more imported series from fellow European nations in prime time than their Western European counterparts, because they cannot easily afford to produce series themselves or acquire them from domestic producers.

Buyers at the Hungarian channels only purchase what are called 'free-television' rights. Occasionally, however, they may partner with local redistributors for both free-television and home video/DVD rights. In some larger markets where broadcasters also have relationships with cable companies and movie theatres, buyers may pick up all rights to a film in the market and redistribute non-broadcast rights to others. In these cases, it seems that the majors are more willing to reduce the size and rigidity of film packages, or to forgo packaging altogether (Fayks, 2004).

Acquisitions decisions at the Hungarian commercial broadcasters, then, are generally independent, even though they are owned in large part by foreign media conglomerates. Of course, the majors try their best to leverage the popularity of their feature films to increase sales of their less popular programming. In genres that air outside of prime time to smaller audience segments, the majors are more successful in their efforts, but competition for advertising dollars is far too fierce to allow them much advantage when trying to push general entertainment series. However, even in feature packages, Hungarian buyers have a degree of flexibility in terms of which series they elect to buy. With non-major distributors, they generally have a rough idea of the kinds of programming they are looking for, but still need to make specific purchasing decisions.

As mentioned, stable relationships with a small number of distributors and a focus on buying their newest programmes help streamline the decision-making process. While larger broadcasters may field larger acquisitions teams, thereby allowing them to keep in touch with more distributors than the Hungarian broadcasters examined here, they still tend to limit the number of distributors from whom they purchase the vast majority of their programming. Furthermore, discussion with other buyers, especially those in the same region of the world and those who are part of the same conglomerate, helps buyers make final decisions. For instance, one of the buyers at RTL Klub explained that she selected specific *telenovelas* from the large number available by asking buyers in the Czech Republic and Poland which series had worked well in their markets.

Buyers and scheduling executives at both RTL Klub and TV2 explained that, while they did not enter into large deals with their sister channels in order to decrease overall prices, they nevertheless did discuss which acquisitions were working well or poorly in other channels' markets.

Acquisitions decisions among Hungarian commercial broadcasters, then, remain largely independent, even as they are shaped by buyers' relationships with a set number of distributors, the differential importance of various audience segments and dayparts for which they are buying programming, the social networks of the global television business, discussion with others in the same parent conglomerate and the power of the Hollywood studios. It would seem that these observations hold for commercial broadcasters in large markets as well, except that such broadcasters acquire fewer programmes, face stiffer competition and hence pay closer attention to acquisitions in off-peak time-slots, drive harder bargains with powerful distributors and may not have sister channels in other markets to discuss acquisitions with.

PROGRAMME IMPORTS AT HUNGARIAN PUBLIC-SERVICE BROADCASTERS

Public-service broadcasters operate in the same global programming markets as commercial broadcasters, and many of them also compete with their commercial counterparts for domestic viewers and advertising revenues. For these reasons, public broadcasters generally face the same kinds of challenges as commercial broadcasters, but at other times they must confront a very different set of problems that arise from the precariousness of their funding and the highly politicised nature of public broadcasting. While not identical to commercial broadcasters, the process of making acquisitions decisions, the barriers to independent decision-making among buyers and even the kinds of programmes acquired from the global television markets are not radically different.

The Hungarian public broadcaster, Magyar Televízió (MTV), operates two channels, a general broadcast channel, M1, and a culturally oriented satellite channel, M2. With the introduction of commercial broadcasting, MTV has faced steep audience declines and currently ranks third in the ratings, well behind its commercial rivals (AGB, 2002). Because MTV is funded by a mix of licence fees and advertising revenues, its poor ratings severely curtail its operating expenses and, thus, its international acquisitions budget. What is more, politicians often use MTV's poor ratings to take the broadcaster to task for not fulfilling its remit as a truly national medium that appeals to all facets of Hungarian society. In essence, then, MTV has suffered an acute identity crisis since the introduction of commercial broadcasting, which puts it into an intractable Catch 22. Since it no longer has the funding to bid for the most popular Western programming and films, MTV cannot maintain ratings and commercial revenues; however, it cannot improve either its advertising- or government-funded operating revenues without popular programming. The unique challenges that buyers at MTV face stem from this basic conflict.

The same buyers acquire programming for both M1 and M2. Hollywood feature films are the most important and sought-after programmes at MTV, because most people who go to the cinema watch American films. Buyers feel that they have to follow this preference when making acquisitions decisions. In addition to the perceived need to serve the audience's preferences, acquisitions officials see the broadcasting of new Hollywood films as part of their remit, which includes introducing the 'best' of all the world's audiovisual culture to Hungarian viewers. MTV is somewhat hobbled in its competition with the commercials for rights to Hollywood films, due to its smaller audience size and fewer advertising slots per hour. At the same time, its programme schedule has little room for US television series, thus diminishing the other bargaining chip MTV might use in its negotiations with the majors. Consequently, MTV typically acquires rights to older or less popular films, although it certainly does carry a number of new Hollywood blockbusters each year. While the commercial broadcasters acquire the newest action films, MTV generally avoids films whose sole purpose is action, sticking more with epics, art films and historical pieces.

As with the commercial broadcasters, an important dimension of MTV's ability to obtain rights to Hollywood films results from the relationships that its buyers have with sales executives at the majors. One buyer had worked as a film buyer for commercial distributors and channels for ten years, where she built close relationships with the Hollywood majors, among other distributors, that allow her to function effectively in acquisitions. 'Sometimes, it's much easier if you have good personal connections [with distributors],' she explains. 'Sometimes, they choose you first.' She cited as an example a recent film deal with a Hollywood distributor that she was able to secure due to her attendance at the Los Angeles Screenings and a long-term relationship with the seller, in which she also picked up the rights to 24 (2001–), a sought-after series that ran in prime time on MTV. MTV also, on occasion, partners with redistributors in the region to acquire multiple kinds of rights to Hollywood films in an effort to compete with the commercial broadcasters.

Much like their commercial counterparts, buyers at MTV list European films as the second most important programming they acquire, although the breadth of European film acquisitions seems to be much wider at MTV, both in terms of programming hours and sources. An analysis of the programme schedules of MTV and the commercial channels confirms that about 60 per cent of the films MTV plays each week are European, while only about 15 per cent of the commercial broadcasters' film programming came from Europe. Not only does MTV acquire films from the larger European countries, including France, Germany, the UK and Italy, but also from other Central European nations, which, again, is seen as part of the public broadcaster's remit. In addition, MTV acquires series and specials from other European nations, in particular documentaries and series produced by other public broadcasters. One of the buyers I spoke with also expressed an interest in acquiring series from other Central European nations, especially the Czech Republic and Poland, but said she has seen few series from these countries recently. Beyond Europe, MTV also followed the trend of the commercial broadcasters by purchasing *telenovelas* from Latin American distributors.

The use of *telenovelas* to appeal to the same demographic as the commercial channels during the day demonstrates well the focus on acquiring primetime programming at MTV, in a fashion similar to the commercial broadcasters. Because MTV's commercial revenues, prestige and subsequent government revenues come primarily from its primetime line-up, its acquisitions strategy continues to place the broadcaster in head-to-head competition with the commercial broadcasters, a battle it is destined to lose.

Some of the most significant challenges facing buyers at the public broadcaster stem from funding uncertainties, political turnover in the organisation's management and the strain that these changes place on relationships with distributors. For instance, when I interviewed a buyer at MTV in 2001, she had been unable to make bids at the Los Angeles Screenings that year because the public broadcaster's funding had been held up in Parliament, as had her acquisitions budget. When I spoke with her again in 2002, the head of the public broadcaster had recently been replaced due to a change in governing parties. Insisting on a less elitist stance, the new director ordered that several documentary slots be replaced by populist programming, forcing the buyer to cancel several long-term contracts with foreign documentary distributors. The damage to this buyer's relationships with those distributors, she told me, was irreparable.

In many ways, the difficulties that buyers from MTV face in international acquisitions are unique to the Hungarian political landscape, not least the broadcaster's inability to reinvent itself after the introduction of commercial broadcasting in 1997, which was due in part to the persistent meddling of bureaucrats. In addition, the fact that MTV is dual-funded makes the job of acquisitions executives who must serve both governmental and commercial masters more difficult, as does the fact that many viewers associate the broadcaster with the former authoritarian state.

Still, the experience of MTV with politically motivated interventions in programming practices, government funding cycles that differ from the business cycles of global television sales and struggles to redefine itself in the wake of privatisation is not dissimilar to the challenges faced by public-service broadcasters around the world. In 2005, for instance, economic problems and identity crises at the Belgian public-service broadcaster, RTBF, prompted the oversight board to alter its profile to include more commercially popular imports, eliminating several educational slots (*Variety*, 2005). In fact, these identity crises shook most of the world's public-service broadcasters in the 1980s and 1990s (Avery, 1993; Groombridge and Hay, 1995; Tracey, 1998). All of these hurdles complicate the job of acquisitions executives, who often are already disadvantaged in their competition with commercial broadcasters for the newest, most sought-after programming because they lack the funds and the purchasing capacity of the commercials.

If we compare the acquisitions priorities and strategies at the Hungarian commercial broadcasters and MTV, we can see a consistent hierarchy of global television programming, which places Hollywood films at the top, regional films in second place, globally popular and culturally proximate series in the third spot and culturally distant or niche-oriented programming on the lowest rung. This pattern is repeated around the world, regardless of the location of broadcasters or their public or commercial status, although the popularity of regional films differs among broadcasters in different regions. Although US series have fallen out of prime time in markets around the world, replaced by locally produced series and shows, local versions of global formats, or programming from linguistically and culturally similar nations, Hollywood films have maintained their primetime positions (De Bens and de Smaele, 2001, p. 60). Even the most powerful public-service broadcaster in the world, the BBC, consistently programmes Hollywood films during prime time (BBC, 2005). How are we to understand such a situation, where television programmers from around the world come to the same conclusions about the fitness of Hollywood films for primetime programming?

The answer lies in the efforts of all of these broadcasters to target an undifferentiated mass audience, and a global business culture that agrees that Hollywood films are the most consistently predictable, economically efficient means of building such an audience. My point here is not that Hollywood films poorly fulfil the role of targeting an undifferentiated audience, but rather that any number of programming strategies could probably do an equivalent or better job. The programming hierarchy of global television is reinforced by the process of dubbing in Hungary, which comes in four price ranges and quality levels: theatrical, broadcast, cable and video. Programming that is expected to perform well will receive a larger budget and better dubbing, which is a significant factor in viewer satisfaction with imported programming, thus making expectations about the performance of top-dollar programming a self-fulfilling prophecy (Havas, 2002).

A final example, drawn from government-funded local channels in Hungary, highlights how pervasive the programming hierarchy of global television is at general entertainment channels, regardless of their funding structure or apparent isolation from the business culture of global television. Kör Media, a consortium of 100 local and regional broadcast and cable channels in Hungary, provides a twenty-four-hour satellite feed, from which its constituents can downlink programming when they lack local productions to fill airtime. Kör Media began operations in spring 2003 with a goal of becoming one-third advertising-supported in the first year of operations. Central to this goal and the need to offer a programming feed that all of its constituents would find useful was an effort to create a general entertainment programming profile that featured US and European films, as well as locally produced series, documentaries and cultural programming (Gáti, 2002). Zoltán Gáti, the director of Kör Media, explains that 'classic' Hollywood films are crucial to bringing a general audience to these local channels during prime time, which may then remain to watch other local programmes. Gáti does not speak English, so he does not read the trade press. He acquires films through Central European redistributors, often rights to the second- or third-run of the film on Hungarian television. Nevertheless, he has internalised the programming hierarchy of global television sales, which dictates that the most popular general entertainment programmes are Hollywood films.

Only the largest general entertainment broadcasters, who are able to self-produce high-quality, local programming can escape the programming logic of the global television marketplace, and even these broadcasters, such as the BBC, typically sell their programming abroad, where it must compete on the open market with Hollywood. Often, these distributors must sell niche-oriented programming or general entertainment series that substitute for Hollywood series. Of course, the programme hierarchy of the global television market is not monolithic, and several buyers, especially those from public-service broadcasters, exhibit different taste regimes. These different tastes are particularly noticeable in the trade in documentary programmes among public-service broadcasters. Nevertheless, given the wide appeal and comparative cheapness of Hollywood's blockbuster films and series, it is difficult for any general broadcaster to resist the tendency to see Hollywood programming as the most universal and desirable in the world.

PROGRAMME IMPORTS AT THEMATIC HUNGARIAN CABLE CHANNELS

Because Hollywood uses its massive economic and discursive muscle to dominate general entertainment programming genres worldwide, thematic channels

that target a segment of the audience operate within very different programming markets and discourses, where the power of Hollywood is much
diminished. Moreover, in order to maintain their positions in their respective
markets, which typically contain both globally branded thematic channels and
other local competitors, all vying for the same audience niche, the programming and acquisitions managers at such channels retain a good deal of control
over acquisitions decisions. In many ways, then, buyers and schedulers at thematic cable channels exhibit the largest degree of independence from
conglomerate ownership or Hollywood's control over the discourses of global
television.

The Hungarian children's channel Minimax is a case in point. In 2002, Minimax was 80 per cent owned by French pay-channel Canal+, itself a subsidiary
of the Vivendi-Universal conglomerate, although changes in corporate strategy
at Vivendi-Universal led the conglomerate to put Minimax Hungary on the auc-
tion block later that year, despite its consistently strong performance among the
two to twelve demographic (*Euromarketing via Email*, 2002). Prevalent political-
economic theories of global media expansion predict that a conglomerate such
as Vivendi-Universal would provide programming 'to their own television networks and cable channels in a privileged manner' (Herman and McChesney,
1997, pp. 68–9). Thus, as a tiny subsidiary of a mammoth conglomerate that
owns a Hollywood studio, Minimax should operate as little more than a pipeline
for excess animated Universal product. Similarly, we would expect little independence on the part of its executives and almost no responsiveness to the local
market. However, in the case of Minimax and, indeed, most television channels
in the world, the identity of the channel and its position within the primary
market for viewers ultimately determines its acquisitions practices, including the
independence of Minimax's executives.

Katalin Radóczy, the general manager of the channel and the person responsible for acquisitions, is a comparative newcomer to the global television
business and the television business in general. In 1999, 'when we started Minimax, nobody had any media experience at our channel', but three years later,
she claimed that she was able to drive a hard bargain with most animation distributors, even the most powerful. 'I never buy programmes in packages,' she
insists. 'I don't like packages, because if you buy a package, you know there are
one or two titles which you cannot use on your channel, so I never buy packages. On the programmes which I really want for the channel, I usually manage
to push down the prices' (2002). Thus, in the two main instances where distributors exercise power vis-à-vis buyers – packaging programmes and setting
high prices – Radóczy claims to have the upper hand. Of course, one might
reasonably question Radóczy's opinion, but both the channel's status as the

main Hungarian-based children's channel and the currently glutted marketplace in television animation lend credence to her claims.

Radóczy, like other buyers of global television programming, works primarily with a handful of distributors with whom she has groomed relationships over the years. These distributors concentrate on animated programming, especially non-violent cartoons. Radóczy mentions as her main distributors Canadian-based Nelvana, French animation house Procidis, Spanish BRB Internacional and British companies Entertainment Rights and Hit Entertainment. As she points out, these are primarily European distributors, but her acquisitions decisions seem to have little to do with cultural similarities between Hungarian children and other European children, except for the fact European societies, including Hungary, are less tolerant of the violence associated with much US and Japanese animation. In addition, Minimax Hungary also owns and pro-grammes Minimax Romania, and typically purchases programming for both territories, which allows it somewhat better prices because distributors can get two sales with one deal. Also, Minimax Hungary's sister channel, Minimax Poland, while independent, sometimes buys programming jointly with Minimax Hungary, allowing distributors access to three markets and again lowering per-country prices. For instance, the Minimax channels in Poland, Hungary and Romania worked together on a deal with Canadian animation house Nelvana in 2002 (ibid.).

Because of its identity as the only channel aimed at young children in the Hungarian market, Minimax faces little competition for either viewers or imported programming. Although Fox Kids, the Cartoon Channel and Nick-elodeon all have Hungarian-language versions of their transnational cable channels, they all skew towards an older audience, leaving Minimax as the only channel for young children. Consequently, Radóczy never finds herself bidding against the transnational channels for programming. Local redistributors such as Twin Media, which brands itself as a children's animation distributor, might be seen as competitors, but the sheer volume of young children's programming on the international markets dampen that competition as well.

Minimax's channel identity also leads it to programme a good deal of local and regional animation. When it began operations, Minimax purchased most of Hungarian Television's animation archive, and it made a similar purchase when it began Minimax Romania. In addition, Radóczy buys animation from Poland, the Czech Republic, and Slovakia, mostly shorts made during socialist times. The main audience for these older animated series, of course, is not the young children, but the parents who are watching with them and recognise not only some of their favourite Hungarian characters from childhood, but also charac-ters from nearby nations that traded children's programming during the socialist era. While this practice lends a distinctly Hungarian and Central European flavour to the channel, it is also important to note that Minimax airs very little new animated programming from regional producers. In other words, its programming strategy may help foster regional and national identities, but it does little to encourage contemporary animation in Hungary or the region.

Although Minimax's identity as the only Hungarian-based children's channel provides a good deal of independence in acquisitions and scheduling, many of Radóczy's programming ideas come from the business culture of global television. When discussing her audience's preferences, she adopts a vaguely developmental model of children's viewing habits, in which the youngest prefer programming with formless characters and a good deal of music and sound, while children under twelve prefer non-violent programming with simple stories and recognisable characters. Older children, meanwhile, prefer more violent programmes. The point to make here is not that this model of programme preferences is wrong, but rather that it obviously comes from others in the global television business, as Radóczy has no training in child development or television. In addition, this model is seen as transferable anywhere. The prevalent attitude in children's programming, which I have often heard and read in trade journals, is that 'kids are the same everywhere' (Hazai, 2001). Thus, although Radóczy's position at the only channel targeted at young children in Hungary appears to give her a good deal of leeway when making acquisitions and programming decisions, she has derived her idea of what kinds of programming will interest Hungarian children from others in the field of global children's television.

The children's animation genre is a buyer's market, which explains the degree of freedom Minimax enjoys in its acquisitions. Low entry barriers for producers, which have sunk even lower with the use of computer animation that saves on labour costs, as well as the growth of cheap animation labour markets in South and Southeast Asia (Russell, 2003), mean that the Hollywood majors cannot dominate the animation genre as they do the feature film genre. Hence, a thematic channel's competitive environment in its domestic market, combined with global market characteristics of its main programming genres, create the degree of independence of its acquisitions and scheduling executives.

PROGRAMME IMPORTS AT GENERAL ENTERTAINMENT HUNGARIAN CABLE CHANNELS

Because the commercial television market in Hungary is comparatively small, new and developing, it is also home to channels that do little more than pump in foreign culture and siphon off local advertising revenues, thus conforming to political-economists' worst fears about media globalisation. The organisational structure of these channels differs in important ways from transnational satellite channels, whose acquisitions practices are explored in Chapter 6, because they retain a degree of local programming control, even though they may share the same brand identity as channels in other nations. These cable channels are owned by transnational media conglomerates that also control similar channels across multiple markets and use the breadth of their holdings to negotiate volume discounts with large US distributors, often improving their revenues and market positions in the more lucrative markets where they operate by dumping programmes onto smaller ones. However, the ability of such channels to survive when markets become more competitive is questionable, as the history of such channels across Europe suggests.

The Hungarian channel Viasat3, which began broadcasting in 2000, fits the description of a general entertainment channel with minimal domestic programming control. Viasat 3 is wholly owned by Swedish newspaper conglomerate Modern Times Group, whose London-based Viasat Broadcasting also owns pay-television and free-to-air channels in Northern Europe, the Baltic region and Russia (MTG, 2004). Viasat3 is carried by the major cable operator in Hungary, UPC, in its basic programming tier. Programmes are dubbed in Budapest and shipped to London, where they are broadcast via satellite from London. Less than twenty people work in the Viasat3 office in Budapest, most of whom sell airtime to Hungarian advertisers. In addition, the channel maintains small programming, channel management and finance departments. Viasat3 identifies itself as 'purely entertainment'.

On my first visit to Viasat3 in 2001, I met with a programming executive who had spent ten years working in television production, radio, advertising sales and programming. By the time I returned in 2002, she had moved on, and her duties had been taken over by an assistant with only a few years' experience in programming at Viasat3, who held a position a step below my original contact. The main office in London had eliminated the higher position, demonstrating the lack of programming independence at Viasat3. Another indicator of the lack of independence is the fact that the assistant speaks very little English, and therefore cannot interact with the international distributors from whom Viasat3 buys programming. Rather, almost all of the decisions regarding programme acquisitions and scheduling are handled by Viasat Broadcasting executives in London. Despite the absence of local decision-makers to respond to the domestic market, Viasat3 has reportedly done well in the ratings for a cable channel that in 2001 reached only 40 per cent of the total national audience (Nadler, 2001).

Responsibility for Viasat3's acquisitions decisions are shared among local and foreign executives, with final decisions resting in the hands of Viasat Broadcasting's London-based headquarters. Viasat Broadcasting acquires almost exclusively from the major Hollywood distributors, buying large packages of films and series for multiple territories from, among others, Twentieth Century Fox, Paramount and Universal. Requests for specific acquisitions originate in the offices of the local Viasat channels, which submit request forms to the London office. When the local channels are interested in specific series, they request them by name, but requests for film acquisitions are done by number of hours, rather than specific titles, because Viasat Broadcasting cannot generally get rights to the newest, most popular films, which most often go first to broadcasters. Consequently, Viasat3 is more interested in acquiring particular genres of feature films that fit its programme schedule. For instance, the channel acquires a number of action films that it airs as part of a branded 'action month' every night in October. US series, on the other hand, are a less coveted commodity in Hungary, and Viasat3 can sometimes get rights to current network series, such as *Sex and the City* (1998–2004).

Viasat3 can compete for films and series with the commercial broadcasters, despite the fact that it reaches a much smaller audience universe and therefore generates significantly smaller advertising revenues, because Viasat Broadcasting buys in bulk. That is, although a distributor might be able to generate higher per-programme prices by selling each title individually in each region, Viasat Broadcasting is able to secure rights because it provides a consistent pipeline for a large amount of product in multiple territories, thereby providing the distributor significant savings on overhead costs. In addition, much as we saw in previous chapters, the relationship that has developed between Viasat Broadcasting and Hollywood distributors as a result of their continued business dealings helps Viasat Broadcasting in its bidding efforts.

After the London headquarters has received request from all of the channels, Viasat Broadcasting's vice president of programming examines all of the requests and makes final decisions about which series and films to pursue. Typically, she buys the same programmes for all of the channels, though sometimes rights are not available for certain programmes in some markets. According to Viasat3's executives, the channel typically gets the acquisitions that it requests, but the channel also receives programming it did not request. In addition, Viasat3 often finds itself bidding against the commercial broadcasters for series and films. Although Hollywood programming is plentiful, the number of new films and primetime series is limited. Combined with the fact that Viasat3 aims at a general entertainment audience, the limited amount of Hollywood programming leads to competition for US imports. However, it also needs to be pointed out that the relatively large volume of programming that the Hollywood majors distribute each year is what makes it possible for a general entertainment channel like Viasat3 to exist in a market where two large commercial broadcasters and a nationwide public broadcaster also rely heavily on Hollywood imports.

Viasat3's executives claim that their acquisitions decisions reflect the preferences of Hungarian viewers, but they are hard-pressed to explain what this means. One programmer, for instance, said that, 'our [acquisitions] recommendations are based on the Hungarian audience and the Hungarian market', but when I asked her to elaborate, she mentioned only that Hungarian viewers follow a single programming trend at a time. At the time, that programming trend was 'fly-on-the-wall' reality series. This phenomenon, as suggested above, probably has more to do with the two-channel market than with the preferences of Hungarian viewers, as well as the fact that Viasat3 is targeting the same eighteen to forty-nine niche. In other words, the trends that executives at Minimax Hungary recognise are likely to be very different than those identified at Viasat3. In a follow-up interview, when I again asked for elaboration of this point, this executive explained that 'viewing habits manifest themselves in when people watch TV, how much TV they watch and what types of programme they are interested in'. Because of the acquisitions practices at Viasat3, however, programme preferences can only be gauged for imported US programming, as no other kinds of programming are available to the channel. At Viasat3, then, programmers' perceptions of local viewing preferences are restricted to understanding which imported US genres are preferred at which times of the day.

Viasat3's reliance on large packages of Hollywood films and series prevent its executives from recognising or capitalising on programming trends that do not involve Hollywood product. For instance, the popularity of Latin American *telenovelas* with women and German crime series with young men on the commercial broadcasters have eluded Viasat3's attention, despite the fact that the executives I interviewed identified these broadcasters as their main competition for viewers. 'Soap operas, *telenovelas* and German series are particularly bad for us,' according to a channel executive.

While Viasat3's acquisitions practices also demonstrate an attempt attract viewers outside of prime time, such efforts are highly circumscribed by the programming available in feature film packages, as well as the perception that Hollywood programming is more universal than other kinds of programming. It is easier, in other words, for Viasat3 to stick with moderately performing series in all dayparts that offer fairly predictable ratings and improve the parent company's ability to strike attractive deals with the Hollywood majors than it is to try to identify different programming trends that audiences might find more relevant.

Of course, in markets where advertising revenues and competition for viewers are greater, even general entertainment cable channels owned by foreign conglomerates exercise higher degrees of independence than Viasat3. VT4, for instance, is a Flemish-language Belgian cable channel, owned by Scandinavian media conglomerate SBS Broadcasting, featuring Hollywood blockbusters and series that it picks up in large packages from Columbia TriStar, Disney, Dream-Works, Paramount and Universal. Despite a skeleton staff, VT4's managing director handles the channel's acquisitions and programming decisions, attending the major sales markets and grooming relationships with distributors, unlike executives at Viasat3 (Johnson, 2001).

VT4's ratings are 300 per cent higher than Viasat3's ratings in Hungary, in part because VT4 reaches almost 100 per cent of the Belgian audience due to the high penetration rates of cable and satellite television in the country, while Viasat3 reaches only about 40 per cent of Hungarian households (Johnson, 2001; Nadler, 2001). Although VT4's higher ratings partially account for the greater independence of its programmers, the affluence of the Belgian population compared to the Hungarian population is probably the main factor. In 2005, the total television advertising spend in Belgium is estimated at $670 million, while the numbers for Hungary are 37 per cent lower at $423 million (Initiative Innovations, 2005). More importantly, the per capita GDP of Belgium in 2004 was more than three times higher than that of Hungary (US Department of State, 2005a, 2005b).

Still, the viability of VT4 as a general entertainment channel remains uncertain. Since 2001, the management has been increasing its domestic programme offerings with imported and domestic reality formats, including Twentieth Television's *Temptation Island* (2001–03), Freemantle Media's *The Apprentice* (2004–) and local series *Peking Express* (2004–), which follows couples racing across Asia on a fixed daily income (Waller, 2004a; 2004b, 2005b). However, the low ratings and subsequent advertising revenues of VT4 make it difficult for the channel to snare the latest Hollywood films and series, which we have seen is the most cost-effective way to attract broad, general audiences. Instead, the channel is left to fill most of its primetime hours with less recent Hollywood films and second-run or second-rate US series (VT4, 2005). At the same time, the channel's modest revenues compared with larger broadcasters restricts its attempts to create or acquire general entertainment domestic programming. Rather, most of its domestic programmes are relatively inexpensive unscripted series that perform moderately well (Johnson, 2001).

Non-broadcast channels that mainly rely on imported Hollywood films and series seem to be most effective in finding audiences when they use Hollywood's prodigious output to create an identifiable niche. The thematic French cable-satellite channel Canal Jimmy, for instance, imports a handful of first-run Hollywood series, which have until recently been notoriously unpopular in

France as general entertainment fair, as well as off-beat British series and 'cult' US series, such as the *Addams Family* (1964–6), *MASH* (1972–83) and *Get Smart* (1965–70), to target teenage and young adult audiences (Blicq, 1999; James, 2004; Tartaglione, 2000).

CONCLUSION

While conventional wisdom suggests that only new channels rely heavily on imports, replacing them slowly with domestic production (Hoskins, McFadyen and Finn, 1997, p. 35; Pool, 1977; Tracey and Redal, 1995, p. 345), this observation is only partly true. Most channels continue to use imports to fill particular holes in their schedules that domestic production cannot meet. Often, these time periods target particularly attractive or disposable audience segments. For instance, general entertainment Hungarian channels programme US features in late prime time in order to attract a large audience to their lead-in programming. These channels also use cheap Latin American *telenovelas* to fill during daytime, when audiences are older, female and less attractive to advertisers. Thus, broadcasters' programme offerings exhibit a constantly changing mixture of domestic and imported programmes.

The intermingling of domestic and imported cultural practices is at the heart of most contemporary theories of media globalisation (see Tomlinson, 1999). This tendency runs throughout the business practices and decision-making procedures of television outlets around the world. On one hand, a channel's acquisitions decisions are based on the viewing habits of national and subnational audiences, as well as the competition among channels for viewers and imported programming. On the other hand, these decisions arise not simply from the needs of domestic viewers, but also from the culture of the global television business – from the identification of viable audience segments and their preferences in other territories, as well as the programming hierarchy of global television sales.

To a large degree, the reliance on the wisdom of others in global television is a matter of institutional efficiency and economy. Rather than shouldering the costs of employing massive teams of acquisitions executives to sift through all of the available programming in the world, not to mention the costs of screening such programming for focus groups to determine which imports would fit the preferences of which audiences most perfectly, television channels have streamlined the process for identifying, evaluating and acquiring new programmes. All of the buyers examined in this chapter, from local, public cable channels to large terrestrial broadcasters rely on a small number of primary distributors for most of their programme acquisitions. Not only does this arrangement help buyers whittle down potential acquisitions to a.manageable

number, it also provides distributors with relative assurance that their new programmes will find buyers. In addition, the various representations of the
audience and its preferences that circulate through the social networks of the
global television marketplace provide ready theories about which programmes
will attract which audience segments. Put simply, the business of global television sales helps reduce risk for channel programmers.

The buyers profiled here demonstrate varying degrees of freedom and restric-
tion when making acquisitions and programming decisions. The animated
children's channel Minimax Hungary and the general entertainment cable channel Viasat3 stand at the two extremes in terms of their decision-making
autonomy, with other thematic and general entertainment channels falling somewhere in between. Again, I want to emphasise that the degree of autonomy does
not seem to be related to the ownership structure of the channel, although in
the case of Viasat3, it certainly matters that the channel is part of an international
consortium of channels. Rather, the most important considerations in determining programming independence are (1) the competitive environment for
programme acquisitions and (2) the competitive environment for viewers in the
national market. Of course, ownership issues are significant for other reasons,
including questions of domestic audiovisual employment and the repatriation of
profits by global conglomerates, but only in rare circumstances does ownership
seem to have a determining effect on programming practices. Instead, concentration of ownership has a more subtle impact on international television
acquisitions, namely that members of the same corporate bodies have more frequent contact with one another than with other executives, so the business lore
of the organisation shapes local television executives' perceptions of audience
preferences and programming options.

5

Scheduling International Television Imports

In the previous chapter, we saw that decisions about international acquisitions typically begin when television executives survey their programming schedules and project future needs. To date, however, critical television researchers have shown little interest in scheduling. Regardless of the origins of this neglect, scheduling practices influence the size and make-up of audiences for imported programmes, their popularity and future acquisitions decisions. Scheduling is a culturally significant act that overdetermines the kinds of television imports audiences watch and the ways in which they make sense of them. Consequently, this last leg of global programme sales feeds back into the overall process of contemporary television trade, as it determines future purchasing decisions and, indirectly, future production choices.

As with the previous chapter, this one concentrates on the Hungarian market because scheduling decisions, like acquisitions, arise primarily from domestic competitive conditions, regardless of whether the programmer in question works for commercial or public-service television outlets. Moreover, this chapter builds on the previous one by providing deeper explorations of some of the acquisitions practices described above. The chapter is not designed as an overview of scheduling practices; neither is it a description of 'best practices'. Rather, it is an attempt to demonstrate in some detail the variety of factors, both foreign and domestic, that come into play in specific scheduling decisions, as well as how such decisions influence the acquisition of international programmes.

UNDERSTANDING PROGRAMME SCHEDULING

The basic idea underlying most programme scheduling is what Owen and Wildman (1992) call the principle of 'adjacency', which suggests that 'viewers are more likely to watch a program if they have watched the previous program or intend to watch the succeeding one on the same channel' (p. 54). Much earlier, Raymond Williams (1974) dubbed scheduling practices that attempt to take advantage of the adjacency principle the 'flow' of television. Both concepts explain the same general phenomenon: once viewers tune to a certain channel, they are more likely to remain with that channel, rather than searching for different programming elsewhere. In other words, television viewing in many parts of the world seems to be governed by its own form of inertia.

Despite the introduction of the remote control, analogue and digital recording and the expansion of channel offerings via new delivery technologies, it still seems that most viewers stick with the channel they are viewing most of the time. Consequently, programmers perpetually try to lure audiences to switch to their channel, or to keep them from switching to other channels. Public-service broadcasters, particularly those partially funded by advertising, are not immune to this persistent contest for viewers. Only premium channels, which make their money not from the size of the viewing audience but from the number of subscribers they have each month, and transnational satellite channels, which are programmed identically regardless of the competitive conditions in the nations where they are operate, demonstrate different programming logics. These different logics will be explored in the following chapter.

In addition to the principle of adjacency, most programme scheduling is based on the assumption that television viewing takes place in real time, so channels are under the constant threat of losing viewers, at the same time they are always in a position to attract new viewers. This observation may seem obvious, but it has profound effects on programme scheduling, especially in a market where ratings companies provide minute-by-minute ratings. Theoretically – and sometimes in practice – this means that scheduling decisions are figured down to the minute, based upon what time a competitor's credits are rolling, what time they begin and end their advertising breaks and so forth. In other words, scheduling often involves more than simply deciding how to order programmes in a particular daypart; it can also involve precise decisions about which moment to begin and end programmes (Kolosi, 2002).

Different dayparts attract different levels of attention, due to their relative importance for advertising revenues and prestige. In prime time, for instance, RTL Klub and TV2 schedule against each other on a minute-by-minute basis. Péter Kolosi (2002), the programme director of RTL Klub, explains how TV2 scheduled a new primetime sitcom, *Szeret, Nem Szeret* (*He Loves Me, He Loves Me Not*) (2002) to coincide precisely with the ending of RTL Klub's local soap opera hit, *Barátok Közt* (*Between Friends*) (1998–): 'You could see exactly that *Barátok Közt* was just over and [*Szeret, Nem Szeret*] just started. So of course, if something is over, people start to zap.' Thus, in order to take advantage of the fact that viewers are most likely to browse other offerings at the end of a programme, TV2 began its new series during the credits of RTL Klub's flagship series. This intense competition leads programmers to yank programmes on and off the schedule quickly if ratings dip for short periods of time, thus speeding the search for new programming trends that have the potential to significantly change a channel's international acquisitions.

During non-primetime dayparts in small markets like Hungary, the competition for viewers is not as fierce, because advertising revenues are significantly smaller. Therefore, early morning, daytime, afternoon, late night and overnight dayparts do not receive the kind of careful scrutiny that prime time does at the commercial broadcasters. Additionally, at other channels, including cable channels and the public broadcaster MTV, this minute-by-minute competition does not exist, even during prime time. Smaller channels lack the staff to follow their competitors' scheduling moves on a minute-by-minute basis, and the net improvement in ratings from adopting such a strategy would probably not be worthwhile. At MTV, on the other hand, both an ethos of non-competitiveness and different restrictions on the allowable amount of advertising per hour keep competition with other channels from getting as fierce as it does at TV2 and RTL Klub. Even in markets where the public broadcaster maintains rough parity with a commercial rival, such as the Slovene market or the Polish market, different advertising regulations work against minute-by-minute scheduling competition (Fayks, 2004; Bergant, 2004). Thus, throughout Europe, such practices are probably uncommon at public broadcasters, but outside Europe, where some public broadcasters are more dependent upon advertising and less restricted in their use of ads, fiercer competition probably exists.

Scheduling requires both structure and flexibility to be successful. Structure provides predictability for the audience, which is one of the governing assumptions underlying the weekly and daily scheduling of the same programmes at the same times. Most television channels set their schedules years in advance, due primarily to the length of rights contracts, which usually include two or three runs of a programme over a three- to five-year period. As a result, most channels know much of their schedule for the near future, because only a fraction of programme rights expire each year and need to be replaced. In addition, since most programmes are bought for specific time-slots and audiences, the part of the schedule for which the programming was bought is generally set. On the other hand, scheduling innovations regularly and unpredictably occur, as channels that are not in first place in a market seek to improve their positions. Scheduling innovations can profoundly alter the landscape of television, as has been seen recently around the world with the introduction of unscripted 'reality' shows as a means for targeting both general and niche audiences. Scheduling innovations can also radically alter a channel's and a nation's television imports, as has happened beginning in 2003 across Southeast Asia, where Korean dramas have replaced Japanese dramas in many nations' television schedules (Schwarzacher, 2004).

Most scholarly research into scheduling comes from applied researchers who examine the impact of various techniques and innovations on audience ratings or attempt to describe changes in prevalent scheduling practices (Eastman, Head and Klein, 1985; Eastman, Neal-Lunsford and Riggs, 1995). This research provides a consistent vocabulary for a variety of common scheduling practices, but it does not illuminate the cultural roots and implications of scheduling, nor does it typically address the influence of globalisation on scheduling.

By contrast, research into international television flows has frequently, if only partially, recognised the importance of scheduling when theorising the impact of foreign television programming on importing cultures, often distinguishing between primetime and non-primetime hours when comparing the volume and kinds of imports in different nations (see De Bens and de Smaele, 2001). However, the distinction between prime time and non-prime time barely scratches the surface of why television scheduling matters, and is built on the assumption that primetime programming is culturally more important than non-primetime programming. This is only the case if we accept the premise that programming that reaches the largest number of people has the most profound impact on the importing culture. If we conceive of television's primary function as the articulation of national audiences, then the programmes that reach the largest number of viewers within the borders of the nation may indeed have the greatest impact on national identity. If, on the other hand, we understand television as articulating together a variety of audience segments, including transnational audiences that coalesce around axes of difference such as sexual, gender, ethnic, or generational identities, then it is just as important to study the programmes that reach these smaller audience segments. More importantly, the tendency to focus only on imports with the largest audiences replicates the bias of the industry, and should be looked upon with suspicion.

SCHEDULING AS A HYBRID CULTURAL PRACTICE

At the most obvious level, scheduling responds to national viewer preferences because decisions are made based on the ratings performance of television programmes in relation to the competitive conditions in which a television outlet finds itself. Despite recent increases in transnational satellite channels, most television channels in most parts of the world continue to operate on a nationwide basis. Scheduling decisions are based upon the number of households viewing television in a given daypart, and what the general make-up of that audience is. For instance, both spouses in most households in Hungary work full time, so the daytime audience is generally composed of retired people, the unemployed and a handful of stay-at-home parents from the upper classes, who tend to watch little television (Koperveisz, 2002). As a result, most of the programming during the day is aimed at an older, mostly female audience. To take another example, Polish families tend to spend a good deal of time together on Saturday afternoons watching television, so the Saturday afternoon time-slot is a competitive one in Poland, filled with domestic, family-centred programmes (Fayks, 2004). This, of course, is the level of scheduling that businesspeople and academics point to when they argue that international programme flows respond primarily to local viewing tastes (see Tracey and Redal, 1995).

The small amount of critical research on scheduling also tends to emphasise its domestic character and authenticity. David Cardiff and Paddy Scannell (1987), for instance, argue that the BBC's radio schedule was constructed around annual national ceremonies rather than the 'fixed point' daily time-slots that characterised the American radio networks. These national ceremonies were the only predictable and massively attended BBC programmes at the time. In their estimation, this programme organisation continues to inform contemporary television schedules and mark them as authentically British.

Similarly, John Ellis (2000) provides a broad overview of scheduling practices in general, and the BBC and ITV in particular, developing the theory that the programme schedule is a sedimented document of the nation's television habits. Ellis identifies several scheduling grids, distinguished by duration, including yearly, seasonal, monthly, weekly and daily schedules, which provide clues about who watches television when, and how television viewing fits in with other leisure pursuits. One of his overriding arguments is that scheduling has a cultural force, which has heretofore been largely ignored, and that this force is largely inward-looking and domestic. 'The character of the national scheduling battle constituted a formidable site of resistance and resilience in the face of any globalising tendencies that might bear down upon it,' he writes. 'Any imported show is imported into this context of scheduling and its cultural identity is significantly altered as a result' (p. 36). Scheduling, in his view, operates as a fortress of authenticity against imported programming that changes the identity of imports into partially domestic cultural entities because industry lore about scheduling comes from local programmers' observations of the domestic market. While this observation may be accurate in largely self-sufficient markets such as the UK, industry lore about scheduling in much of the world increasingly derives from both unique local conditions and imported ideas.

Echoing Ellis' characterisation of the domestic character of the programme schedule, Cunningham and Jacka (1996) liken scheduling to a semiotic code, in which 'the time slot is the paradigmatic aspect [while] ... the sequence of program ... flow is the syntagmatic element'. Much like language differences, differences in 'the mix of programs, the favored genres, the way they are grouped into time slots and blocks' continue to 'mark a television service as local' (p. 19). The strength of this insight is that it reminds us that television as a phenomenon refers not just to programmes, but to the varied and complex ways that television viewing fits in with other social activities and pastimes. These other activities, in turn, indirectly influence acquisitions decisions.

Unlike the syntax of a language, however, broadcast schedules have been intentionally international since the beginning. In some instances, the schedules of foreign broadcasters were simply copied, such as the Australian Broadcasting Company's former practice of beginning programmes at ten minutes to and twenty-five minutes past the hour, like the BBC (ibid.). In other instances, such as the BBC's disdain for American-style fixed-point radio schedules prior to the mid-1930s, foreign scheduling practices have served as the 'other' against which domestic scheduling practices developed (Hilmes, 2003, p. 66). In both examples, the syntagmatic dimension of the programme schedule is more deeply inflected with foreign practices than linguistic syntax. Furthermore, scheduling practices change much more rapidly than linguistic syntax, especially when institutional, economic, or technological changes occur. Over the past twenty years, for instance, due to the rapid, worldwide expansion of broadcasting hours and channel capacity, countless new scheduling practices have become necessary, and many have been imported from abroad along with programming. How, for instance, does one programme a twenty-four-hour music channel or the overnight hours at a terrestrial broadcaster? The answers to such questions often come from a mixture of domestic and imported scheduling lore. While such hybridity is most common in less self-sufficient markets, it seems to mark scheduling practices almost everywhere.

Certainly, even in young television markets, programmers sometimes make thoroughly domestic scheduling decisions based on local cultural and political conditions. In the mid-1980s, for instance, Bophuthatswana Television (Bop-TV), which broadcast from the South African homeland of Bophuthatswana to the black Tswana-speaking residents of Soweto, programmed a mix of imported US series, black-oriented news and interviews with radical political figures, often 'hammocking' interviews and news between two imported series in an effort to increase the reach of its original programming (*TV World*, 1984). Bop-TV particularly sought out US programming that featured both African American and white actors, such as *Benson* (1979–86) and *Diff'rent Strokes* (1978–86), something banned on South African television. Because the channels of the South African Broadcasting Corporation (SABC) programmed few imported or domestic entertainment shows, Bop-TV became an instant hit, even among white viewers, who were legally forbidden to receive the channel and had to pay hundreds of dollars for equipment to bring in the station's weak signal (Spiller,

1990; Van Slambrouck, 1984). The channel became so popular with white viewers that, when the SABC took steps to block the signal from reaching them, they petitioned the government, eventually collecting more than 60,000 signatures (*TV World*, 1984).

Thus, through creative scheduling of US imports to draw in viewers to news and opinion from a different viewpoint than that of the South African government, Bop-TV carried out a radical political agenda. By placing interviews with political radicals adjacent to *Benson*, which featured African-American actor Robert Guillaume as a cabinet officer for an inept, white governor in the South, the channel managed not only to expand the audience for its interviews, but to use the apparent racial harmony and equality of *Benson* to underscore the backwardness of South Africa's racial regime of apartheid. Furthermore, by counter-programming the SABC, Bop-TV was able to identify itself as the voice of modernity, while simultaneously identifying the SABC – and, by association, the South African government – as anachronistic (Spiller, 1990).

At the opposite end of the spectrum from the Bop-TV case are instances where foreign programmers design a channel's schedule. For instance, when channels that are part of a global media conglomerate are first launched, the parent company may send representatives to 'teach' local programmers how to schedule effectively. Katalin Radóczy (2002), the general manager of the children's cable channel Minimax Hungary, describes how her channel's programme schedule was designed by foreign professionals. 'When we started with this channel with the help of Canal + [a French pay-channel that owned the Minimax brand], there were two French colleagues who came here and showed everything to us, how to work in Hungary.' In such instances, of course, foreign executives are likely to design programme schedules that fit the programming strengths of their parent company's production and distribution holdings.

Ágnes Havas (2002), a former programmer at the now-defunct TV3, a Hungarian cable channel owned by US-based Central European Media Enterprises (CME), which owns several channels throughout the region, tells a similar story:

> *Married with Children* was the first [sitcom on commercial television in Hungary].
> ... Basically *Married with Children* was required programming by CME. And the
> cassette arrived, and he looked at the tape, the general director, and said, 'Oh my
> God! This is crap! What are we going to do with this?' ... Of course we had the
> acquisition and programming experts from London and from Amsterdam, from
> NovaTV in the Czech Republic, and they said that, 'You should have this show in
> your prime time. Lead [with it] in your prime time.'

TV3 followed the advice of CME and its other affiliates, and led prime time with *Married with Children*, where it became the channel's largest success and a local phenomenon whose popularity continues to this day.

Though troubling, such instances of direct foreign interference in programme scheduling in Hungary are rare and usually limited to a channel's launch or sudden bad fortune. Too much concentration on them can deflect attention from the more subtle ways in which foreign scheduling practices make their way into the domestic market, including discussions among television professionals in the same transnational media conglomerates and geographical regions, as well as the monitoring of foreign television channels. Each example below explores the different routes through which foreign scheduling practices make their way into the industry folklore of Hungarian programmers, paying particular attention to how these hybrid practices influence foreign acquisitions decisions.

THE ROLE OF THE REGIONAL IN DOMESTIC SCHEDULING: DAYTIME *TELENOVELAS*

As in much of Central and Eastern Europe, imported Latin American *telenovelas* have a long history in Hungarian television. In the late 1980s, the Brazilian *telenovela Escrava Isaura* (1976) attracted strong ratings during prime time on MTV. Such a performance in prime time, however, was a rarity, and most *telenovelas* have been scheduled in off-peak hours since. When the commercial channels began broadcasting in 1997, they scheduled multiple *telenovelas* in daytime. This practice, repeated at commercial broadcasters across Central and Eastern Europe, led to a region-wide upsurge in *telenovela* trade. The story of how *telenovelas* came to dominate Hungarian daytime and how they were replaced offers us a window into the development of region-wide scheduling trends, the uncertainties that surround daytime scheduling decisions in a newly commercialised market and the practical constraints that acquisitions practices place on scheduling choices.

From 1997–2001, *telenovelas* continued to be popular daytime fair in Hungary. Commercial and public broadcasters programmed the serials in both morning and afternoon time-slots each weekday. Some even block-scheduled *telenovelas* back-to-back in daytime, generating a need for a large number of programming hours (Fraser, 2002). While not ratings blockbusters, *telenovelas* performed well enough to remain in the programming schedules year-in and year-out during time periods that were not very aggressively programmed. One buyer at TV2 whom I interviewed in 2001 claimed that, in terms of the number of programming hours acquired each year, one-third were Latin American *telenovelas*, another third comprised US movies and series and the final third were European products. Other buyers and programmers at the rival commercial network and the public broadcaster confirmed the *telenovela* trend, as did industry trade journals. *Telenovelas* even found their way into access prime time and primetime slots (ibid. 2002).

The use of block-scheduling and the placement of *telenovelas* in access prime time demonstrate Central European scheduling innovations that utilise the genre more flexibly than elsewhere in the world: in their domestic markets, *telenovelas* were mainly scheduled in prime time until the early 2000s, and primarily filled morning and afternoon dayparts in Western European markets, except for Spain, Portugal and Italy, where they occasionally found their way into prime time (Biltereyst and Meers, 2000, p. 403). While it is impossible to reconstruct the historical roots of these Central European scheduling innovations, their prevalence in markets across the region and the uniqueness of the phenomenon compared to markets in other regions of the world suggest that they stemmed primarily from regional sources. One Hungarian buyer I interviewed confirmed that she had several discussions with colleagues in the Czech Republic, Slovakia and Poland about which *telenovelas* to purchase and how to schedule them effectively, demonstrating how acquisitions and scheduling decisions often travel together in the global programme markets (Balogh, 2001).

By the time I returned to Hungary in 2002, several programmers informed me that the *telenovela* 'bubble' had burst (Balogh, 2002; Balázs, 2002; Havas, 2002). Bianca Balázs (2002), an acquisitions executive at TV2, explained, 'We had some time when we had a lot of *telenovelas* from Mexican companies, and it was a big hit for a while. And after one-and-a-half years, we had it slowly change. And now we can only use these programmes in the morning.' According to both programme buyers and programme sellers, the reason for the genre's decline between 2001 and 2002 was a change in viewers' preferences, who had grown tired of the genre. In fact, the main reason for the altered fortunes of *telenovelas* in Central Europe probably lies in changes at the largest television broadcasters in Mexico and Brazil, which also own the main production and distribution houses. As we saw in Chapter 2, these broadcaster-producers responded to increased competition from cable and satellite channels in their domestic markets by creating more *telenovelas* for niche audiences, which led to discrepancies among the primary audiences in the domestic and Hungarian markets. The resulting decline in *telenovela* acquisitions across the region hit distributors hard, and the slump in sales continued through 2004 (Sahab, 2004). As Figure 5.1 makes clear, *telenovelas* moved from primarily afternoon and evening slots to morning slots, where audiences and advertising revenues are both lower.

Regardless of the reasons for the dissipation of the *telenovela* trend in Hungary and the region, the perception of that change among programme schedulers

Figure 5.1: Comparison of Daytime Programme Schedule for TV2

Monday 6 August 2001		Monday 12 August 2002	
9:00	*Milady* (Arg. telenovela)	9:00	*Friends and Lovers* (Mex. novela)
9:25	Egy puha fészek (local talk show)	9:30	*Loving with Passion* (Sp.-Arg. novela)
10:10	Napló (local magazine show)	10:00	*Sonadoras* (Mex. novela)
11:00	Közvetlen ajánlat (home shopping)	10:30	Közvetlen ajánlat (home shopping)
12:05	News	11:15	*Wild Angel* (Arg. novela)
12:15	Riviéra (European co-produced serial)	12:00	Claudia (local talk show)
12:40	*Marimar* (Mex. novela)	12:45	Champion's Academy (UK teen series)
13:10	Lighting, the White Stallion (US feature, 1986)	13:10	Superstar (US feature, 1999)
14:50	Step by Step (US sitcom)	14:40	Kapcsoltam (local game show)
15:20	Treasures of the South Sea (Fr-Austral series)	15:15	F/X: The Series (US series)
16:10	*Bruised Hearts* (Mex. novela)	16:10	Melrose Place (US serial)
16:40	*Fiorella* (Peru. novela)	17:05	Yago (Argentine adventure series)
17:35	*Lucecita* (Arg. novela)	17:55	Aktív (local game show)
18:00	*Beauty of Acapulco* (Mex. novela)	18:30	Tények (local newsmagazine)
18:30	Tények (local news magazine)	19:05	Friends (US sitcom)
19:00	Szerencsekerék (local game show)	19:30	Tequila & Bonetti (US series)
19:30	*Wild Angel* (Arg. telenovela)		

Sources: Színes Kéthetes Tévéműsor (2001: p. 34 and 2002a: p. 4)

Notes:
Non-US titles are translated from the Hungarian and are not necessarily the original titles.
Titles of telenovelas are in bold italic.

led to a problem: what other kinds of programming might appeal to daytime viewers? Both TV2 and RTL Klub turned first to Hollywood series that they had acquired in film packages, especially teen dramas such as *Beverly Hills 90210* (1990–2000) and *Melrose Place* (1992–9) (see Figure 5.1). Normally, such series might have been 'burned' in overnight time-slots. In addition, both channels began to programme talk shows centred on personal relationships and social deviance that, collectively, have improved daytime ratings among younger male and female viewers and decreased imports in the time period (AGB Hungary, 2002; Balogh, 2002).

Decisions about how to programme *telenovelas* in Hungary and across Central Europe, as well as decisions about how to replace them, seem to have taken place outside the shadow of both the conglomerates who own the channels and the large *telenovela* distributors who sell the programming. The initial scheduling decisions were regional, rather than domestic in origin, facilitated by region-wide commercial organisations and industry conferences, while the replacement decisions were domestic in character. However, the economic realities of the Hungarian market severely limited programmers' options because they could only afford to schedule self-produced talk shows or unwanted acquisitions that were already 'on the shelves' in these time-slots. Thus, less profitable dayparts, such as daytime, are particularly open to regional and global trends in Hungary simply because they aren't worth the time or the cost that more tailored scheduling practices would require. Even when Hungarian programmers make their own decisions during daytime, those decisions are deeply influenced by Hollywood's dominance of the global programme markets, which have placed unwanted series from film packages on the broadcasters' shelves and diminished their capacity to purchase more relevant programming.

These observations, of course, refer only to the Hungarian market, and perhaps the other nations of Central Europe, but the general principle may have wider application. While programmers in different markets may define these less profitable dayparts differently, such dayparts exist in all markets, during which less money and effort are expended on developing the schedule. These are the dayparts that may be most open to regionally and globally standardised scheduling solutions, such as the use of *telenovelas* as daytime programming by many Western European broadcasters in the 1990s (Biltereyst and Meers, 2000). Such standardised scheduling practices, in turn, can lead to upsurges in the global sales revenues for the genres and the distributors that fill them.

INDIGENISING FOREIGN SCHEDULING PRACTICES: PRIMETIME REALITY SHOWS

Primetime schedules, at least at large commercial broadcasters, are the most carefully tailored to domestic viewer preferences, due to the economic importance of primetime advertising revenues. While this fact would seem to guarantee a large amount of home-grown scheduling practices and autonomy among domestic programmers, non-domestic scheduling practices can still find their way into domestic markets, where they may become commonplace. For instance, when a foreign-owned broadcaster's performance falters, foreign programme executives can become deeply involved. Moreover, because all broadcasters respond to domestic competitive conditions, successful foreign programming practices can influence domestic programmers at other channels as well.

Hungarian primetime programme schedules have undergone considerable change since the collapse of socialist state broadcasting and the introduction of private television channels with foreign investors. Although programmers also relied on imported programmes during socialism, they came mostly from other

Figure 5.2: Comparison of Hungarian Primetime Broadcast Schedules

MTV – 28 October 1988		MTV – 11 November 2002	
19:05	Workout series	19:00	*The Flintstones* (US animated series)
19:10	Children's cartoons	19:30	News
19:30	News	20:05	*Blue Light* (local crime magazine show)
20:05	Talk show	20:50	*Highlander 2* (US feature, 1991)
21:20	*Panorama* (world current affairs)		
22:05	*My Little Village* (Czech film, 1986)	22:45	News

Sources: Magyar-Szovjet Baráti Társaság (1988: p.28) and *Színes Kéthetes Tévéműsor* (2002d: p.34)

socialist nations and furthered political goals of cohesion among Eastern bloc nations, as opposed to current primetime schedules, where programmes from advanced capitalist nations serving commercial goals predominate. Moreover, while earlier schedules were certainly influenced by foreign practices, notably the BBC's avoidance of fixed-point scheduling, current primetime schedules demonstrate quite a few imported practices, including daily strip-scheduling, relatively fixed-point starting and ending times and the frequent use of US features during prime time (Figure 5.2). The scheduling of reality shows in Hungary provides a case study of how imported scheduling practices can spread throughout the domestic programme schedule, as well as how they get indigenised and can profoundly alter the acquisitions profile of a country.

Because of the size of the Hungarian market and the comparatively high production costs of fly-on-the-wall reality shows like Endemol's *Big Brother*, reality shows were slow to come to Hungary. Cable channel Viasat3 was the first to air such a series, *The Bar*, in 2000, which focused on contestants' efforts to successfully manage a local Budapest pub, and achieved quite good ratings for a small cable channel (Nadler, 2001). As a result of Viasat3's success, RTL Klub commissioned a study examining the feasibility of launching its own reality show. However, due to global instability in the advertising markets beginning in late 2000, which picked up speed throughout 2001, the broadcaster decided against creating a reality show, preferring to stick with less financially risky programming (Kolosi, 2002). At the same time, TV2 had fallen persistently out of the first-place ranking it had enjoyed since the launch of commercial television in 1997. As a result, senior executives from TV2's Scandinavian majority-owner, SBS Broadcasting, took a much more active role in the broadcaster's day-to-day operations, including an attempt to refocus the programming to target eighteen- to thirty-nine-year-old, urban viewers. As part of its new identity, TV2 decided to produce a local version of *Big Brother*, *Nagy Testvér*, to serve as the centre-piece of its 2002 primetime schedule (Balázs, 2002; Szőllőssy, 2002). Perhaps predictably, *Big Brother* became the opening salvo in a reality show battle that spread throughout Hungarian television.

Nagy Testvér arrived in Hungarian prime time accompanied by months of hype, including promotional features in magazines about the contestants, billboards that simply announced the starting date and countless promotional spots on TV2. Premiering on 1 September 2002, the show immediately shot to the top of the ratings, where it would remain until RTL Klub knocked it out in November with its own reality show. Rather than purchase an international format, RTL Klub resurrected the programme it had abandoned only a year earlier, dubbing the series *Való Világ* and promoting it as the 'Hungarian' reality show (Kolosi, 2002). However, even a less-than-casual observer could be forgiven for

Figure 5.3: Primetime Programme Schedules RTL Klub and TV2
(15 August 2002)

	RTL Klub	TV2
19:00	*Fókusz* (local magazine show)	*Friends* (US sitcom)
19:30	*The Clown* (German drama series)	*The Sentinel* (US drama series)
20:30	*Cover Up* (US feature, 1991)	*Spiders* (US feature, 2000)
22:00	National News	
22:30	Movie preview show	National News

Source: *Színes Kéthetes Tévéműsor* (2002a: p. 16)

Note: All times are approximate.

seeing little difference between the two programmes. *Nagy Testvér* featured ten strangers living together and enduring a variety of challenges, while the audience voted one of the contestants off the show each week until a single contestant remained. *Való Világ*, on the other hand, featured twelve contestants. The main difference among the shows was that the audience also voted contestants into the *Való Világ* house.

From the outset, *Big Brother* and *Való Világ* became the backbones of TV2's and RTL Klub's primetime schedules, muscling imported US series out of primetime hours. Spanning two or three distinct 'episodes' per day, instalments of the comings and goings of the contestants in both houses were used as 'hammocks' to support weaker shows, as lead-ins to build audiences for ensuing programming and as 'tent-poles' to support the entire primetime line-up. Prior to the beginning of reality shows, Hungarian prime time spanned 7pm–11 pm and was typically populated by local versions of international game shows, such as *Who Wants to Be a Millionaire?* (*Legyen Ön Is Milliomos?*), local infotainment magazines, and imported films and series, mostly from the US, Europe and Canada (see Figure 5.3). Initially, TV2 programmed a promotional, ten-minute *Nagy Testvér* teaser at 7pm, followed by a thirty-minute game show and an hour of the main episode of *Nagy Testvér* edited down from the previous day's happenings. Afterwards, TV2 aired a film or series, followed by a twenty-minute 'live', studio-based episode of *Nagy Testvér* at the end of prime time that recapped the earlier episode and included interviews with contestants and viewers' comments via phone and text messages (see Figure 5.4). Scheduling the

Figure 5.4: TV2's Initial Scheduling of *Nágy Testvér*
(9 September 2002)

19:00	*Nágy Testvér*
19:10	*Aktív* (local game show)
19:45	*Nágy Testvér*
20:45	*Frei-dosszié* (local tabloid show)
21:45	*Nyom nélkül* (local current affairs show)
22:45	*Nágy Testvér*
23:15	Late Evening News

Source: *Színes Kéthetes Tévéműsor* (2002b: p. 4)

show each night during prime time repeats the format's scheduling in its native Netherlands and throughout Western Europe, a practice that was obviously imported along with the format.

RTL Klub, on the other hand, initially programmed *Való Világ* against the main episode of *Nagy Testvér*, using *Való Világ* as a tent-pole for the lead-in info-tainment magazine *Fókusz* (see Figure 5.5). By October, however, the broadcaster moved *Való Világ* to the beginning of prime time and hammocked its infotainment magazine between *Való Világ* and the broadcaster's popular local soap opera, *Barátok Közt* (see Figure 5.6). This move demonstrated the growing popularity of *Való Világ*, which became the first locally produced reality show in the world to beat an adaptation of *Big Brother* in head-to-head competition (Kolosi, 2002). At one point, RTL Klub began using two full hours of *Való Világ* in prime time.

As these scheduling practices make clear, reality shows rather suddenly became a powerful force in Hungarian television, causing imported series to all but disappear from prime time. In the two weeks prior to the beginning of *Való Világ*, RTL Klub programmed seven imported series and seventeen imported films during primetime hours. During the first two weeks of *Való Világ*, RTL Klub had scaled back to using only fourteen imported films during prime time and no imported series. In the two-week period running from 21 October to 3 November 2002, RTL Klub programmed only eleven imported films during prime time and two imported series, both of which were episodes of *ER* (1994–). Marginal series, including the German series *Kommisar Rex* (1994-2004) and the US series *Third Watch* (1999–2005) were bumped out of prime time into late-night, late-afternoon and access primetime hours. Meanwhile the blockbuster series *ER*, which had been purchased to form the backbone of RTL Klub's primetime schedule, was relegated to a filler position between the local soap opera *Barátok Közt* and the Tuesday night movie. Non-blockbuster films likewise moved from prime time into the beginning of late-night and overnight hours. Therefore, although scheduling may not immediately influence the amount of imported programming at a channel, because all imported programming must eventually be shown, scheduling does influence the performance, importance and future of imported programming. The reality show boom in Hungary continues through the autumn of 2005 (at the time of writing), which

Figure 5.5: RTL Klub's Original Scheduling of *Való Világ*
(16 September 2002)

18:55	*Fókusz* (local magazine show)
19:30	*Való Világ*
20:10	*Barátok Közt* (local soap opera)

Source: *Színes Kéthetes Tévéműsor* (2002b: p. 34)

Figure 5.6: Changes in RTL Klub's Scheduling of *Való Világ*
(9 October 2002)

19:00	*Való Világ*
19:40	*Fókusz* (local magazine show)
20:10	*Barátok Közt* (local soap opera)

Source: *Színes Kéthetes Tévéműsor* (2002c: p. 12)

means that the decreased need for imported series and films has persisted for more than three years now.

While the steady expansion of reality shows throughout prime time on both major broadcasters may be unique to the Hungarian market, we may draw from it more general lessons about the relationship between scheduling practices and programme acquisitions, namely that programme schedules are potentially highly volatile and give distributors little guarantee from year to year that their programming will continue to be popular with buyers. In fact, these kinds of sudden changes are the reason why redistributors familiar with small markets are able to make a living from the global programme markets, as even the largest global distributors lack the staff necessary to keep up with all such changes in every market.

The volatility of programme schedules and their subsequent influence on acquisitions have led many distributors to begin 'educating' buyers on how to properly schedule their programmes (Sahab, 2004). This education entails advice on how to schedule acquisitions where they will find the greatest favour with viewers and how to adapt them to fit changing programming needs. The overall impact of all of these discussions among global programme merchants has led television channels in many parts of the world to adopt similar scheduling solutions, which has increased the spread of worldwide programming trends, even in the most advanced television markets. In the US, for instance, strip-scheduling in prime time was virtually unheard of at the national broadcast networks until the strategy was imported along with reality shows from Europe.

LEARNING FROM INTERNATIONAL CHANNELS: REALITY SHOWS IN LATE-NIGHT TIME-SLOTS

To influence domestic scheduling practices and acquisitions decisions, foreign programmers need not have direct interaction with domestic executives. In fact, most programmers of internationally distributed cable and satellite channels are probably unaware of the impact that their scheduling practices have on broadcasters in nations such as Hungary. Nevertheless, as this final case study examining the scheduling of 'adult' outtakes from Hungarian reality shows in late-night time-slots makes clear, domestic scheduling innovations often respond to pre-existing scheduling practices on international cable and satellite channels, again setting the scene for the circulation of programming trends abroad.

As mentioned above, TV2 began programming a twenty-minute daily recap and live interview episode of *Nagy Testvér* on the day after the show's premiere at the end of prime time, running from 10.50–11.10pm. The main purpose of this episode was not only to promote the show for those who had missed the primetime episode, but also to increase discussion of the show in internet chat rooms, to promote the show's premium website and to make additional revenues from mobile phone text messages. Similarly, RTL Klub began a late-night episode of *Való Világ* during the show's second week, by which time all of the contestants had moved into the house. This late night episode moved around in the schedule quite a bit during the show's fifteen-week run, appearing initially after midnight, then stripped at the end of prime time Monday through Thursday and finally settling into a Monday through Thursday midnight slot, with an earlier slot on Friday (Figure 5.7). RTL Klub's later episode, which was quickly copied by TV2, included many of the 'steamier' outtakes from the cameras in the home, including grainy, night-vision footage of contestants involved in sexual encounters, women and (less frequently) men taking showers and heated arguments among contestants, laced with profanity.

RTL Klub's scheduling of the late-night episode of *Való Világ* reflects an awareness of the episode's drawing power. The Hungarian Media Law of 1996 prevents broadcasters from airing sexually explicit or excessively violent programming such as the adult episodes of *Való Világ* before 10pm (ORTT, 1996), but such restrictions still allowed the broadcasters a good deal of play in deciding how best to schedule the episodes. Initially isolated after midnight, the adult episodes moved up in the schedule to a position on the cusp between prime time and late night, where it operated as a lead-in to such US series as *The Sopranos* (1999–) and *The West Wing* (1999–), as well as late-night movies. The episode also countered erotic programming on international cable and satellite channels, such as soft-core movies and HBO's *Real Sex* (2000–) and

Figure 5.7: Scheduling of *Való Világ* and *Nágy Testvér*
(12 November 2002)

	RTL Klub	TV2
19:00	*Fókusz* (local magazine show)	*Aktív* (local game show)
19:30	*Való Világ*	*Szeret, nem Szeret* (Can. sitcom)
20:00		*Nágy Testvér*
21:00	*Barátok Közt* (local soap opera)	*Universal Soldier 3* (US film, 1998)
21:30	*ER* (US series)	
22:30	*Való Világ*	*Nágy Testvér – Élö* (live)

Source: *Színes Kéthetes Tévémüsor* (2002d: p. 38)

Note: All times approximate.

Shock Video (2001–) on Viasat3, a nationwide cable channel primarily programmed in London; erotic movies on imported commercial German broadcasters; and a non-premium cable pornography feed from the UK's Private Network (Figure 5.8).

These scheduling changes altered late-night programming in a manner similar to the way that reality shows changed Hungarian prime time. Underperforming series and unexceptional films were pushed further into late-night and overnight hours, where fewer and fewer viewers would watch them. The resulting poor ratings for these programmes gives Hungarian buyers added clout when negotiating package deals with Hollywood distributors, because they now have ratings data to back up their claims that certain kinds of series and movies will underperform, and also because they simply cannot use as many programmes.

On one hand, then, the use of reality show outtakes in late-night time-slots has helped increase local production and decrease broadcasters' reliance on imported programmes in Hungary. On the other hand, it would be a mistake to see this change as evidence of greater cultural autonomy on the parts of the broadcasters, and not only because they have become reliant on imported programme formats. Perhaps more importantly, this final case study demonstrates how the very conception of the audience and its pleasures is a hybrid of local and imported ideas, regardless of whether the programming is domestically produced or imported. That is, while the idea of scheduling adult outtakes of *Való Világ* after midnight is a Hungarian programming innovation, the ideas underlying the innovation regarding the make-up of the late-night audience and how best to target that audience were borrowed from foreign sources. The fact that RTL Klub conceived of using outtakes that were unsuitable for prime time as a way to target young men demonstrates how schedulers' ideas about the possibilities of television, its various audiences and the pleasures they seek are influenced by their surveillance of other channels, regardless of whether those channels are domestic or foreign. Of course, the decision to use erotic programming to attract young male viewers may seem like an obvious choice. My point is not that this perception of the audience and its pleasures is inaccurate,

Figure 5.8: Comparison of RTK Klub and Viasat3 Late Night Programme Schedules
(11 November 2002)

	RTL Klub	Viasat3
23:00	*Die Hard* (US feature, 1988)	*Witchblade* (US series)
23:30		*Jerry Springer* (US talk show)
0:00	*Való Világ*	*The Simpsons* (US series)
0:30	*Deadly Intentions* (US TV movie)	*Real Sex* (US erotic series)

Source: *Színes Kéthetes Tévéműsor* (2002: p. 34)

Notes: All times approximate.

but rather that there are probably an infinite number of ways of conceiving of the audience and its preferences. The fact that these particular conceptions determined scheduling practices at RTL Klub demonstrates how the broadcaster's interpretation of its audience depended as much on imported models as it did on home-grown ones. Again, we see that hybrid Hungarian scheduling practices help create the conditions necessary for the development of transnational programming trends, even in the absence of direct influence from abroad.

Of course, depending upon the size and buying power of the market, programme schedules at international cable and satellite channels exhibit varying degrees of localisation, regardless of the national origin of the channel's owners. Thus, foreign-owned cable and satellite channels in the US, such as BBC America and Reality TV, have adopted the US cable practice of block scheduling episodes of the same series back-to-back throughout the day (Cole, 2004; BBC America, 2005). As foreign-owned cable and satellite channels in smaller markets such as Hungary develop, they are likely to design more tailored scheduling practices, as they currently do when they open channels in larger markets. At present, however, these channels continue to constitute a major route by which foreign scheduling practices and programming trends enter the domestic market and alter the country's acquisitions profile.

CONCLUSION

The cases analysed here make it clear that both local and imported forms of knowledge about viewers' behaviours and preferences constitute contemporary scheduling practices at the Hungarian commercial broadcasters. While such hybridity has been recognised as a significant element in the indigenisation and impact of cultural imports, its presence and significance in the institutional cultures and industrial practices of media organisations typically goes unnoticed. These institutions function as screens between the strategies of large multinational media conglomerates and the tactics of local viewers, as domestic executives with varying degrees of clout in international programming circles strive to match the perceived preferences of their audiences with available and affordable offerings.

Although the Hungarian experience may be unique in some ways, not least because it lacks a larger linguistic partner with whom to trade programming and ideas, several of the observations here may apply equally well to broadcasters elsewhere. Regions and transnational conglomerates probably provide conduits for the dissemination of knowledge about scheduling for broadcasters everywhere. In every nation, the competitive structure of the market for viewers profoundly influences scheduling practices and the pace of scheduling change, which create worldwide programming trends and increasingly volatile programme schedules.

Of course, significant portions of the scheduling grid remain predominantly domestic in their origins. In Hungary, for instance, the nightly news on the public-service broadcaster remains, as always, at 7.30 p.m. (see Figure 5.1), and prime time on New Year's Eve is dominated by live variety shows. Such traditional scheduling practices retain a good deal of their domestic character, whereas newer practices that have developed since the globalisation of media ownership and programming markets tend towards hybridity. This hybridity, moreover, mirrors the unequal power relations among the world's economies, such that richer nations and corporations tend to have more power to define programming trends, in part because higher potential profits in these markets encourage greater experimentation, but also because those practices are more widely reported in the trade journals, spread through Western-programmed channels and frequently seen by industry insiders as international best practices.

Of course, as with other forms of discourse, alternative ideas and practices also circulate and dominant practices are never secure. In all likelihood, scheduling practices operate much as programming practices, with telecasters relying heavily on imports in their early years of operation and increasing domestic content later on. However, the point that I want to emphasise is that scheduling is both dynamic and hybrid in today's world, and even the most powerful television markets are not immune to imported scheduling practices.

The hybrid nature of programme scheduling has a profound influence on the global television marketplace. When scheduling practices change, they profoundly alter a channel's and a nation's programme import profile. Each of the innovations described above altered the flow of programming into Hungary. The shift from using *telenovelas* throughout daytime severely decreased Latin American imports. The spread of the reality show *Való Világ* during prime time on RTL Klub caused a 42 per cent drop in the number of hours of imported prime-time programmes within two months. Finally, the use of adult outtakes in late-night time-slots bumped second-rate films and TV series picked up in package deals further into the overnight hours, a fact that is likely to give Hungarian buyers more power to be choosy when putting packages together.

Scheduling drives not only the decision-making process in global television sales, but also the structure of the industry. For instance, the reason that small, regional or thematic redistributors can exist in the global television marketplace is because scheduling practices worldwide change so quickly that even the largest distributors cannot keep up with the schedules everywhere, whereas small redistributors can track such changes more closely because of their familiarity with the market. Thus, the relationships among scheduling practices, programme trade and the globalisation of ownership and programme markets deserve much closer attention from scholars seeking to understand the cultural sources and consequences of the global television marketplace.

6

Programme Acquisitions at Transnational Channels

Our discussion about acquiring international programming has thus far concentrated on nationwide channels because much of the industry still conceives of the audience as a national mass, and because the global television programme business continues to define each nation as a unique market with unique pricing structures. While broadcasting never neatly obeyed national boundaries, satellite channels opened the possibility to cover much larger geographical areas than broadcasting, particularly satellite channels that are delivered via cables, which are cheaper for consumers than satellite dishes. We saw in Chapter 1 how prevalent industry conceptions of the audience as a national bloc stymied the growth of transnational satellite channels for many years, but with the expansion of demographically targeted satellite and cable channels in the 1990s, the global television industry needed to revise many of its long-standing business practices to accommodate these non-national buyers. However, despite the growing numbers of transnational buyers, only those channels that concentrate on lower-prestige genres or that have close ties with large distributors fair well when competing in the global television programme markets.

While transnational channels have the benefit of offering one-stop shopping for global advertisers and programme distributors, their Achilles heel is their general lack of audience appeal. To begin with, most transnational channels are carried on cable, which generally has a smaller audience reach than broadcasting. In addition, most transnational channels target a single audience segment with niche-oriented programming, again limiting their potential appeal. Finally, many transnational channels are programmed from abroad, and do not fit as well into the competitive environment of other channels or viewers' behaviour patterns as well as channels that are programmed locally. In fact, Jean Chalaby (2002) reports that transnational satellite channels rarely attract more than 1 per cent of the nationwide audience share in Europe. Still, in 2000, such channels attracted nearly $500 million in advertising revenues (ibid., p. 199).

The reasons why such poorly performing channels can still attract a moderate amount of advertising revenue are twofold: first, they attract specific demographics from multiple territories, potentially offering advertisers a highly attractive and engaged segment of the audience, whose composite size across the various nations where they operate is substantial; second, the sheer reach of transnational channels can make them attractive for smaller-calibre advertisers or programme distributors who want to reach the largest possible audiences with the smallest possible investment of time, effort, or capital. In other words, for advertisers and distributors whose primary interests are keeping costs down, transnational channels can offer an attractive alternative.

Transnational channels range from localised versions of globally branded channels, such as MTV Italy, MTV Poland and MTV Spain, to channels that transmit a single programme feed in a single language across several markets, such as BBC World. Obviously, both the acquisitions and scheduling practices of such channels differ markedly depending on the form of transnationalisation that they take. According to Chalaby (ibid.), in Europe, transnational channels operated by public broadcasters and those with distinctly European-wide remits are less likely to engage in localisation than channels that are part of the globalising strategies of transnational corporations. In addition, the degree of localisation that transnational channels need in order to compete effectively with national channels depends upon the geolinguistic make-up of the regions they operate in. Some channels, such as Sony's AXN channel, which targets young male audiences with action films and action series, requires a good deal of localisation because it operates in several different language markets across Asia, Latin America and Central Europe (AXN, 2004). Others, such as the Latin American women's channel GEMs, require little localisation because all of the members of its target audiences speak the same language (Whitefield, 1999).

In a related manner, the level of localisation at a transnational channel depends on the intended target market and its importance for the channel and its advertisers. Thus, BBC World targets elite professional viewers across Europe who can understand English (Chalaby, 2002, p. 196). Fox Kids in Slovenia, on the other hand, broadcasts in English not because it targets English-speaking children but because dubbing into Slovenian would not be a profitable venture. Finally, as Chalaby notes, the level of localisation of a transnational channel seems to be related to its primary programming genres. Thus, news programming is 'less deeply rooted in one culture' than entertainment genres, and transnational news channels experience a smaller cultural discount as compared with, say, children's programming (ibid.).

In this chapter, we will focus on both niche and general entertainment transnational channels that operate in both linguistic and non-linguistic markets. For purposes of this chapter, I will define transnational channels as only those channels that have some degree of multinational audience reach and programme acquisition strategy, rather than nationally branded versions of international channels, such as MTV Italy, which may have management overlap but that buy and programme their channels independently from their parent companies. The reason I make this distinction is that I want to diagnose how such channels compete in the markets for global programming and viewers, which are dominated by nationally bound channels.

Chalaby distinguishes among European transnational channels based upon four degrees of localisation: the use of local advertising; the dubbing or subtitling of programme feeds in local languages; the scheduling of some local programming; and local opt-out, or 'fully regionalized operations and production facilities' (ibid. p. 194). Often, however, the same transnational channel engages in each of these strategies in different markets or regions of the world. For our purposes, it makes more sense to distinguish between transnational channels based upon the geographic reach of their programming feeds, since this fact influences the channel's capacity to compete in international programme markets and to schedule effectively against competing channels. Some channels are nearly global in their reach, and only split their feeds into multi-continental regions to account for worldwide time-zone differences. Others cover a smaller transnational area, taking advantage of regional satellite or cable operations and multinational discounts from distributors. This chapter addresses one global satellite channel, Reality TV, and two regional channels, HBO Central Europe and the Hungarian-language channel Duna TV, which, respectively, operate in the mainstream and at the margins of the global television marketplace.

The main argument of this chapter is that, despite the increase in transnational channels in recent years, markets for viewers and imported programming remain primarily national in orientation, making the jobs of acquisitions and scheduling uniquely challenging. Moreover, those channels that conform to dominant industry perceptions of what a transnational channel should be have an easier time acquiring programming and, consequently, attracting viewers.

PROGRAMMING STRATEGIES AT GLOBAL SATELLITE CHANNELS
Global satellite channels operate a handful of different programming feeds, whose programming comes primarily from low-cost genres that are widely available in the global marketplace. Each feed has its own programme schedule and varying degrees of language localisation. For instance, commercial transnational channels such as Discovery, Fox Kids, Animal Planet, VH1, Cartoon Network and Viva all rely on lower-end documentary, animation and music video genres to fill airtime. Part of the reason such channels can thrive relates to the cheapness and ubiquity of programming that they have to choose from on the global programme markets. However, since they must compete for rights with buyers in multiple markets, acquisitions are more complicated and relationships with

distributors perhaps even more important than they are for nationally bound channels.

Global satellite channels tend to proliferate in large markets that are saturated with channel capacity or in smaller markets where costs are low and multichannel operators are looking for cheap channels to fill bandwidth. In large markets, programme offerings and schedules are carefully tailored to local competitive conditions and audience behaviour, whereas programme feeds that reach across multiple small territories are scheduled from abroad with only a general sense of what other channels may be offering or what viewers might want to watch. Obviously, the degree of localisation depends upon the perceived economic importance of each market, and that status can change over time. In fact, many global channels employ a gradual localisation process, slowly tailoring their language of operation, their acquisitions decisions and their schedules as they gain audience share and advertising revenues.

The distribution of global satellite channels is analogous in many ways to the distribution of global programming. One common way that these channels expand into new markets is by securing a carriage deal with a cable or satellite operator in a major Western nation, especially the US or the UK. Much as a sale in a major territory can help a programme and its distributor gain global visibility and credibility, carriage deals in such markets can provide transnational channels and their distributors with crucial prestige that can help them negotiate agreements in other territories. Consequently, the kinds of global channels that are commercially viable today tend to be those whose programming appeals to viewers in affluent nations and that operate in commonly traded global genres.

Reality TV, a global satellite channel specialising in unscripted vérité reality programming, offers a prime example of the acquisitions challenges that global satellite channels face. Reality TV is owned by Zone Vision Networks, a formerly independent European satellite channel distributor that was taken over in 2005 by multinational cable operator UnitedGlobalCom. Like many satellite channels, Zone Vision is located in the UK because of that nation's liberal laws governing transnational satellite transmission and the renewal of satellite licences (ibid., p. 185). In addition to Reality TV, Zone Vision programmes Romantica, a *telenovela*-based channel concentrated in Central Europe, and Europa Europa, a channel dedicated to European films carried mostly by European cable operators. All of these channels build their brands around abundantly available and generally cheap programme genres. Zone Vision also represents some of the largest transnational channels in their negotiations with cable operators and advertising agencies, including Hallmark, MTV Music Television and Discovery (Zone Vision, 2004b).

Reality TV is Zone Vision's signature channel, reaching 35 million cable and satellite viewers in 125 territories in 2004, including the US (Brennan, 2004). Reality TV began in 1999, when Zone Vision secured a carriage agreement with cable MSO United Pan Cable (UPC), the largest MSO in Central Europe (Major, 2001). Initially limited to the Polish market, Reality TV spread to Hungary, Turkey, Israel, Russia, the Czech Republic, Slovakia and Bulgaria in late 2000 and early 2001, before breaking into Scandinavia and the Netherlands in late 2001. In 2002, the channel launched in Latin America, Latvia, Lithuania, Estonia, Romania, Croatia, Macedonia, Serbia, Greece and Africa, as well as the UK, where it is carried on both digital direct-to-home (DTH) satellite and cable. The next markets were Ireland, the Philippines, Thailand, Singapore, Hong Kong, Taiwan, Portugal, Germany and the US in 2003, with discussions currently under way to launch in France, Spain and Italy (Brennan, 2004; *Channel 21*, 2001; *Channel 21*, 2002; *Channel 21*, 2003; *Channel 21*, 2004a; Holmes, 2004; Meils, 2000; Newbery, 2002; Stewart, 2003; Turner, 2002; Waller, 2002).

The list of nations where Reality TV has launched seems to support the company's vision of the channel as 'the first commercial global network to be created from outside the US' (*PR Newswire*, 2003). Zone Vision particularly targets digital terrestrial television (DTT) systems that have high channel capacity (Holmes, 2004). The overhead costs of DTT are markedly lower than digital DTH or digital cable services, which require massive investments in infrastructure and satellite transponder rents, and usually target higher-income audiences with higher-end channels, such as movie and cultural channels. In many ways, Reality TV represents the future of global programme trade, which will likely entail the buying and selling of rights to include entire channels in various national and transnational digital television platforms. These channels, in turn, will feature transnational programming from a limited number of programme genres, thus restructuring programming windows and relationships among programme buyers and sellers profoundly.

Zone Vision follows a dual strategy of national and regional devolution, customising some channels to national audiences and some to regional audiences. The company retains five different programme schedules for Reality TV, including feeds for the UK, the US, Latin America, EMEA (Europe, the Middle East and Africa) and Asia/India (Reality TV, 2004; *Television Business International*, 2004). In countries covered by a regional feed, some channels are broadcast in local languages, while others are broadcast in English. In Europe, for instance, the Czech Republic and Germany receive local-language versions, while Macedonia and Portugal receive English-language feeds (*Channel 21*, 2003; *Broadcast*, 2004; Waller, 2002). All of these regional feeds rely on programming purchased from the global markets. The US and UK markets, on the other hand, have devoted channel management executives and distinct acquisitions practices. As much as 10 per cent of the programming on Reality TV in the US has been specifically commissioned by Zone Vision for that market (Reynolds and Donohue, 2003).

Reality TV acquires a reported 3,000 hours of reality programming per year from global television distributors, typically purchasing worldwide rights for programming, which it then televises across its five feeds (*Television Business International*, 2004). Its main distributors come from the US, the UK and other English-speaking territories, including US producers Universal, MGM, Twentieth Television, CBS, GRB Entertainment, RDF Media and Rive Gauche International Television, as well as UK producers BBC Worldwide and Carlton International. Several independent Canadian, British and Australian distributors also consistently sell programming to Reality TV. Beyond the English-speaking nations, the Netherlands and Spain supply the largest amount of Reality TV's schedules (Abraham, 2004; *Hollywood Reporter*, 2004b; *PR Newswire*, 2003).

Reality TV relies on the economies of scope offered by its worldwide operations and the cheapness of reality programming for its survival as a commercial venture. Dermot Shortt, CEO of Zone Vision, explains, 'The only way super-niche channels such as Reality ... can make the numbers work is if you leverage the costs over more than one market. ... You have to be able to leverage your program rights and playout costs, marketing and promotional costs across several markets' (Marsh, 2003). Chris Wronski, Zone Vision's president and CEO, concurs: 'With every new country, the company becomes a better deal. Channels are cheaper per subscriber' (Major, 2001). In other words, the more channels Reality TV opens worldwide, the more its per-viewer costs for programme rights, satellite time, translation and marketing decrease. Despite these economies of scope, as a relatively small, independent channel operator, Zone Vision has tight profit margins that it protects fiercely. For instance, all dubbing and subtitling, graphics and promotional materials are developed in Warsaw, in order to save on equipment and labour costs (Cole, 2004; Major, 2001).

The reason that a niche channel based on reality programming is viable worldwide has as much to do with programme costs as it does with the universal appeal of the genre. Not only are the programme costs associated with reality programming low because no actors or writers need to be paid, but the costs of portable technology continue to decrease, making it even cheaper to produce reality shows. As Zone Vision's Shortt puts it, 'the advantages of reality TV are that the genre unit price actually falls by the day as the number of CCTV cameras increases. The supply of footage is exponentially going up, while the cost of editing it is also collapsing' (Marsh, 2003).

As with buyers from nationally oriented channels, personal relationships among distributors and buyers from global satellite channels shape worldwide flows of television programming. In addition, these relationships influence the development and operations of global channels. Zone Vision began as a Central European redistributor, purchasing and reselling programme rights from moderate-sized Western European companies. As its executives built relationships with programme suppliers and buyers throughout the 1990s, the company moved into channel representation in Central Europe for some of the best-known transnational channels, taking advantage of both its relationships with the channels and with regional cable and satellite providers (Zone Vision, 2004a). Romantica, Zone Vision's *telenovela* channel, and Reality TV were natural outgrowths of the relationships that Zone Vision established in its channel representation business. Not only did the company have an inside track when it came to selling new channels to Central European cable and satellite operators, it also had long-standing relationships with programme producers that it could draw on to fill its new channels' broadcasting schedules (Cole, 2004). Thus, the relationships that develop within the global programme markets inevitably spread to other areas of the television industry, as programming executives interact with executives in a variety of other areas of the business.

In addition to giving Reality TV access to programme distributors and cable operators, personal relationships also help the channel get clearance in all of the markets where it operates, which is one of its primary acquisitions considerations. That is, in order to buy programming for its EMEA feed, Reality TV must be certain that programme rights are available in almost every territory across three continents. Because of Reality TV's relationships with its distributors, the channel can sometimes convince distributors to renegotiate settled deals with other buyers when Reality TV needs a particular programme in a particular market. Steve Cole, vice president of Reality TV, explains the process in more detail: 'At Carlton, ... one of their sales managers ... went to all the stations where there were little issues of rights and cleared them, and that netted them a significant deal' (ibid.). In some instances, distributors do not have individual sales agents that can cover the entire area for which Reality TV wants rights, complicating some deals and making others impossible. This is especially the case with large companies, where Cole often needs to negotiate with numerous sales agents in order to secure rights for all of Reality TV's feeds. 'If I've got a show that I want to take across every feed, a small company is going to have, normally, one person or two people dealing with their portfolio,' he explains, 'whereas at the bigger companies, they obviously split up into territories,' and different sales executives deal with each different territory (ibid.). Thus, the large distributors' organisational structure conflicts with the acquisitions and scheduling needs of a transnational channel like Reality TV.

ACQUISITIONS AND SCHEDULING AT PREMIUM SATELLITE CHANNELS

At the other end of the spectrum from global channels that feature bargain-price genres are highly devolved regional channels that serve as pre-broadcast windows for premium programming. Offered via subscription or top-end digital cable and satellite packages, these channels take advantage of multi-territory programme rights discounts, even as they maintain separate feeds for each language community served, and often provide nationally tailored programme schedules, since they require viewers to pay premium prices to receive the channels. Ironically, although these channels primarily rely on Hollywood product to attract viewers, in their effort to maintain subscribers they often programme a good deal of local and regional fare that may not otherwise find its way onto television.

HBO International is perhaps the quintessential channel operator in this category. HBO's internationalisation strategy began as one that combined both localisation and regionalisation, with national pay channel HBO Hungary launching only days before HBO Olé in 1991, which covered all of Spanish-speaking Latin America. Throughout the 1990s, HBO introduced HBO Asia, HBO India, HBO Poland, HBO Czech, HBO Slovakia, HBO Romania and HBO Brazil, continuing its dual practice of localisation and regionalisation. In 1999, in an instance of reverse-localisation, the Central European channels were combined under a single umbrella, HBO Central Europe. In a similar vein, HBO India has expanded to serve viewers in Bangladesh, Maldives and Pakistan. In 2004, HBO International claimed 16 million subscribers in more than fifty countries, not including the US (HBO, 2004). Although HBO in the US is owned by AOL-Time Warner, its international channels are typically owned by a variety of co-operative arrangements with other major Hollywood studios (*Multichannel News*, 2004). HBO Central Europe, for instance, is owned by a consortium that includes Disney, Sony and Time Warner.

The spread of HBO's international channels around the world reflects its efforts to find markets that were powerful enough to support premium channels, yet new enough that the Hollywood majors did not have output deals in the region. Indeed, of the top ten television programme rights markets in the world outside the US, HBO International has channels in only two, Italy and Spain. In most of Western Europe, HBO still does not operate channels. In the early 1990s, HBO channels could not have been introduced in these large markets because a new competitor in the pay-television window would have soured relationships with terrestrial broadcasters who had signed massive volume deals for Hollywood product. By the mid-1990s, when those volume deals ran out, Western European groups such as KirchMedia aggressively fought to renew them because they had created their own pay-television services, including digital bouquets of movie channels that promised to take significantly more product than a channel like HBO.

It is not, then, by accident that Hungary, Poland and the Czech Republic were three of the first markets where HBO International expanded. As these societies lurched from state-planned economies to rampantly capitalist ones in the late 1980s and early 1990s, a number of well-placed party functionaries and entrepreneurs profited handsomely from the privatisation of formerly state-run businesses. In addition, advertising money began to pour into these markets, which were the strongest in the former Soviet bloc and promised rapid economic growth. Finally, national media laws were revised in the transition and often welcomed Western investment and businesses, including channels like HBO (Downing, 1996; Petkovič, 2004). Thus, Central European markets offered HBO International a chance to target a newly created economic elite with premium programming at a premium price. Here, there were no large terrestrial buyers to offend by introducing a pay-television window. Still, in its early years, HBO Hungary primarily programmed low-budget action movies because it lacked the resources to compete with the public broadcaster MTV for new releases.

On the other hand, HBO channels developed in the Latin American and Asian regions for slightly different reasons. Here, Hollywood distributors lacked volume deals due to a large amount of self-production by broadcasters in the regions. Furthermore, in the early 1990s, predictions about the growth of pay-television throughout Latin America and Asia were rosy, and HBO's introduction of region-wide channels demonstrates its attempt to be one of the first channels to capitalise on those trends (de la Fuente, 1997; Langdale, 1997). The later creation of locally devolved versions of these regional channels in Brazil and the Indian subcontinent reflect a strategy similar to NewsCorp's SkyAsia services and Music Television's (MTV) international channels, where efforts to blanket an entire region with a single transnational channel are eventually replaced by more locally targeted channels when local competition arises (Chalaby, 2002). Thus, not unlike the example of Reality TV above, the contractual and personal relationships among global television merchants determined the timing and placement of HBO International's channels.

As with all devolved transnational channels, HBO International's channels each handle their own programme acquisitions and scheduling. In addition to the conventional mix of recent Hollywood blockbusters, HBO International channels typically programme imported series and local films that they help co-produce. For instance, HBO Hungary has screened *Falcon Crest* (1981–90), *Melrose Place* (1992–9), *Friends* (1994–2004) and *South Park* (1997–), and has co-produced and aired such Hungarian films as *Szamba* (1996) and *Rosszfiúk* (2000) (Burman, 1995; *Electronic Media*, 1995). Meanwhile HBO original series, such as *The Sopranos* and *Sex and the City*, do not necessarily appear on HBO International channels, because they are sold on the open market by distributors such as Paramount International Television (Marenzi, 2004).

In order to explore the specific acquisitions practice of HBO International in more depth, it is helpful to concentrate on a single channel. HBO Central Europe, which presently comprises HBO Bulgaria, HBO Czech, HBO Hungary, HBO Poland, HBO Romania and HBO Slovakia, and was formed in 1999 when the acquisitions, programming and transmission functions of the constituent channels were centralised, with the exception of HBO Bulgaria, which began operations in 2004. Prior to 1999, each of the five Central European HBO channels fielded its own acquisitions team, although they had frequent contact with one another in order to help facilitate region-wide discounts for particularly expensive product. Since evolving its regional organisation, HBO Central Europe's purchasing decisions have been made by a board of executives representing each of the constituent channels.

Despite the fact that acquisitions decisions are made as a group, HBO Central Europe maintains separate feeds and separate profiles for each of its national channels. In part, this practice of using different programming and scheduling on the various national channels results from the fact that the availability of rights to programming differs among nations. Furthermore, the channels have somewhat different profiles, because each channel developed independently for several years before being consolidated under one roof. HBO Poland, for instance, shows a good deal more domestic programming than its counterparts.

As mentioned, HBO channels in the region initially had trouble acquiring recent Hollywood blockbusters, because those movies were either promised to others in output deals or too expensive for the upstart channels to afford. Since the mid-1990s, however, a pay-television distribution window has existed throughout the region, and HBO Central Europe has few if any competitors in this window. Instead, because film distribution windows in the region move from theatrical release to video release before entering the pay-television window, HBO Central Europe's primary competition for viewers comes from video stores, which rent new releases at relatively low prices before they appear on HBO Central European channels, thereby threatening HBO Central Europe's subscriber base. In addition, with the gradual introduction of DTH satellite services such as Sony's AXN in the region, HBO Central Europe has begun to face stiffer competition for pay-television rights to new releases.

HBO Central Europe acquires region-wide pay-television rights to Hollywood films and series, Western European films, Central European films and a small number of films from other areas. The organisation buys packages from Hollywood distributors, which typically contain films and a small number of cult or blockbuster series. HBO Hungary, for instance, has recently aired *Friends*, *South Park* and *Six Feet Under* (2001–5). From Western European producers, HBO Central Europe also buys film packages, though in lesser quantities than it buys from Hollywood. Generally, HBO Central Europe works with about fifteen Western European distributors from whom it acquires most of its European films, but it frequently finds new producers as well. In Central Europe, on the other hand, HBO Central Europe primarily programmes co-productions in which it has an interest, as well as films that win national or international awards.

In terms of the diversity of genres and sources of Western and Central European content, then, HBO Central Europe fairs better than most broadcasters or cable channels, whether publicly or commercially supported. In addition, much like HBO in the US, HBO Central Europe's executives claim that the channel broadcasts 'quality' programming in comparison with the unimaginative, populist fair on other channels. Of course, as students of popular culture would remind us, definitions of 'quality' in television are riddled with aesthetic judgments that reflect the preferences, desires and worldviews of the socially powerful (for example, Fiske, 1987). Furthermore, the most common measure of quality in film and television production – the size of the production budget – does little more than reinforce the bias that richer is better. Finally, executives' claims that their programming is superior in quality to their competitors must surely be questioned. Still, it is undoubtedly true that many of the imported series and regional films shown on HBO Central Europe's channels differ from other television outlets and do increase the diversity of Central Europe's television cultures.

Much of the reason that HBO Central Europe can provide different kinds of programming is that, like its US counterparts, it is subscription-based, rather than advertiser-supported, which causes its acquisitions and programming practices to differ greatly from advertiser-supported services. The goal of HBO International channels is not to attract the widest possible audience to sell to advertisers, but rather to attract new subscribers and retain them from month to month. The main commodity that HBO International sells is access to recent films and blockbuster television series, which are available to subscribers earlier and more frequently than on other channels, giving subscribers not only privileged access to certain programmes but also more control over when they watch them. Secondarily, HBO International offers a venue for cult programming and local programming that otherwise might not find a television audience. HBO Central Europe's avoidance of output deals reflects these priorities, as the organisation tries hard to minimise the amount of unwanted programming it picks up from the major distributors because its schedule of programme rotation allows for far fewer undesirable time-slots during which unwanted programmes can be burned. Ironically, this lack of capacity is a large part of what forced the HBO channels in Central Europe to regionalise: since the channels were not bulk-buyers, they had to take rights for a larger number of territories in order to make it worthwhile for the majors to maintain a pay window in Central Europe, especially as prices at the commercial broadcasters increased in the mid- and late 1990s.

The regional organisational structure of HBO Central Europe and its centralised manner of making acquisitions decisions detracts somewhat from the freedom of its constituent channels, as such decisions must be weighed against the economic and programming needs of the organisation as a whole. To a large extent, these observations apply to the kinds of programming HBO Central Europe specialises in, which are generally high-ticket items. As noted, the prices of such programming and the sales practices of the major distributors, especially in pay-television windows, require buyers either to take a large amount of programming or to purchase rights for a variety of territories. In this way, transnational channels such as HBO Central Europe have one more bargaining chip in their negotiations with the majors than nationally based outlets which, as we saw in Chapter 4, are limited to either paying higher prices or taking larger quantities to get the programming they want.

In an ironic twist, the very uniqueness of the acquisitions practices at subscription-based channels, which help bring diverse programming into the market, also dampen that diversity because no local knowledge, history, or experience in programming such channels exists for executives to draw upon. Local executives first needed to learn the regimens of the HBO programming model and its acquisition strategies before they could be trusted with independent decisions. Unlike the head of programming at TV3 Hungary, discussed in the previous chapter, who agreed to schedule *Married with Children* as a prime-time lead-in against his best instincts, the executives at HBO Central Europe's channels did not even possess such instincts, because the programming models they were working with were so foreign.

ACQUISITIONS AND SCHEDULING AT MINORITY SATELLITE CHANNELS

Thus far, the transnational channels we have examined are speciality channels built primarily around a small number of programming genres. By contrast, some transnational channels acquire more generically diverse programmes in an effort to address a broader audience, particularly channels targeted at ethnic or linguistic minorities in multiple nations. Channels that target large minority groups, especially those from nations with active television industries, such as European Turks, can fill their schedules with self-produced programming or programmes sourced from the home-state (Aksoy, n.d.). Others, such as the transnational Hungarian-language channel Duna TV, must rely on the global programme markets to help fill their schedules.

Because general entertainment programmes are usually sold to large broadcasters in each nation, the acquisitions aims of non-niche minority channels work against the grain of the global television marketplace. In addition, some distributors treat transnational satellite channels as a premium distribution window prior to terrestrial broadcasting and therefore charge more for acquisitions in this window, often driving up prices beyond what minority channels can afford. Thus, because the programme formats of these channels do not fit the business practices of global television, it can be difficult for them to operate effectively. Instead, channels that target minority niches in multiple territories are better positioned to compete for programming, and hence viewers, because niche genres are generally more abundant and cheaper. For instance, Zone Vision Networks was exploring the idea of launching Turkish-language channels in Europe and Turkey aimed at young male viewers before the channel was taken over by UnitedGlobalCom in 2005 and the project was shelved (Major, 2001; Webdale, 2005). In this way, the global programme markets influence the kinds of transnational communal bonds that can and cannot be forged through television.

Duna Televízió is a typical European public-service channel, focusing on general entertainment, educational and cultural programmes, except that Duna TV is a satellite broadcaster targeted at Hungarian-speakers throughout the Carpathian Basin, particularly the Hungarian minorities in Romania, the former Yugoslav countries and Slovakia. Outside Hungary, Duna TV is not generally transmitted via cable, so viewers must have a satellite dish to receive it. The channel is funded by a combination of federal and private grants as well as advertising revenues. In 1999, Duna TV received UNESCO's Camera Prize, which is awarded to the best cultural television channel in the world (Duna Televízió, 2001).

The Control Board, a body consisting of twenty-five representatives from Hungary and Hungarian-speaking communities abroad, has final approval of Duna TV's programme schedule and acquisitions, although in practice the programme director and acquisitions department make decisions, which the Board then approves (Petrovszky, 2001). According to my interviews, political considerations often influence the Board's decisions, especially in terms of how much programming should be devoted to children, what kinds of programming children should watch and how the editorial profile of the newscasts might affect relations between Hungary and its neighbours. Few of the Board's members live in the international communities that Duna TV targets any longer, having long since emigrated to Hungary, so their understanding the needs of the communities they represent is questionable.

Despite this somewhat heavy-handed government oversight, Duna TV operates relatively independently in most of its acquisitions decisions. One of the main reasons for its independence is that Duna TV is not a nationwide broadcast channel but a far less widespread satellite channel, which reaches only about 60 per cent of the Hungarian viewing audience via cable (Duna Televízió, 2001). Unlike its terrestrial public cousin MTV, which frequently has to deal with changes in ownership and programming profile that can damage its relationships with distributors and viewers, Duna TV has a much more consistent management structure and more predictable programming budgets and needs (Tóth, 2002).

Duna TV's primary acquisitions genres are feature films, television series, documentaries, animation and cultural programming, most of which come from European distributors. Duna TV acquires feature films from the UK, France, Germany, Spain, Italy and across Europe, including Central and Eastern European films. It also takes films from the Middle East, Asia, Latin America and Africa, though these usually come to Duna TV through a European-based redistributor. In terms of television series and cultural programming, Duna TV acquires primarily from European public broadcasters. In particular, the channel looks for 'classic' series, such as the BBC's *Yes, Minister* (1980–4, 1986–7). Documentaries and children's programming come mostly from European and Canadian sources, both public and commercial (ibid.).

Like the other channels we have examined, Duna TV has a small cadre of about twenty distributors from whom it acquires most of its programming each year, including the BBC, Carlton International, Granada and Channel 4 in the UK. However, Duna TV's buyers also keep their eyes open for individual series, films, or specials from other distributors. For instance, in 2002, Duna TV's buyers attended the Barcelona Television Festival for the first time, where they met Spanish producers and distributors from whom they acquired several properties (ibid.).

Duna TV's acquisitions season begins when Zoltan Petrovszky, the programme director, assesses the performance of each programme and the amount of new programming needed to replace those whose licence periods have expired. Petrovszky draws up an acquisitions plan that indicates how many hours of each genre the channel will need in the upcoming year, after which acquisitions executives make specific purchasing decisions. Duna TV employs four or five acquisitions executives, each of whom is responsible for a different territory, mostly in Europe. Thus, one executive works with UK companies, one with

French companies and another with German companies. This organisation reflects the relative importance of European programme sources, as compared with the commercial Hungarian terrestrials that assign a single acquisitions officer to cover all of Europe (ibid.; Petrovszky, 2001).

The biggest hindrance that Duna TV faces when acquiring programming comes from the distribution window in which it operates and the transnational reach of its satellite footprint. As a satellite channel, Duna TV operates in what the global television business defines as a pay-television window, despite the fact that the channel is publicly funded and receives no carriage fee from cable operators, who are obliged to carry the channel within Hungary. In addition, because Duna TV transmits to several surrounding countries and is receivable across Europe, distributors often want the channel to pay for multi-territory programming rights, even though the channel is dubbed into Hungarian and not understood by non-Hungarian speakers. Therefore, Duna TV finds itself lumped together in the same window with such transnational powerhouses as HBO International and Discovery Channel Europe. However, the small size of its budget precludes Duna TV from bidding on highly sought-after programming, such as Hollywood feature films, despite the fact that it does see such programmes as fitting its remit to bring the best of the world's audiovisual culture to Hungarian-speaking minorities worldwide (Tóth, 2002).

Duna TV's lack of ability to compete effectively for viewers or programming with commercial broadcasters in Hungary or commercial transnational channels means that it attracts mostly children and older viewers, giving the channel a unique identity in comparison with other channels (ibid.). When Duna TV does attract an eighteen to forty-nine audience, it is primarily a small but elite 'art-film' audience, who watch the channel's late-night art films (Petrovszky, 2001). Obviously, this audience make-up attracts mostly downscale advertisers, which further limits the channel's budget and its ability to compete for more popular programmes and films.

Not surprisingly, then, Duna TV's programme schedule shows a good deal more diversity than public-service or commercial Hungarian broadcasters or other transnational channels, due largely to its limited acquisitions capabilities. In addition to time-slots reserved for Hungarian feature films, Hungarian classical music, children's game shows and documentaries for women, Duna TV programmes a good deal of news and current affairs programming, as well as imports (Duna Televízió, 2001). Nevertheless, Duna TV still succumbs to the lure of large advertising dollars in prime time by programming general entertainment programmes, including feature films primarily purchased from Hollywood.

Because Duna TV has difficulty acquiring new Hollywood releases, the channel primarily acquires 'classic' Hollywood films to air in prime time. In an

instance of how Duna TV turns this necessity to its advantage, in 2001 the channel acquired rights to a package of classic MGM films, which it programmed as
a 'great-directors' series, featuring weekly films devoted to a single director each
month. Still, executives at the channel admitted to wanting newer Hollywood
releases, such as the 1999 blockbuster *Titanic* (Tóth, 2002). Obviously, Duna
TV's location on the fringes of the global television business restricts its ability
to acquire the programming it wants, at the same time that perceptions about
how to attract a general audience have filtered into the channel's scheduling
practices from elsewhere, as demonstrated by the channel's efforts to attract
more eighteen to forty-nine-year-old viewers with primetime feature films on
Tuesdays, Thursdays, Fridays and Saturdays.

Thus, Duna TV's identity as a transnational satellite channel targeted at a general, Hungarian-speaking audience in Central Europe and beyond provides both
flexibility and constraints. Because Duna TV is a satellite channel aimed primarily at Hungarians living abroad, it does not attract the kind of close
governmental scrutiny that the Hungarian broadcaster MTV does, which can
wreak havoc with programme suppliers and viewers. This freedom has allowed
the channel to develop a number of consistent and clearly defined programming
blocs that target segments of the audience often ignored by commercial channels, and even the public-service broadcaster, with predominantly imported
programming. Moreover, Duna TV's lack of heavy dependence on advertising
revenues, and the fact that it does not actively compete against other channels
at home or abroad, free the channel to target whom it wants in the ways that it
wants. Of course, the channel is not free of outside influence, most notably the
interference of its Control Board in acquisitions and programming matters,
which often comes from people who are more interested in currying political
favour than in maintaining the channel's cultural integrity. In fact, while out-
siders may find laudable the channel's efforts to maintain Hungarian cultural
identity abroad, the image of a greater Hungarian community, which was dis-
membered after World War I, finds its strongest domestic supporters among
political and cultural conservatives.

In addition to the Control Board's influence, the structure and economics of
global television trade prevent Duna TV from acquiring the programming it
wants. Much like any other channel in the world, Duna TV must take packages
of programming from the Hollywood majors in order to gain access to their
programmes. Duna TV's acquisitions choices, however, are even more limited
than most channels because it operates in a distribution window normally
reserved for high-end commercial ventures. Even many smaller distributors that
do not sell programming in different windows nevertheless insist that Duna TV
buy programme rights not just for Hungary, but for every territory in the chan-

nel's footprint, making rights prohibitively expensive. Finally, industry-wide assumptions about how to programme for different audiences have filtered into Duna TV's programming practices, as evidenced by its reliance on feature films to reach general, primetime viewers. Despite the fact that the programme director does not keep track of industry trade journals, and his English is poor enough that he preferred to speak to me through a translator, Duna TV's acquisitions and scheduling practices still reflect these conventional industry assumptions because he bases his decisions in part on how other channels have solved the riddle of audience appeal.

CONCLUSION

Transnational television channels have opened up new distribution windows for suppliers of premium audiovisual product and infused the global television sales business with a new crop of buyers. Most of these channels are commercially funded niche operations specialising in genres that glut the global programme markets, such as fly-on-the-wall reality shows, *telenovelas*, documentaries and children's animation. They are profitable only because the supply of these genres outstrips demand, and because production costs are low, keeping the price of programme rights down. Still, these channels can only break even if they operate across numerous territories, customise their programme offerings only in the most lucrative markets, and target audience niches desirable to transnational advertisers. Thus, Zone Vision recently redesigned its *telenovela* channel, Romantica, to include talk shows and do-it-yourself reality shows aimed at attracting more eighteen- to forty-nine-year-old women (*Television Business International*, 2004).

At the other end of the spectrum, transnational channels that buy primarily from Hollywood often provide new distribution windows for premium US product, particularly feature films. The channels of HBO International, for instance, rely on a subscriber-funded model to generate high enough prices to make it worthwhile for the major studios to hold off selling rights to larger commercial broadcasters for a few months. Paradoxically, this model also forces the channels to customise both their acquisitions and their programme schedules to a fair degree in order to maintain their paying customers, opening opportunities, for instance, for more Central European films to be screened on television. However, the commercial viability of these operations outside the largest markets is questionable: HBO Central Europe was formed in an effort to cut costs at national HBO channels across the region, and scepticism in the industry about the profitability of HBO Central Europe's operations is widespread. If this trend bears out, it is possible that we will soon see a television world where economically powerful nations and audience segments enjoy a wide range of rel-

evant programming, while others will have to make do with transnationally controlled channels with little cultural relevance.

Regardless of the degree to which commercial transnational television channels help foster local production, their impact is likely to be one of solidifying a
common set of industry-wide assumptions about the proper uses of satellite television. Much as our investigations of programme scheduling have revealed that
certain, standard ideas about viewers' behaviours and pleasures have become
commonplace among programme officials worldwide, so may conventional
assumptions about transnational audience segments and the programming that
can attract them. I do not mean to suggest that transnational channels will come
simply to duplicate conventional broadcasting, but rather that the range of possibilities that satellite broadcasting opens up for thinking creatively about
viewers, their relationships to television and the expressive possibilities of the
medium could be short-circuited as a fairly standard type of channel becomes
dominant. Of course, satellite channels need not succumb to the operating priorities of the global television markets, but those that do not succumb face the
challenge of reconciling costs with programme offerings that are capable of
interesting viewers.

Conclusion: Imagining Post-national Television

Common sense suggests that the largest hurdle faced by global television merchants is cultural difference. Cultural difference impedes the flow of both programming and profits. It is hostile to the very goals of global commercial television. On the other hand, the research here has shown how cultural difference also forms the basis of global television sales, as buyers and sellers strive to distinguish themselves from their competitors based upon genre, nationality, ethnicity and the like. This is why the Indian producer-distributor Zee TV used traditional Indian puppets and a puppeteer to help brand its programming on the sales floor of MIP-TV. This is also why the children's cable channel, Minimax Hungary, uses Central European animation to distinguish itself from its rivals. Understood in this light, cultural difference becomes a conduit for global television sales, creating identifiable links among distributors, genres, buyers and audience segments. This is some of the primary cultural work that the business of global television carries out: imagining how to conceptualise the make-up of mass, transnational audiences and the cultural sensibilities that supposedly bind them together. This is not cultural homogenisation on a grand scale. Rather, as we have seen, the forces of homogenisation and differentiation interact at each stage of programme trade.

Although numerous scholars have recognised that the globalisation of television has led to cultural hybridity among viewers (Ang, 1996; Gillespie, 1995; Tomlinson, 1999), this study discovers hybridity *within* the global television business as well, as buyers and sellers trade ideas about how to reconcile textual pleasure with viewers' tastes and behaviours. In a similar vein, Chris Barker suggests that global television leads to confrontations with 'capitalist modernity' among media professionals around the world. 'Though television as both technology and cultural form is a western-originated project, and continues to be dominated economically by western and, particularly, American economic powers,' he writes, 'the global spread of television may be inflected and configured in different ways under different local circumstances' (1997, pp. 204–5). In other words, television industry practices exhibit a mixture of local and Western ideas. Likewise, David Hesmondhalgh sees the 'complex professional era' (2002, p. 51) of cultural industry organisation spreading worldwide. Unlike earlier forms of cultural production, such as the era of patronage, the present era is characterised by complex institutional arrangements and divisions of labour among cultural producers, distributors and funding sources. I would add that we are also witnessing the encounter on a global scale between transnational media-capitalism, new communications technologies and cultural difference, which encourages the creation of certain forms of post-national 'imagined communities' (Anderson, 1991).

Benedict Anderson has shown how the imagined community of the modern nation was the product of 'print-capitalism', which includes 'a system of production and productive relationships (capitalism), a technology of communications (print), and the fatality of human linguistic diversity' (ibid. pp. 42–3). Print-capitalism took advantage of the capacity of a single written code to encompass a variety of spoken dialects, uniting different linguistic communities into a single, national language market. At the same time, linguistic diversity also limited the size of these markets, establishing boundaries between language groups that were equally as important as were linkages for imagining national identity.

By contrast, as we saw in Chapter 1, contemporary media-capitalism organises television production and audiences on a post-national basis, seeking to unite people in groupings based upon age, gender, ethnicity, sexual preference and so forth that transcend national and linguistic division. Media-capitalism, then, integrates and differentiates consumers as much along *cultural* lines as along linguistic ones. Of course, language and national differences continue to organise the structure of television markets, but they are no longer the only organising principles. Thus, media-capitalism strives not only to overcome linguistic differences, but also establishes boundaries among culturally defined groups within the same national-linguistic community.

Part of the reason media-capitalism can achieve this alternate grouping is because the televisual code contains visual signifiers that reach across linguistic boundaries. The public good nature of television programming also encourages its global circulation. Whereas print-capitalists exploited the printed code to integrate different language cultures, media-capitalists use genre and branded audiovisual elements to bring together television audiences worldwide. Genres permit the standardised targeting of specific segments of the audience from around the world, including animation for children, soap operas for women and action dramas for men. Meanwhile, branded audiovisual elements, such as the standard logo, theme music and set design of the different local versions of *Who Want to Be a Millionaire?*, mark programming as simultaneously local and global, allowing cosmopolitan viewers to participate imaginatively in global media events.

Of course, these newer groupings do not replace national identities, nor do they possess the kinds of deep emotional appeals to primordial human community that national identities often do. In addition, as Michael Curtin has shown regarding transnational media portrayals of feminine desire, the industry's capacity to imagine and exploit transnational audiences is 'immature and incoherent if not inadequate' (1999, p. 70). Still, several ways of bringing together post-national audience segments have been institutionalised and, as we saw in Chapter 6, transnational satellite channels that go against the grain of how post-national audiences are conventionally imagined and targeted face problems acquiring programmes.

In fact, throughout this study, we have seen that post-national textual and institutional practices tend to collect around the upper and lower rungs of each nation's social ladder. The competition for the most lucrative audience segments leads to more sophisticated and costlier productions that require worldwide circulation in order to make them economically feasible. These coveted consumers are members of what Eileen Meehan (1990) terms the 'commodity audience', referring to those members of society who spend most heavily on media-related commodities. High-end forms of post-national television are designed to appeal to such audiences in as many territories as possible. Moreover, new television technologies help consolidate the global commodity audience even further. Premium video services permit affluent viewers around the world privileged access to the same programmes. In addition, digital video recorders that allow users to skip through advertisements have prompted global advertisers to buy product placements in certain high-end, internationally traded programmes (Marenzi, 2005a). Meanwhile, among less desirable audiences, post-national television proliferates because commercial television outlets simply won't put forth the expense of producing relevant programming, relying instead on cheap imports that perform moderately well. In this way, post-national television seems to be encouraging the development of distinct transnational taste-cultures, which are roughly akin to social classes. Whether these class sensibilities will erode cross-class national alliances remains to be seen.

The post-national aspects of television involve more than just efforts to target specific audiences across national lines. As we have seen throughout this study, several business practices exhibit a hybridity of domestic and imported ideas that work to standardise how television professionals around the world conceptualise and target the audience. These include the segmentation of audiences into standard age, gender and income groups, as well as the trading of ideas at sales markets, within media conglomerates, and through the trade press about how to select and schedule programmes for each segment. Some of these ideas circulate worldwide, such as the use of erotic programming to attract young male viewers in late-night hours; others, such as the scheduling of *telenovelas* for older women during daytime across Central Europe, are limited to

particular regions of the world. However, even successful, locally derived strategies, such as the Dutch strategy of stripping voyeuristic reality shows in prime
time to attract broad, eighteen- to forty-nine-year-old audiences, get copied
quickly by commercial channels elsewhere.

We have also seen that the hybridity of contemporary television business practices is heavily weighted toward richer, Western nations, such that Western
practices, like Western programmes, are more likely to get adopted abroad than
those that originate elsewhere. One of the most striking instances of this
inequity is the global programming hierarchy that values Hollywood-distributed
films and series above all others, and that many television executives in a variety of places and roles seem to have internalised. This bias is owed in part to
the business culture of global television sales and the uncertainties of trade,
which lead programmers everywhere to trust the programming and scheduling
strategies of the most prestigious global companies. As we saw in Chapter 3,
perceptions of prestige in global television depend in large part on a company's
ability to cultivate an aura of exclusivity at programme sales markets, which
comes easier to Western companies with deep pockets. This prestige extends
not only to Western programming, but to a host of Western business practices,
including the use of English in screening tapes and rights contracts, the promotional strategies that distributors adopt and the programming strategies that
buyers borrow from other channels or learn about through the trade press.

Thus, much as print-capitalism privileged linguistic groups with large numbers and access to social power, media-capitalism encourages certain forms of
post-national identity to the exclusion of others, specifically those forms that are
both lucrative and consistent with Western cultural frameworks. For instance,
among North American and European executives, it is commonly accepted that
programmes featuring white actors are inherently more universal than those that
feature non-whites, while the opposite tends to be true among executives in
Latin America, the Middle East and Africa (Havens, 2002, 2003). However,
because, on the whole, white European and American viewers are more affluent than their non-white counterparts, and because the ideology of whiteness
universalises white cultural values while particularising others, television trade
among non-white groups in Europe and North America is minimal and generally goes unnoticed by the trade journals (Ross, 1996).

Despite the dominance of Western values, companies and programming in
the global television marketplace, these practices and discourses do not fully
control transnational programme exchanges. Rather, like any dominant discourse, these discourses face a variety of counter-discourses that imagine global
television flows differently. To return to the example of the worldwide circulation
of non-white programming cited above, a prominent Jordanian redistributor

claims that, 'Most of the black situation comedies are about middle-class or lower-middle-class people. For many people in the Middle East, they associate and sympathise with that kind of life ... and if they see these [white] situation comedies always with the high-brow politicians or the millionaires, they don't sympathise as much' (Hajjawi, 1999). Thus, although Hollywood executives view whiteness as a neutral racial and cultural category that facilitates global exchanges, Middle Eastern professionals see non-white characters and cultures as more translatable, due to the shared economic conditions of many non-white people worldwide. However, while two distinct discourses about race and global television flows exist among programme merchants, trade journals have covered only the discourse of Hollywood, due to their exclusive reliance on executives at the most successful companies as sources.

The problems that alternative discourses face within global television sales are those of legitimacy and access, which academic research can help remedy. With our access to alternative publications that are more than willing to publish research examining silenced and alternative voices within the belly of global corporate capitalism, academics have a rare chance to nurture and give voice to alternative ideas and practices in global television sales. While American critical scholars, who have been socialised to look upon all forms of business warily, may find such a suggestion quaint, or even dangerous, our counterparts abroad, who are accustomed to having far more input into the regulations and business operations of domestic television organisations, are likely to be less sceptical.

A wide array of buyers and sellers utilise the global television markets to trade vastly different kinds of programming worldwide. As we saw above, the British Film Institute relies on global sales markets to distribute its catalogue of experimental European films within and beyond Europe. The United Nations audiovisual department and UNESCO both sell programming at the major global markets, as does a boutique British company, Digital Classics Distribution, which specialises in 'performance programmes and documentaries about the performing arts for television' (Digital Classics, 2002). Each of these distributors, and scores of others like them, has experience in global television sales that may differ markedly from dominant practices. While this volume has tried to remain attentive to such differences, its summary nature has required a broader analysis that only scratches the surface of the myriad discourses and practices that make up the global television marketplace.

In addition to academics, students who go on to pursue careers in the media can become agents of change by understanding the roots of cultural difference and similarity in ways that are more nuanced than those that predominate in the global marketplace. Current cultural relations are the result of a variety of struggles for dominance and survival, yet, as we have seen, the basis for cross-cultural trade often gets explained by dominant Western notions of universal human nature. Roland Barthes has warned that such appeals to human nature often mask a profound Western bias. 'Classic humanism postulates that, in scratching the surface of the history of men a little … one very quickly reaches the solid rock of human nature,' he writes. 'Progressive humanism, on the contrary, must always … scour Nature, its "laws" and its "limits" in order to discover History there' (1972, p. 101). An appreciation of the ways in which contemporary cultural trade shapes and is shaped by history can help lead to cross-cultural television exchanges that are more meaningful and equal. What is more, as the television industries confront an increasingly multicultural world, both at home and abroad, television professionals may have to rethink some of their most basic assumptions about the universal appeal of Western cultural values.

The orientation towards the global television marketplace that I am advocating necessarily deflects attention away from the dominant global players. Of course, it is necessary to study the strategies of the major distributors and buyers as well as the tactics of the smaller companies, but an exclusive focus on large corporations risks oversimplifying what we have seen is a complex process of trade, at the same time that such analyses replicate the biases of the global television business. That is, a focus on how Western media conglomerates dominate global television sales risks reifying and naturalising those practices through a lack of attention to other practices. Moreover, arguments stressing the dominance of US and Western media conglomerates play into the hands of those conglomerates who, as we have seen, work very hard to maintain the impression that Western programming is more successful and universally accepted than other kinds of programming. Thus, I believe it is crucial to balance analyses of Western dominance with research that continues to verify and theorise alternative flows and practices.

Bibliography

Abraham, Raphael (2004), 'Zone Picks up Five Titles for US Channel', *Channel 21*, 27 April, <http://www.c21media.net/news/ detail.asp?area=4&article=20184> (downloaded 27 September 2004).

Advertising Age (1958), 'Boasting 25% of TV Film Income from Abroad, CBS Aims to Hold Sales Lead', 20 October, p. 30.

Advertising Age (1965), 'State Control Stunts TV's Growth as Medium in Europe, Though Sets Soar', 30 August, pp. 247–8.

AGB Hungary (2002), 'AGB News, Anniversary Issue', Budapest: AGB Hungary.

Aksoy, Asu (n.d.), 'The Possibilities of Transnational Turkish Television', <http://www.photoinsight.org.uk/text/aksoy/aksoy.pdf> (downloaded 3 June 2005).

Akyuz, Gün (1996), 'Forever Young', *TV World*, January, pp. 15–21.

Albiniak, Paige (2003), 'Deficit Disorder', *Broadcasting & Cable*, 5 May, p. 1.

Alleyne, Mark (1995), *International Power and International Communication*, New York: St Martin's Press.

Al-Mugaiseeb, Khalid (1998), CEO of Kuwait TV 2. Personal interview.

Amin, Hussein (1996), 'Egypt and the Arab World in the Satellite Age', in John Sinclair, Elizabeth Jacka and Stuart Cunningham (eds), *New Patterns in Global Television: Peripheral Vision*, Oxford and New York: Oxford University Press, pp. 101–25.

Anderson, Benedict (1991), *Imagined Communities: Reflections on the Origin and Spread of Nationalism*, London and New York: Verso.

Ang, Ien (1985), *Watching Dallas: Soap Opera and the Melodramatic Imagination*, trans. Della Couling, London and New York: Methuen.

Ang, Ien (1990), 'Culture and Communication: Towards an Ethnographic Critique of Media Consumption in the Transnational Media System', *European Journal of Communication*, 5, pp. 239–60.

Ang, Ien (1991), *Desperately Seeking the Audience*, London and New York: Routledge.

Ang, Ien (1996), *Living Room Wars: Rethinking Media Audiences for a Postmodern World*, London and New York: Routledge.

Appadurai, Arjun (1990), 'Disjuncture and Difference in the Global Cultural Economy', *Theory, Culture & Society*, 7, pp. 295–310.

Atkinson, Claire (1998), 'Days of Wine and Pre-Sales', *Realscreen*, 1 October, p. 74.

Avery, Robert K. (ed.) (1993), *Public Service Broadcasting in a Multichannel Environment: The History and Survival of an Ideal*, White Plains, NY: Longman Press.

Avis, Tim (2001), 'Hispanic TV – the Fine Art of Partnership', *Channel 21*, 15 March, <http://www.c21media.net/features/detail.asp?area=2&article=521> (downloaded 26 September 2004).

AXN (2004) Untitled, <http://www.axn.com> (downloaded 26 September 2004).

Balázs, Bianca (2002), Acquisitions Director, TV2 (Hungary). Personal interview.

Balogh, Edina (2001), Acquisitions Editor, RTL Klub (Hungary). Personal interview.

Balogh, Edina (2002), Acquisitions Editor, RTL Klub (Hungary). Personal interview.

Barker, Chris (1997), *Global Television: An Introduction*, Oxford: Blackwell.

Barthes, Roland (1972), 'The Great Family of Man', *Mythologies*, trans. ed. Annette Lavers, New
    York: Hill and Wang, pp. 100–2.

Bathelt, Harald, Anders Malmberg and Peter Maskell (2004), 'Clusters and Knowledge: Local
    Buzz, Global Pipelines, and the Process of Knowledge Creation', *Progress in Human
    Geography*, 28, no. 1, pp. 31–56.

BBC (2005), 'BBC One Listing', <http://www.bbc.co.uk/bbcone/listings/> (downloaded
    29 May 2005).

BBC America (2005), 'BBC America Schedule', <http://www.bbcamerica.com/schedule/
    schedule.jsp> (downloaded 29 June 2005).

Bednarski, P. J. (2001), 'The Low Spark of Vegas', *Broadcasting & Cable*, 29 January, p. 21.

Berciano, Rosa A., Charo Lacalle and Lorenzo Vilches (2000), 'Playing It Safe: Spanish TV
    Fiction in 1998', in Milly Buonanno (ed), *Continuity and Change: Television Fiction in Europe*,
    Luton: University of Luton Press, pp. 63–82.

Bergant, Boris (2004), Deputy Director General of International Relations, Radio-Television
    Slovenia. Personal interview.

Bielby, Denise D. and C. Lee Harrington (2002), 'Markets and Meanings: The Global
    Syndication of Television Programming', in Diana Crane, Nobuko Kawashima and Ken'ichi
    Kawasaki (eds), *Global Culture: Media, Arts, Policy, and Globalisation*, New York and
    London: Routledge, pp. 215–32.

Bielby, Denise D. and C. Lee Harrington (2004), 'Managing Culture Matters: Genre, Aesthetic
    Elements, and the International Market for Exported Television', *Poetics: Journal of Empirical
    Research on Culture, Media, and the Arts*, 32, no. 1, pp. 73–98.

Biltereyst, Daniël and Philippe Meers (2000), 'The International *Telenovela* Debate and the
    Contra-Flow Argument: A Reappraisal', *Media, Culture & Society*, 22, pp. 393–413.

Blicq, Annette (1999), Head of Acquisitions, Canal Jimmy (France). Personal interview.

Bortin, Meg (1998), 'US Producers Seek Euro Help', *Hollywood Reporter*, 26 February,
    <http://web.lexis-nexis/universe> (downloaded 17 June 2004).

Boyd, Douglas (1998), 'The Arab World', in Anthony Smith (ed.), *Television: The International
    View, 2nd edn*, Oxford: Oxford University Press: pp. 182–7.

Brennan, Steve (1997), 'Pay Dirt: Par Hooks up with Spain's Sogecable', *Hollywood Reporter*,
    10 October, <http://web.lexis-nexis/universe> (downloaded 6 September 2004).

Brennan, Steve (1999a), 'As an Epilogue, Execs Weigh the Market Value', *Hollywood Reporter*,
    16 April, p. 6.

Brennan, Steve, (1999b), 'Col TriStar at High Tide for Overseas Production', *Hollywood
    Reporter*, 22 July, p. 1.

Brennan, Steve (1999c), 'MIP-TV Fights For its Future: Riviera Mart Vows to Press on Even if
    Hollywood Bails Out', *Hollywood Reporter*, 20 April, p. 64.

Brennan, Steve (1999d), 'MIP-TV May Fall off US A-List: Timing and Belt Tightening Reduce
    Studios' Interest in Cannes Market', *Hollywood Reporter*, 30 March, p. 48.

Brennan, Steve (1999e), 'TV's "Largo" Open for Business', *Hollywood Reporter*, 23 November, <http://web.lexis-nexis/ universe> (downloaded 14 June 2004).

Brennan, Steve (2000), 'Midseason is in Season for MIP-TV Buyers', *Hollywood_Reporter*, 11 April, p. 54.

Brennan, Steve (2004), 'Sharper Picture', *Hollywood Reporter*, 6 January, <http://web.lexis-nexis/universe> (downloaded 7 September 2004).

Brennan, Steve (2005), 'Global Ratings Grabbers', 20 May, <http:www.hollywoodreporter.com> (downloaded 29 May 2005).

Broadcast (2004), 'Reality TV Channel Launched in Portugal', 23 July, p. 8.

Broadcasting (1959a), 'Films for South of the Border', 9 February, p. 146.

Broadcasting (1995b), 'Rich Getting Richer in TV Film', 2 February, pp. 39–42.

Broadcasting (1960), 'TV Overseas Market Limited', 1 February, pp. 89–90.

Broadcasting (1962a), 'Distribution Rights Vital', 15 October, p. 82.

Broadcasting (1962b), 'Foreign Broadcasting Interests of US Firms', 15 October, p. 76.

Broadcasting (1962c) 'Overseas Program Sales Hit $52 Million', 15 October, pp. 78–82.

Broadcasting (1972), 'ABC is Next to Divest Program-Sales Operations', 21 August, pp. 32–3.

Broadcasting (1975a), 'Escalating Costs Putting Squeeze on TV Networks' Program Suppliers', 13 January, pp. 17–18.

Broadcasting (1975b), 'Producers Say Crunch Hurts in their Networks' Pay', 21 July, p. 22.

Broadcasting (1977a), 'MIP-TV Cannes: Starting Point for a Worldwide Grand Prix in Television', 9 May, pp. 88–94.

Broadcasting (1977b), 'The US as TV Programer [*sic*] to the World', 18 April, pp. 48–54.

Broadcasting (1978), 'Springtime in France and Thoughts Turn to TV Programming', 17 April, pp. 81–5.

Broadcasting (1979), 'Television Goes Global at MIP-TV', 30 April, pp. 42–6.

Broadcasting (1980), 'TV: The One Language Spoken at MIP', 28 April, pp. 65–72.

Brockmeyer, Dieter (2002), 'Kirch's Crisis', *Multichannel News International*, April, pp. 22–6.

Brown, Kimberly (2001), 'Worth the Trip to MIP?', *Realscreen*, 1 September, pp. 43–5.

Buonanno, Milly (2000), 'A Comparative Overview', in Milly Buonanno (ed.), *Continuity and Change: Television Fiction in Europe*. Luton: University of Luton Press, pp. 7–28.

Burman, John (1995), '"Szamba" First in HBO Hungary Local Prod'n Plan', *Hollywood Reporter*, 1 August, <http://web.lexis-nexis.com/univers> (downloaded 25 September 2001).

Burnett, Kate (2002), 'Happy Endings: Asia's Position on the *Telenovela* Distribution Roster is Rising', *Television Asia*, October, p. 52.

Business Week (1960a), 'TV Abroad Thrives on US Ways', 3 September, pp. 105–7.

Business Week (1960b), 'World Laps Up US TV Fare', 23 April, pp. 129–31.

Business Week (1962), 'Second Life for TV Films Abroad', 8 December, p. 58.

Cantor, Muriel G. and Joel M. Cantor (1986), 'American Television in the International Marketplace', *Communication Research*, 13, pp. 509–20.

Cardiff, David and Paddy Scannell (1987), 'Broadcasting and National Unity', in James Curran, Anthony Smith and Pauline Wingate (eds), *Impacts and Influences: Essays on Media Power in the Twentieth Century*, London and New York: Methuen, pp. 157–73.

Caughie, John (1990), 'Playing at Being American: Games and Tactics' in Patricia Mellencamp (ed.) *Logics of Television: Essays in Cultural Criticism*, Bloomington: Indiana University Press, pp. 44–58.

CBS (1968), 'CBS International Television Catalogue', Pamphlet Collection, #332, Broadcast
    Pioneers Library of American Broadcasting, College Park, MD.
Chalaby, Jean (2002), 'Transnational Television in Europe: The Role of Pan-European Channels',
    European Journal of Communication, 17, pp. 183–204.
Chan, Joseph Man (1996), 'Television in Greater China: Structure, Exports, and Market
    Formation', in John Sinclair, Elizabeth Jacka and Stuart Cunningham (eds), *New Patterns in
    Global Television: Peripheral Vision* Oxford and New York: Oxford University Press,
    pp. 126–60.
Channel 21 (2001), 'Zone's Reality TV Expands Euro Footprint', 19 December,
    <http://www.c21media.net/news/detail.asp?area=4&article=2252> (downloaded
    27 September 2004).
Channel 21 (2002), 'Zone Adds Yugoslavia to Reality Footprint', 28 May,
    <http://www.c21media.net/news/detail.asp?area=4&article=3394> (downloaded
    27 September 2004).
Channel 21 (2003), 'German Debut for Zone's Reality TV', <http://www.c21media.net/news/
    detail.asp?area=4&article=18682> (downloaded 26 September 2004).
Channel 21 (2004a), 'Asian Expansion for Reality TV', 2 March,
    <http://www.c21media.net/news/detail.asp?area=4&article=19438> (downloaded
    26 September 2004).
Channel 21 (2004b), 'Programme Prices Map', <http://www.c21media.net/resources/
    index.asp?area=45> (downloaded 24 September 2004).
Charvadze, Alexander (2004), International Sales Representative, TV Channel Russia. Personal
    interview.
Cohen, Bert (1999), Executive Vice President and COO, Worldvision Entertainment. Personal
    interview.
Cole, Steve. (2004), Vice President, Reality TV. Personal interview.
Couldry, Nick (2003), *Media Rituals: A Critical Approach*. London and New York: Routledge.
Cunningham, Stuart and Elizabeth Jacka (1996), *Australian Television and International
    Mediascapes*, Cambridge: Cambridge University Press.
Curtin, Michael (1996), 'On Edge: Culture Industries in the Neo-Network Era', in Richard
    Ohmann (ed.), *Making and Selling Culture*, Hanover, NH: Wesleyan University Press,
    pp. 181–202.
Curtin, Michael (1997), 'Dynasty in Drag: Imagining Global Television', in Lynn Spigel and
    Michael Curtin (eds), in Lynn Spigel and Michael Curtin (eds), *The Revolution Wasn't
    Televised: Sixties Television and Social Conflict*, New York and London: Routledge,
    pp. 245–62.
Curtin, Michael (1999), 'Feminine Desire in the Age of Satellite Television', *Journal of
    Communication*, 44, no. 2, pp. 55–70.
Darwish, Maha (2004), International Marketing Director for Television and Satellite, Egyptian
    Radio & TV Union. Personal interview.
Davies, Jonathan (1998), 'World Affairs: Cisneros Set to Snuggle up with Playboy', *Hollywood
    Reporter*, 22 December, p. 3.
Deal, Helen (1997), 'Emerging Identities', *TV World*, April, pp. 81–4.

De Bens, Els and Hedwig de Smaele (2001), 'The Inflow of American Television Fictions on European Broadcasting Channels Revisited', *European Journal of Communication*, 16, pp. 51–76.

de la Fuente, Anna Marie (1997), 'National Subscriptions', *TV World*, May, pp. 43–4.

De Pablos, Emiliano (2002), 'Spain Takes Reins on *Telenovelas*', *Variety*, 19 August, p. 33.

Dewi, Torsten (1999), Commissioning Producer of International Co-productions, Prosieben (Germany). Personal interview.

Digital Classics (2002), 'New Programmes 2002–2003', London: Digital Classics Distribution.

Dinerman, Ann S. and Dom Serafini (1997), 'The World's 95 Power TV Buyers', *Video Age International*, Industry Overview Section, pp. 1–3.

Downing, John (1996), *Internationalizing Media Theory: Transition, Power, Culture*. London: Sage.

Du Gay, Paul and Michael Pryke (2002), *Cultural Economy: Cultural Analysis and Commercial Life*, London: Sage.

Duna Televízió (2001), Promotional Materials. Budapest: Duna Televízió.

Dupagne, Michel (1992), 'Factors Influencing the International Syndication Marketplace in the 90s', *Journal of Media Economics*, 5, no. 3, pp. 3–29.

Duran, Igancio (1999), Vice President of International Affairs, TV Azteca. Personal interview.

EAO (2000), 'European Films on European Televisions', <http://www.obs.coe.int/ online_publication/reports/films_in_tv.pdf> (downloaded 7 June 2005).

EAO (2003), 'American Fiction and Feature Films Continue To Dominate Western European Television Channel Programme Imports', <http://www.obs.coe.int/about/oea/pr/a02vol5.html> (downloaded 7 June 2005).

Eastman, Susan Tyler, Sydney W. Head and Lewis Klein (1985), *Broadcast/Cable Programming: Strategies and Practices, 2nd Ed*. Belmont, CA: Wadsworth.

Eastman, Susan Tyler, Jeffrey Neal-Lunsford and Karen E. Riggs (1995), 'Coping with Grazing: Prime time Strategies for Accelerated Program Transitions', *Journal of Broadcasting and Electronic Media*, 39, pp. 92–108.

Edmunds, Marlene (2001), 'Modern Times Group: Rolling with the Times', *Television Europe*, January, p. 34.

Egan, Jack (1990), 'Hollywood's Numbers Game', *US News & World Report*, 2 April, p. 39.

Electronic Media (1995), 'HBO International Widens Reach in Eastern Europe', 3 April, pp. 22ff.

Ellis, John (2000), 'Scheduling: The Last Creative Act in Television?', *Media, Culture and Society*, 22, pp. 25–38.

Escalante, José (2004), Vice President and General Manager, Coral International. Panel discussion at DISCOP 2004, Budapest, Hungary, 26 June.

Eugster, Ernest (1983), *Television Programming Across National Boundaries: The EBU and OIRT Experience*, Dedham, MA: Artech House.

EurodataTV (1999), 'One Television Year in the World: Audience Report', Levallois-Perret Cedex, France: Eurodata TV and Mediametrie.

Euromarketing via Email (2002), 'Vivendi Puts Hungary's Minimax Up for Sale', 25 October, <http://web.lexis-nexis.com/ universe> (downloaded 20 September 2004).

Ewing, Jack (2002), 'The Fall of Leo Kirch', *Businessweek Online*, 11 March, <http://www.businessweek.com/magazine/content/02_10/b3773007.htm> (downloaded 14 May 2005).

Fair, Jo Ellen (2003), 'Francophonie and the National Airwaves: A History of Television in Senegal', in Lisa Parks and Shanti Kumar (eds), *Planet TV: A Global Television Reader*, New York and London: New York University Press, pp. 189–210.

Fayks, Piotr (2004), Programme Director, Polsat TV (Poland). Personal interview.

Feiwell, Jill (2002), 'Par Int'l TV Ups Ottinger', *Variety*, 14 May, <http://web.lexis-nexis/universe> (downloaded 14 June 2004).

Fejes, Fred. (1981), 'Media Imperialism: An Assessment', *Media, Culture & Society*, 3, pp. 281–9.

Financial Times (1984), 'Sales of British-Made TV Programmes Abroad', 5 January, p. 4.

Fineshriber, William H (1960), 'Interim Report on Television', Pamphlet Collection, #3477, Broadcast Pioneers Library of American Broadcasting, College Park, MD.

Fiske, John (1987), *Television Culture*, London and New York: Routledge.

Flahive, John (2004), Sales Manager, British Film Institute. Personal interview.

Ford, Jeff (1999), Controller of Acquisitions, Channel 5 Broadcasting (UK). Personal interview.

Fox, Elizabeth (1997), *Latin American Broadcasting: From Tango to Telenovela*, Luton: University of Luton Press.

Fraser, Fiona (2002), '21-on-21: Novela Revolution', *Channel 21*, 1 July, <http://www.c21media.net/features/detail.asp?area=2&article=3626> (downloaded 26 September 2004).

Fry, Andy (2002), 'Euro drama: Menage à Trois, Quatre, Cinq ...', 10 May, http://www.c21media.net/features/detail.asp?area=2&article=3263 (downloaded 24 September 2004).

Gálik, Mihály (2004), 'Hungary', in Brankica Petkovič (ed.) *Media Ownership and its Impact on Media Independence and Pluralism*, Ljubljana: Peace Institute, pp. 191–218.

Gáti, Zoltán (2002), Director, Kör Media Hungary. Personal interview.

Gillespie, Marie (1995), *Television, Ethnicity, and Cultural Change*, London and New York: Routledge.

Gopalakrishna, Srinath, Gary L. Lilien, Jerome D. Williams and Ian K. Sequeira (1995), 'Do Trade Shows Pay Off?', *Journal of Marketing*, 59, no. 3, pp. 75–84.

Gordon, Mitchell (1960), 'TV Abroad: US Video Producers Step Up Foreign Sales of Filmed Programmes', *New York Times*, 20 October, Eastern Edition, pp. 1ff.

Groombridge, Brian and Jocelyn Hay (1995), *The Price of Choice: Public Service Broadcasting in a Competitive European Market Place*, Luton: University of Luton Press.

Guback, Thomas (1977), 'The International Film Industry', in George Gerbner (ed.) *Mass Media Policies in Changing Cultures*, New York: Wiley and Sons, pp. 15–26.

Guider, Elizabeth (2004), 'Purchase Prowess', *Variety*, 29 March, p. 6.

Guider, Elizabeth and Eileen Tasca (2000), 'Pearson TV Looks South', *Variety*, 22 May, p. 1.

Hajjawi, Bassam (1999), President and CEO, International Distribution Agency (Jordan). Personal interview.

Hara, Yumiko (2004), 'Import and Export of Japanese Television Programs', <http://www.jamco.or.jp/2004_symposium/en/hara> (downloaded 2 June 2005).

Harverson, Patrick (1998), 'TC takes guard at C4 crease', *Financial Times*, 30 December, p. 16.

Harwood, Kenneth (1961), 'The International Radio and Television Organization', *Journal of Broadcasting*, 6, no. 1, pp. 61–72.

Harvey, David (1990), *The Condition of Postmodernity: An Enquiry into the Origins of Cultural Change*, Cambridge, MA, and Oxford: Blackwell.

Hatch, Mary Jo and Majken Schultz (2000), 'Scaling the Tower of Babel: Relational Difference Between Identity, Image, and Culture in Organizations', in Majken Schultz, Mart Jo Hatch and Mogens Holten Larsen (eds), *The Expressive Organization: Linking Identity, Reputation, and the Corporate Brand*, Oxford and New York: Oxford University Press, pp. 11–35.

Havas, Ágnes (2001), Acquisitions Manager, TV2 Hungary. Personal interview.

Havas, Ágnes (2002), Independent producer-distributor. Personal interview.

Havens, Timothy (2002), '"It's Still a White World out There": The Interplay of Culture and Economics in International Television Trade', *Critical Studies in Media Communication*, 19, pp. 377–98.

Havens, Timothy (2003), 'African American Television in an Age of Globalization', in Lisa Parks and Shanti Kumar (eds), *Planet TV: A Global Television Reader*, New York: New York University Press, pp. 423–38.

Hazai, Cecilia (2001), President, Twin Media (Hungary). Personal interview.

Hazai, Cecilia (2002), President, Twin Media (Hungary). Personal interview.

HBO (2004), 'HBO International'. <http://www.hbo.com/corpinfo/international.shtml> (downloaded 27 September 2004).

Hecht, John (2003a), 'Televisa, Azteca Lay Plans for Worldwide Incursions', *Hollywood Reporter*, 19 December, <http://web.lexis-nexis.com/universe> (downloaded 7 September 2004).

Hecht, John (2003b), 'Televisa Renames Sales Division', *Hollywood Reporter*, 11 November, <http://web.lexis-nexis.com/universe> (downloaded 7 September 2004).

Herbig, Paul, Fred Palumbo and Bradley S. O'Hara (1996), 'Differences in Trade Show Behavior Between North American-Focused Firms and Worldwide-Oriented Firms', *International Journal of Commerce and Management*, 6, nos. 1–2, pp. 97–110.

Herman, Edward and Robert McChesney (1997), *The Global Media: The New Missionaries of Global Capitalism*, London and Washington: Cassell.

Herman, Melissa (2002), 'Forever Young: Now Almost 50 Years Old, the *Telenovela* Genre's Appeal Shows No Sign of Winding Down', *Television Asia*, January, Special Section 3.

Hesmondhalgh, David (2002), *The Cultural Industries*, London: Sage.

Hilmes, Michelle (2003), 'Who We Are, Who We Are Not', in Lisa Parks and Shanti Kumar (eds), *Planet TV: A Global Television Reader*, New York: New York University Press, pp. 94–110.

Hindu Business Line (2003), 'Zone Vision Unfolds Reality TV', 30 January, <http://www.factiva.com> (downloaded 7 September 2004).

Hirsch, Paul (1972), 'Processing Fads and Fashions: An Organization-Set Analysis of Cultural Industry System', *American Journal of Sociology*, 77, pp. 639–59.

Hollywood Reporter (1995), 'Color Our World!', 3 October, p. A3.

Hollywood Reporter, Anniversary Issue, (1998a), 'Global Influence – America's Piece of the Pie', p. 17.

Hollywood Reporter, (1998b), 'Worldwide Reach', 26 May, p. S-27.

Hollywood Reporter, (2004a), 'Mixed 03 for French TV Exports', 3 September, p. 6.

Hollywood Reporter, (2004b), 'New cable network Reality TV', 10 February, <http://web.lexis-nexis.com/universe> (downloaded 7 September 2004).

Holmes, Mark (2004), 'Zone Vision to Launch Second Reality TV Channel?', *Inside Digital TV*, 21 January, <http://web.lexis-nexis.com/universe> (downloaded 10 August 2004).

Hong, Junhao (1998), *The Internationalization of Television in China: The Evolution of Ideology, Society, and Media Since the Reform*, Westport, CT: Praeger.

Hoskins, Colin and Stuart McFadyen (1991), 'The US Competitive Advantage in the Global Market: Is it Sustainable in the New Broadcast Environment?', *Canadian Journal of Communication*, 16, pp. 207–24.

Hoskins, Colin, Stuart McFadyen and Adam Finn (1997), *Global Television and Film: An Introduction to the Economics of the Business*, New York and Oxford: Oxford University Press.

Hoskins, Colin, Stuart McFadyen, Adam Finn, and Anne Jackel (1995), 'Film and Television Co-Production: Evidence from Canadian-European Experience', *European Journal of Communication*, 10, pp. 221–43.

Hoskins, Colin and Rolf Mirus (1988), 'Reasons for the US Dominance of the International Trade in Television Programming', *Media, Culture, and Society*, 10, pp. 499–515.

IMDB (2005), 'Le Comte de Monte Cristo', <http://www.imdb.com/title/tt0167565> (downloaded 16 March 2005).

Initiative Innovations (2005), 'Spheres of Influence: Global Advertising Expenditure, 2005', <http://www.interpublic.com/read_file.php?did=282> (downloaded 29 May 2005).

Jacka, Elizabeth and Lesley Johnson (1998), 'Australia', in Anthony Smith (ed.), *Television: The International View, 2nd edn*, Oxford: Oxford University Press, pp. 208–22.

James, Alison (2004), 'Gauls Gunning for More Laffers Apres "Friends"', *Variety*, 24 May, p. A5.

Jenkinson, David (2005a), 'Endemol's Dramatic Development', *Channel 21*, 5 May, <http://www.c21media.net/features/detail.asp?area=2&article=24645> (downloaded 13 June 2005).

Jenkinson, David (2005b), 'Transmedia and 3DD launch iConcerts Channel', *Channel 21*, 11 April, <http://www.c21media.net/news/detail.asp?area=4&article=24305> (downloaded 13 June 2005).

Johansen, Bruce (1999), President and CEO, NATPE. Personal interview.

Johansen, Bruce (2001), President and CEO, NATPE. Personal interview.

Johansen, Bruce (2002), President and CEO, NATPE. Personal interview.

Johnson, Debra (2001), 'All Change for Belgium's VT4', *Channel 21*, 5 November, <http://www.c21media.net/features/detail.asp?area=2&article=1919 > (downloaded 29 May 2005).

Johnson, Debra (2002), 'Blighty Notches up Show Sales O'seas'. *Variety*, 17 June, p. 20.

Kaner, Mark (1999), President of International, Twentieth Century-Fox Television Distribution. Personal interview.

Kato, Hidetoshi (1998), 'Japan', in Anthony Smith (ed), *Television: The International View, 2nd edn*, Oxford: Oxford University Press, pp. 169–81.

Keller, Kevin Lane (2000), 'Building and Managing Corporate Brand Equity', in Majken Schultz, Mart Jo Hatch and Mogens Holten Larsen (eds), *The Expressive Organization: Linking Identity, Reputation, and The Corporate Brand*, Oxford and New York: Oxford University Press, pp. 115–37.

Kelly, Brendan (1995), 'Facing up to the Future', *Variety*, 16 January, p. 50.

Kingsley, Simon (2001), 'TV Movies: Small Screen, Big Boot', *Television Europe*, April, p. 52.

Kintner, Robert E (1965), 'The Public's Stake in Global Television', presented at the Ohio State Institute for Education by Radio-Television, 3 June. Pamphlets Collection, #3470, Broadcast Pioneers Library of American Broadcasting, College Park, MD.

Kirschbaum, Erik (1996), 'Rising Costs Co-Prod Ufa into Par, P&G Pact', *Variety*, 29 April, p. 42.

Kolosi, Péter (2002), Programme Director, RTL Klub (Hungary). Personal interview.

Koperveisz, Ágnes (2002), Director of Research, TV2 (Hungary). Personal interview.

Kraidy, Marwan (2002), 'Hybridity in Cultural Globalization', *Communication Theory* 12, pp. 316–39.

Kriek, Kaisa (2004), Programme Sales Manager for Netherlands Public Broadcasting. Personal interview.

Kroeger, Albert E. (1966), 'A Long, Hard Look at the Genealogy of Network TV', *Television Magazine*, 16 April, pp. 33–9.

Ladouceur, Roland (1984), 'The Challenge of Producing for Transnational Audiences', *EBU Review*, 35, pp. 12–14.

Langdale, John V. (1997), 'East Asian Broadcasting Industries: Global, Regional, and National Perspective', *Economic Geography*, 73, pp. 305–21.

Lau, Tuen Yu (1998), Former Adviser, Indosiar Visual Mandiri (Indonesia). Personal interview.

Lawrence, Deborah (2002), Managing Director, Lippin Group London. Personal interview.

Licis, Girts (1999), Head of Acquisitions and Sales for Latvian Television. Personal interview.

Lindlof, Thomas R. (1995), *Qualitative Communication Research Methods*, Thousand Oaks, CA and London: Sage.

McCrone, David, Angela Morris and Richard Kiely (1995), *Scotland – the Brand: The Making of Scottish Heritage*, Edinburgh: Edinburgh University Press.

Mahamdi, Yahia (1992), 'Television, Globalization, and Cultural Hegemony: The Evolution and Structure of International Television', dissertation, University of Texas at Austin.

Mahoney, William (1991), 'Global Ratings: More Important, More Accessible', *Electronic Media*, 25 March, p. 12.

Major, Rose (2001), 'East European Programmer Targets Growth in UK', *New Media Markets*, 29 June, <http://web.lexis-nexis.com/universe> (downloaded 11 August 2004).

Margolis, Mac (1997), 'Soaps Clean Up', *Latin Trade*, 5, <http://www.rdsinc.com> (downloaded 16 May 2004).

Marich, Robert (1992), 'Col TriStar TV Shoots "Berlin"', *Hollywood Reporter*, 9 June, <http://web.lexis-nexis.com/universe> (downloaded 2 May 2005).

Marenzi, Gary (1999), President of International Television, Paramount International Television. Personal interview.

Marenzi, Gary (2004), President of International Television, Paramount International Television. Personal interview.

Marenzi, Gary (2005a), Former President of International Television, Paramount International Television, 1997-2004. Personal interview.

Marenzi, Gary (2005b), Former President of International Television, Paramount International Television, 1997-2004. Personal interview.

Marsh, Sarah (2003), 'Survival of the Fittest', *Cable and Satellite Europe*, March, <http://www.factiva.com> (downloaded 15 August 2004).

Mato, Daniel (2002), 'Miami in the Transnationalization of the Telenovela Industry: On Territoriality and Globalization', *Journal of Latin American Cultural Studies*, 11, pp. 195–212.

Mattelart, Armand, Xavier Delcourt and Michele Mattelart (1984), *International Image Markets: In Search of an Alternative Perspective*, London: Comedia.

Meehan, Eileen (1990), 'Why We Don't Count: The Commodity Audience', in Patricia Mellencamp (ed.), *Logics of Television: Essays in Cultural Criticism*, Bloomington and Indianapolis: Indiana University Press, pp. 117–37.

Meehan, Eileen (1999), 'Commodity, Culture, Common Sense: Media Research and Paradigm Dialogue', *Journal of Media Economics*, 12, no. 2, pp. 149–63.

Meils, Cathy (2000), 'Zone Vision Looking to Turkey, Israel Ops', *Variety*, 14 June, p. 14.

Merton, Robert K. (1968), *Social Theory and Social Structure*, New York: Free Press.

Meza, Ed and Christian Kohl (2003), 'On the Right Track', *Television Business International*, August, <http://web.lexis-nexis.com/universe> (downloaded 1 September 2004).

Miller, Daniel (1992), '*The Young and the Restless* in Trinidad: A Case of the Local and the Global in Mass Consumption', in Roger Silverstone and Eric Hirsch (eds), *Consuming Technologies: Media and Information in Domestic Spaces*, London and New York: Routledge, pp. 163–82.

Miller, Toby, Nitin Govil, John McMurria and Richard Maxwell (2001), *Global Hollywood*, London: BFI.

Miller, Toby, Nitin Govil, John McMurria, Richard Maxwell and Ting Wang (2005), *Global Hollywood 2*, London: BFI.

MIPTV (2004a), *MIPTV and MILIA Guide*, Paris: Reed-Midem.

MIPTV (2004b), 'MIPTV 2004 Statistics', Paris: Reed-Midem.

Moore, Päivi (2004), Head of Export, YLE, Finish Broadcasting Company. Personal interview.

Moran, Albert (1998), *Copycat TV: Globalization, Programme Formats, and National Identity*, Luton: University of Luton Press.

Morley, David (1992), *Television, Audiences, and Cultural Studies*, New York and London: Routledge.

Morley, David and Kevin Robins (1995), *Spaces of Identity: Global Media, Electronic Landscapes, and Cultural Boundaries*, New York and London: Routledge.

MTG (2004), 'Modern Times Group (MTG)', <http://www.mtg.se> (downloaded 4 March 2004).

Mulder, Frank (1999), Director of Programme Acquisitions and Sales, Netherlands Public Television. Personal interview.

Multichannel News (2004) 'An Overview of Time Warner's Business', 31 May, p. 41.

Myers, Harold. (1957), 'A Lion's Share for Britain', *Variety*, 31 July, p. 31.

Nadler, John (2001), 'Hungary Catching on to Cable', *Variety*, 1 October, p. 66.

NATPE (2004), 'About NATPE', <http://www.natpe.org/about/> (downloaded 24 September 2004).

NCTA (2005), 'History of Cable Television', National Cable and Telecommunications Association, <http://www.ncta.com/Docs/pagecontent.cfm?pageID=96> (downloaded 13 May 2005).

Negrine, Ralph M. and Stylianos Papathanassopoulos (1990), *The Internationalization of Television*, London and New York: Pinter.

The New York Times (1957), 'Soviet Bloc to Exchange TV', 17 December, p. 3.

Newbery, Charles (2002), 'Reality TV Launches in Latin America', *Variety*, 25 November, p. 21.

Nordenstreng, Kaarle and Tapio Varis (1974,) *Television Traffic – a One-way Street? A Survey and Analysis of The International Flow of Television Programme Material*, Paris: UNESCO.

O'Hara, Bradley S. (1993), 'Evaluating the Effectiveness of Trade Shows: A Personal Selling Perspective', *The Journal of Personal Selling & Sales Management*, 13, no. 3, pp. 67–78.

Okigbo, Charles (1998), 'Africa', in Anthony Smith (ed.), *Television: The International View, 2nd edn*, Oxford: Oxford University Press, pp. 234–46.

Olins, Wally (2000), 'How Brands Are Taking Over the Corporation', in Majken Schultz, Mart Jo Hatch and Mogens Holten Larsen (eds), *The Expressive Organization: Linking Identity, Reputation, and The Corporate Brand*, Oxford and New York: Oxford University Press, pp. 51–65.

Olson, Scott Robert (1999), *Hollywood Planet: Global Media and the Competitive Advantage of Narrative Transparency*, Mahwah, NJ, and London: Lawrence Erlbaum.

Ooi, Kok Hong (Andrew), (2004) Producer, Inspedia (Malaysia). Personal interview.

O'Regan, Tom (1990), 'Too Popular By Far: On Hollywood's International Popularity', *Continuum: The Australian Journal of Media and Culture*, 5, no. 2, <http://wwwmcc.murdoch.edu.au/ReadingRoom/5.2/O'Regan.html> (downloaded 24 September 2004).

ORTT (1996), 'Act on Radio and Television Broadcasting, Act I', Országos Rádió és Televízió Testület, <http://www.ortt.hu/index_angol.htm> (downloaded 26 September 2004).

O'Shaughnessy, John and Nicholas Jackson O'Shaughnessy (2000), 'Treating the Nation as a Brand: Some Neglected Issues', *Journal of Macromarketing*, 20, no. 1, pp. 56–64.

Owen, Bruce M. and Steven S. Wildman (1992), *Video Economics*, Cambridge, MA, and London: Harvard University Press.

Paoli, Pascale and Michael Williams (1996), 'Local TV Crossing Language Barrier', *Variety*, 2 December, p. 53.

Parkes, Christopher (1996), 'Kirch Buys 7.5% Stake in US Film Producer', *Financial Times*, 5 October, p. 11.

Parks, Lisa (2003), '*Our World*, Satellite Televisuality, and the Fantasy of Global Presence', in Lisa Parks and Shanti Kumar (eds), *Planet TV: A Global Television Reader*, New York: New York University Press, pp. 74–93.

Paxman, Andrew (1996), 'Roots of Form Trace to Cuba', *Variety*, 7 October, p. 61.

Paxman, Andrew (1998), 'Televisa Reduces Export Arm, Drops Plan to Sell Pub Subsid', *Variety*, 24 December, p. 4.

Paxman, Andrew (1999), 'Novela Excess Puts Distribs in Distress', *Variety*, 3 May, p. 74.

Penacchioni, Irene (1984), 'The Reception of Popular Television in Northeast Brazil', *Media, Culture & Society*, 6, pp. 337–41.

Penaloza, Lisa (2001), 'Consuming the American West: Animating Cultural Meaning and Memory at a Stock Show and Rodeo' *Journal of Consumer Research*, 28, pp. 369–98.

Petkovič, Brankica (ed.), (2004) *Media Ownership and its Impact on Media Independence and Pluralism*, Ljubljana: Peace Institute.

Petrovszky, Zoltán (2001), Director of Programming, Duna Televízió (Hungary). Personal interview.

Pollack, Donald K. and David Lyndon Woods (1959), 'A Study in International Communication: Eurovision', *Journal of Broadcasting*, 3, no. 2, pp. 101–18.

Pool, Ithiel de Sola (1977), 'The Changing Flow of Television', *Journal of Communication*, 27, no. 2, pp. 39–49.

PR Newswire (2002), 'Sony Pictures Entertainment Renames Television Operations', 16 September, <http://web.lexis-nexis.com/universe> (downloaded 30 June 2005).

PR Newswire (2003), 'DISH Network Adds Zone Vision's Reality TV Channel', 22 September, <http://web.lexis-nexis.com/universe> (downloaded 10 August 2004).

Puopolo, Michael (1999), Manager of International Research, Warner Bros. International Television. Personal interview.

Radóczy, Katalin (2002), General Manager, Minimax Hungary. Personal interview.

Ray, Manas and Elizabeth Jacka (1996), 'Indian Television: An Emerging Regional Force', in John Sinclair, Elizabeth Jacka and Stuart Cunningham, (eds), *New Patterns in Global Television: Peripheral Vision*, Oxford and New York: Oxford University Press, pp. 83–100

Reality TV (2004), Homepage, < http://www.realitytvchannel.com > (downloaded 27 September 2004).

Renaud, Jean-Luc and Barry R. Litman (1985), 'Changing Dynamics of the Overseas Marketplace for TV Programming', *Telecommunications Policy*, 9, pp. 245–61.

Reynolds, Mike and Steve Donohue (2003), 'Dish Adds Reality Import', *Multichannel News*, 29 September, p. 1.

Rice, Gillian (1992), 'Using the Interaction Approach to Understand International Trade Shows', *International Marketing Review*, 9, no. 4, pp. 32–46.

Robertson, Roland (1994) 'Globalisation or Glocalisation?', *The Journal of International Communication*, 1, pp. 33–52.

Robertson, Virginia (1999), 'Latin America's Terrestrials Take on International Kids Fare', *Kidscreen*, May, p. 60.

Ross, Karen (1996), *Black and White Media: Black Images in Popular Film and Television*, Cambridge, MA: Blackwell.

Roxborough, Scott (2002), 'Kirch an Enigma Until the End', *Hollywood Reporter*, 9 April, <http://web.lexis-nexis.com/universe> (downloaded 21 May 2003).

Roxborough, Scott and Charles Masters (2001), 'MIPCOM Defies Dire Forecast', *Hollywood Reporter*, 16 October, <http://web.lexis-nexis.com/universe> (downloaded 16 October 2003).

Russell, Mark (2003), 'Korean Animation Thrives on Foreign Contracts but Lacks Identity', *Hollywood Reporter*, 26 August, <http://web.lexis-nexis.com/universe> (downloaded 9 September 2004).

Sahab, Claudia (2004), Director of European Sales, Televisa. Panel discussion at DISCOP 2004, Budapest, Hungary, 26 June.

Sakamoto, Hideaki (2004), Senior Executive Manager of Sales, Media International Company. Personal interview.

Sarnoff, Robert W. (1968), 'Global Television: A Proposal', presented at the European Broadcasting Union Conference, 22 October 1962, New York. Reprinted in Harry J. Skornia and Jack William Kitson, (eds), *Problems and Controversies in Television and Radio: Basic Readings*, Palo Alto: Pacific Books, pp. 489–94.

Schapiro, Mark (1991), 'Lust-Greed-Sex-Power: Translatable Anywhere', *The New York Times*, 2 June, Section 2, p. 29.

Schiller, Herbert (1969), *Mass Communication and American Empire*, New York: A. M. Kelley.

Schiller, Herbert (1991), 'Not Yet the Post-Imperialist Era', *Critical Studies in Mass Communication*, 8, pp. 13–28.

Schlessinger, Philip (1986), 'Trading in Fictions: What Do We Know About British Television Imports and Exports?', *European Journal of Communication*, 1, pp. 263–87.

Schwarzacher, Lukas (2004), '"Scent" of Success'. *Variety*, 15 March, p. 18.

Scott, Walter D. (1967), 'A Perspective on Global Television', presented to the Detroit Economic Club, 6 February, Detroit. Pamphlet Collections, #4257, Broadcast Pioneers Library of American Broadcasting, College Park, MD.

Screen Digest (1992), 'Transformation Scene in World Television'. February: 33-40.

Screen Digest (1997a), 'European TV Programmeme Budget: Acquisitions on the Rise', April, pp. 81–5.

Screen Digest (1997b), 'Europe's "Other" Channels: Numbers Double Every Three Years'. March, pp. 57–64.

Screen Digest (1998), 'World Television, Cable, and Satellite Homes 1995–1997', May, pp. 111–12.

Screen Digest (2001), 'Euro-Japan High Definition Production First', November: <http://search.rdsinc.com> (downloaded 19 June 2004).

Screen International (2000a), 'Action, Comedy Worldwide Winners', 18 August, p. 10.

Screen International (2000b), 'Europe's Broadcasters Give European Films a Hard Time', 5 May, p. 16.

Seagrave, Kerry (1998), *American Television Abroad: Hollywood's Attempt to Dominate World Television*, Jefferson, NC, and London: McFarland and Company.

Sinclair, John (1999), *Latin American Television: A Global View*, New York and Oxford: Oxford University Press.

Sinclair, John, Elizabeth Jacka and Stuart Cunningham (eds) (1996), *New Patterns in Global Television: Peripheral Vision*, Oxford and New York: Oxford University Press.

Smithard, Pam (2002), Managing Director of Europe for NATPE. Personal interview.

Sofley, Kris (2002), 'Out Foxing the Competition?' *M21*, Autumn, pp. 14–16.

Sofley, Kris (2004a), 'Making Kids TV Pay', *Channel 21*, 9 November, <http://www.c21media.net/features/detail.asp?area=2&article=22434> (downloaded 8 June, 2005).

Sofley, Kris (2004b), 'Wild at Heart', *Channel 21*, 26 October, <http://www.c21media.net/features/detail.asp?area=2&article=22263> (downloaded 8 June 2005).

Spiller, Nancy (1990), 'Bop TV is Free from S. African Censorship', *Chicago Tribune*, 18 June, p. 5.

Sponsor (1961), 'Worldwide TV: A Dynamic Fact', 19 June, pp. 40–56.

Standard & Poors (1997), 'Grupo Televisa: Annual Report', 2 July, <http://web.lexis-nexis.com/universe > (downloaded 23 May 2005).

Steemers, Jeanette (2004,) *Selling Television: British Television in the Global Marketplace*, London: BFI.

Stephenson, Donald (1967), 'The BBC's Foreign Relations', presented at the Second of the
    Sixth Series of Lunch-Time Lectures in the Concert Hall of Brodacasting House,
    15 November, Pamphlets Collection, #751, College Park, MD: Broadcast Pioneers Library
    of American Broadcasting.
Sterling, Christopher P. and John Kittross (2002), *Stay Tuned: A History of American
    Broadcasting, 3rd Edition*, Manwah, NJ: Lawrence Erlbaum Associates.
Stewart, Lianne (2003), 'Zone Vision Expands in Asia', *Channel 21*, 8 September;
    <http://www.c21media.net/news/detail.asp?area=4&article=17123> (downloaded
    27 September 2004).
Stilling, Erik (1995), 'The History of Spanish-Language Television in the United States and the
    Rise of Mexican International Syndication Strategies in the America', *Howard Journal of
    Communication*, 6, pp. 231–49.
Straubhaar, Joseph (1991), 'Asymmetrical Interdependence and Cultural Proximity', *Critical
    Studies in Mass Communication*, 8, pp. 39–59.
Straubhaar, Joseph (2004), 'The Multiple Proximities of *Telenovelas* and Audiences', paper
    presented at the International Communication Association Convention, 27–30 May, New
    Orleans.
Straubhaar, Joseph D. and Gloria Viscasillas (1991), 'The Reception of *Telenovelas* and Other
    Latin American Genres in the Regional Market: The Case of The Dominican Republic',
    Studies in Latin American Popular Culture, 10, pp. 191–215.
Stronach, Bruce (1989), 'Japanese Television', in Richard Gid Powers and Hidetoshi Kato (eds),
    Handbook of Japanese Popular Culture, New York, Westport and London: Greenwood Press,
    pp. 127–61.
Strover, Sharon (2004), 'Coproduction, International', in Horace Newcomb (ed.), *Encyclopedia
    of Television, 2nd edn*, New York and London: Fitzroy-Dearborn Publishers, pp. 588–91.
Sutter, Mary (2002), 'Mexican Sidekick: Grupo Televisa Fights Typecast as Supporting Actor in
    the Growing US Hispanic Market', *Latin Trade*, July, p. 48.
Syvertsen, Trine and Skogerbø (1998), 'Scandinavia, Netherlands, and Belgium', in Anthony
    Smith, *Television: The International View, 2nd edn*, Oxford: Oxford University Press,
    pp. 223–33.
Szőllőssy, Gábor (2002), Acquisitions Director, TV2 (Hungary). Personal interview.
Tartaglione, Nancy (2000), 'Niche Channels', *Variety*, 3 April, p. M6.
Tegal, Simeon (2001), 'New Momentum at Televisa', *Television Latin America*, January, p. 36.
Televisa Estudios (2004), 'Contact Us',
    <http://www.televisaestudios.com/asp/contacto/frame_contact0?IntSecID=0&IntDubSecID
    =&cve_clase_producto=1&lan=2> (downloaded 26 September 2004).
Television Asia (2001), 'Star Movies in Dream Works Output Deal for South Asia', September,
    p. 11.
Television Asia (2003), '24-Hour Reality TV Rolls in Asia', May, p. 6.
Television Business International (2003), 'Leading the Charge', 1 March,
    <http://www.factiva.com> (downloaded 15 August 2004).
Television Business Internationa (2004), 'Zone Vision Channels Broaden Their Outlook', 1 May,
    p. 28.

Television International (1999), 'Program Exports from France, Germany, UK', 15 November, p. 2.

Television International (2002), 'Price Guide', October, p. 58.

Television Magazine (1966), 'The Global Market: Tough Nut', August, pp. 68–89.

Thomas, Pradip (1998), 'South Asia', in Anthony Smith (ed.) *Television: An International History*, 2nd edn, Oxford and New York: Oxford University Press, pp. 201–7.

Tinic, Serra (2003), 'Going Global: International Coproductions and the Disappearing Domestic Audience in Canada', in Lisa Parks and Shanti Kumar (eds), *Planet TV: A Global Television Reader*, New York: New York University Press, pp. 169–85.

Tinic, Serra (2005), *On Location: Canada's Television Industry in a Global Market*, Toronto: University of Toronto Press.

Tobin, Betsy (1990), 'The Language of Laughs', *TV World*, October, pp. 29–33.

Tomlinson, John (1991), *Cultural Imperialism: A Critical Introduction*, Baltimore: Johns Hopkins University Press.

Tomlinson, John (1999), *Globalization and Culture*, Chicago: University of Chicago Press.

Tóth, Erika (2002), Acquisitions Assistant, Duna Televízió (Hungary), Personal interview.

Tracey, Michael (1998), *The Decline and Fall of Public Service Broadcasting*, Oxford and New York: Oxford University Press.

Tracey, Michael and Wendy W. Redal (1995), 'The New Parochialism: The Triumph of the Populist in the Flow of International Television', *Canadian Journal of Communication*, 20, pp. 343–65.

Turner, Mimi (1999), 'Unfriendly Time for British TV', *Hollywood Reporter*, 17 December, <http://web.lexis-ncxis.com/universe> (downloaded 17 August 2004).

Turner, Mimi (2002), 'Reality TV Check: Factual Channels into More Homes', *Hollywood Reporter*, 16 April, <http://web.lexis-nexis.com/universe> (downloaded 11 August 2004).

Turow, Joseph (1997), *Media Systems in Society: Understanding Industries, Strategies, and Power*, 2nd edn, New York: Longman.

TV World (1984), 'Bop-TV Petition Fails', December: p. 8.

TVB (2004), 'Corporate Information', <http://www.tvb.com/affairs/faq/tvbgroup/tvb_e.html> (downloaded 24 September).

Tyler, Ralph (1966), 'Television Around the World', *Television Magazine*, October: pp. 32–60.

US Department of State (2005a), 'Belgium', <http://www.state.gov/r/pa/ei/bgn/2874.htm> (downloaded 29 May 2005).

US Department of State (2005b), 'Hungary', <http://www.state.gov/r/pa/ei/bgn/26566.htm> (downloaded 29 May 2005).

USIA (1962), 'Overseas Television Developments in 1961', United States Information Agency. Pamphlets Collection, #2590, Broadcast Pioneers Library of American Broadcasting, College Park, MD.

Valaskakis, Gail (1988), 'Television and Cultural Integration: Implications for Native Communities in the Canadian North', in Rowland Lorimer and Donald Wilson (eds), *Communication Canada: Issues in Broadcasting and New Technologies*, Toronto: Kagan and Woo, pp. 124–38.

Van Slambrouck, Paul (1984), 'South African Whites Clamor to Tune in Black TV', *Christian Science Monitor*, 3 February, p. 7.

Variety (1959), 'Global Cinematic TV Market', 15 April, p. 113.

Variety (1960), 'Snail's Pace for US Features on O'Seas Channels', 6 July, p. 31.

Variety (1962), 'Foreign Syndie Biz: 50% Mark', 21 November, p. 23.

Variety (1963a), 'Features Abroad Play Minor Role', 13 March, p. 33.

Variety (1963b), 'O'Seas Pix-to-TV Expansion', 27 February, pp. 25ff.

Variety (1964), 'O'Seas Mart Shun US Pix', 24 June, p. 29.

Variety (1981), '"Volume Sales" Moves Goods in Small Mkts', 6 May, pp. 1ff.

Variety (1996), 'Soapmeisters: The Big Four Exporters', 7 October, p. 64.

Variety (1997a), 'Kirch Group at 40', 13 January, p. 134.

Variety (1997b), 'Sudsers Scoring with Latino Neighbors', 8 December, p. 54.

Variety (2005), 'Belgium: Pubcasters Eye New Product', 4 April, p. A14.

Varis, Tapio (1985), *International Flow of Television Programmes*, Paris: UNESCO.

Vörös, Csilla (2002), Managing Director, AGB Hungary. Personal interview.

VT4 (2005), 'TV-Gids', <http://www.vt4.be/html/gids.asp> (downloaded 27 May 2005).

Waisbord, Silvio (2004), 'McTV: Understanding the Global Popularity of Television Formats',
    Television & New Media, 5, pp. 359–83.

Waller, Ed (2002), 'Reality TV Builds East Euro Footprint', *Channel 21*, 8 April,
    <http://www.c21media.net/news/detail.asp?area=4&article=2942> (downloaded
    27 September 2004).

Waller, Ed (2004a), 'Fremantle Formats Go to Greece, France, Denmark', *Channel 21*,
    28 September: <http://www.c21media.net/news/detail.asp?area=4&article=21892>
    (downloaded 29 May 2005).

Waller, Ed (2004b), 'SBS Renews Kanakna's Asian Odyssey', *Channel 21*, 19 October,
    <http://www.c21media.net/news/detail.asp?area=4&article=22183> (downloaded 29 May
    2005).

Waller, Ed (2005a), 'TV Formats Business at War', *Channel 21*, 21 April,
    <http://www.c21media.net/features/detail.asp?area=2&article=24466> (downloaded 9 May
    2005).

Waller, Ed (2005b), 'Turkish Delight for Fox Formats', *Channel 21*, 1 February,
    <http://www.c21media.net/news/detail.asp?area=4&article=23332> (downloaded 29 May
    2005).

Walley, Wayne (1995), 'US Distributors Say Business Back on Track', *Electronic Media*, 7 April,
    p. 3.

Wasko, Janet (1994), *Hollywood in the Information Age: Beyond the Silver Screen*, Austin:
    University of Texas Press.

Webdale, Jonathan (2005), 'Zone Vision Poised for Growth', *Channel 21*, 24 June,
    <http://www.c21media.net/features/detail.asp?area=2&article=25319> (downloaded
    8 August 2005).

Wheldon, Huw (1971), 'Competition in Television', presented to a Joint Meeting of the Faculty
    of Royal Designers for Industry and the Royal Society of Arts. Uncatalogueued collections.
    Pioneers of Broadcasting Library of American Broadcasting, College Park, MD.

Whitefield, Mimi (1999), 'GEMS Strategy Shifts to Enter Key Hispanic Market'. *Miami Herald*,
    8 February, <http://web.lexis-nexis.com/universe> (downloaded 15 March 2003).

Wildman, Steven S. and Stephen E. Siwek (1988), *International Trade in Films and Television Programs*, Cambridge, MA: Ballinger Publishing Company.

Wilkins, Karen Gwinn (2004), 'Hong Kong', in Horace Newcomb (ed.), *Encyclopedia of Television, Second Edition*, New York and London: Fitzroy-Dearborn Publishers, pp. 1129–32.

Williams, Phil (1994), 'The Evolution of the Television Rerun', *Journal of Popular Film and Television*, 21, no. 4, pp. 162–76.

Williams, Raymond (1974), *Television: Technology and Cultural Form*, Glasgow: Fontana.

Woodcock, Andrew (1997), 'Double Delight as Sky Swoops For Top Shows', *Press Association*, 21 June, <http://web.lexis-nexis.com/universe> (downloaded 22 June 2003).

Worldscope (2005), 'Grupo Televisa', 23 May, <web.lexis-nexis.com/universe > (downloaded 23 May 2005).

Worth, Robert F. (2005) 'Tragicomedy of Life in Baghdad is Brought Home in a TV Series'. *The New York Times*, 14 May, <http://web.lexis-nexis.com/universe> (downloaded 29 June 2005).

Wünsche, Jochen (1984), 'International Television Coproduction in Europe', *EBU_Review*, 35, pp. 29–31.

Zaras, Andrea (2001), Acquisitions Manager, RTL Klub (Hungary). Personal interview.

Zone Vision (2004a), 'History', <http://www.zonevision.co.uk/corporate/history.php> (downloaded 24 February 2004).

Zone Vision (2004b), 'Profile'. <http://www.zonevision.co.uk/corporate/profile.php> (downloaded 24 February 2004).

Index